# CALIBAN WITHOUT PROSPERO

# CALIBAN

# ESSAY ON QUEBEC AND BLACK LITERATURE

# WITHOUT PROSPERO

## MAX DORSINVILLE

PRESS PORCEPIC ERIN ONTARIO

# CALIBAN

The book has been published with the help
of a grant from the Humanities Research
Council of Canada, using funds provided
by the Canada Council.

Printed and Published by Press Porcépic
70 Main Street, Erin, Ontario N0B 1T0


ISBN   0-88878-034-6   hard
ISBN   0-88878-035-4   soft

# WITHOUT PROSPERO

FOR MY MOTHER AND FATHER

# PREFACE

Max Dorsinville set two formidable objectives for himself when he undertook to write this book. First, he wanted to analyze in parallel the whole evolution of Quebec and Black American culture and literature. Secondly, he proposed to examine the development of these two cultures and literatures in the light of an extended metaphor from Shakespeare's *Tempest*, with a view to formulating a new concept which could then be applied to the literatures of all emerging national or ethnic groups. He felt that the Caliban and Prospero metaphor, long recognized as an instrument of insight into the complexities of cultural confrontation in a colonial context, would provide the key to the rationales underlying the literatures of Black America and French Canada.

Both objectives have been realized in brilliant scholarly fashion. Dorsinville's analysis of the two bodies of literature is thorough and penetrating, the fruit of an extensive knowledge of both primary and secondary materials. His familiarity with Third World literature, African and West Indian, allows him to elucidate the philosophy of "Négritude" and to relate it to Black American thought. He also explores the views of Fanon and the Marxist critics, tracing their influence in Quebec and the U.S.A. In many respects his study of the evolution of the literature of French Canada is vastly superior to any of the existing literary histories, for he is able to consider this literature in a broad and illuminating perspective, moving far beyond the cataloguing of works and trends to an objective evaluation of motivating forces.

Max Dorsinville's premise that literature is not an isolated or sterile phenomenon, but rather an expression of collective psychological and philosophical aspects of cultural experience, is to my mind patently valid. Otherwise, literary criticism is an intellectual exercise in stylistics or aesthetics, an old-timers' hockey game without slap shots or bodychecks. The premise, however, requires of the analyst a great deal of para-literary information. Dorsinville demonstrates that he has this information, bringing to bear on his subject a strong sense of history and a wide knowledge of current events.

This book is an important contribution to several fields of study, including Canadian, American, Third World and comparative literatures, not to mention literary history, sociology and philosophy. It is entirely original in approach, the first attempt at parallel analysis of Black American and Quebec literature. And the value of such a parallel analysis is made obvious. The fundamental conditioning ideas of both literatures emerge clearly when the literatures are viewed side by side, each providing a foil for the other. The place of religious practice, remarkably similar in each, is one striking example. But more important perhaps, parallel examination permits Dorsinville to avoid the subjectivity and emotionalism so often associated with critiques of Quebec and Black American writing.

Dorsinville's observations of the "miniaturization" of the concept of culture and on the phenomenon of duality (hybridity) in a dominant-subservient social context are of particular significance. It is here that the metaphor of Caliban and Prospero provides a key, a framework of interpretation, allowing Dorsinville to bring forth a number of valuable insights, especially with regard to dialect and Quebec "joual". He is able to transcend the specific aspects — the sexual myth of the Black man, the Quebec girl as avenger, fractured language as a form of protest, and so on —which have caught up many critics in the past. By examining the two cultures together, Max Dorsinville succeeds in moving behind the superficial specifics to the common conditioning ideas, to the real implications of cultural domination and juxtaposition. And in so doing he offers a fresh and perspicacious interpretation of what is happening now and of what will happen in Black American and French-Canadian society and literature.

Ronald Sutherland
Université de Sherbrooke

# INTRODUCTION

In 1945, shortly before departing for expatriation in France, Richard Wright, the Black American novelist, spent two months living on a picturesque little island east of Quebec City. (1) Witnessing the extent to which rural French Canadian life was wedded to tradition, Wright reflected upon the contrast with the urban industrialized landscape of Chicago and New York and marveled at this "close, organic, intimate, ... way of life." (2) Earlier, in the twenties, Marcus Garvey, the nationalist leader of Jamaican descent, had travelled also to Canada; but, because his purpose was to find Black Canadian disciples for his United Negro Improvement Association, his relationship was of that somewhat narrow political nature which has long marked any rapport between Quebec and Black America. (3)

Since the nineteenth century at least, French Canadians have been concerned with the Black situation in the United States. (4) In our time, however, it is not the few streets around Windsor Station, in Montreal (where there is a tentative Black ghetto), the fact that Jackie Robinson played for a Montreal baseball team, on his way to break the "colour bar" in the Major leagues, nor the presence throughout Quebec of a small, integrated middle class of teachers, engineers, doctors and other professionals, composed mainly of Blacks of West Indian descent — which sensitized Quebec culture to the Black experience.    Rather, the emergent "Québécois" identity of the late fifties and sixties drew definite parallels between its own social experience and that of Blacks in America and Africa.

It may be said that the 1954 Supreme Court school decision, or the 1955 Montgomery bus boycott, is a watershed for any understanding of modern Black assertiveness. 1959, when a notoriously autocratic Church-dominated political regime ended, is the corresponding crucial date for the articulation of modern Quebec. But it is in the early sixties, when the politics

9

of Canada and the United States become radically affected by the aggressive affirmation of the French Canadians and the Blacks, (5) that the figure of the Black man, as symbol, image and myth, emerges in the French-Canadian consciousness. A young poet expresses this novel identification: "(quand j'irai à New York c'est vers Harlem que j'appareillerai et non par exotisme j'ai trop le souci de parentés précises je connais le goût de la matraque à Alabama il y a des fraternités dans le malheur que vos libertés civiles savent mal dissimuler)." (6) And a would-be revolutionary entitles his political memoirs, *Nègres Blancs d'Amérique,* dramatizing experience of submissiveness, alienation and long-repressed anger.

Politics, then, seems to be a major common ground between Quebec and Black America. But the correct basis for attempting to analyze two literatures apparently so foreign to each other lies, I believe, in the spectrum of Western culture understood, historically speaking, as a unified experience. (7)

The twentieth century has witnessed the growth and fruition of a socio-cultural phenomenon that arose with the Renaissance and was stressed in the age of Romanticism. The breakdown of a common religious belief and an outlook said to be God's design, traditionally articulated in a universal language (Latin), (8) brought forth philosophical concerns about Nature and man, and encouraged fiction rooted in close analytical descriptions of milieu, character and societal, bourgeois values. This preoccupation with man's immediate environment and his role in it, augmented by the taste for folklore, local colour, and the cult of the 'self', undoubtedly finalized, in the nineteenth century, the disintegration of the unity of European culture. (9)

The rise of self-conscious bourgeois literature, and the continuation of its radical, secular stance ushering in a concept of "national" literature, lead directly to an increasing affirmation, in the twentieth century, of so-called minor literatures. (10) What is the critical student of literature to do when faced with a body of literature coming from Africa, the Caribbean, French Canada and Black America? Is he to stress the filiation of writers such as Achebe, Ngugi, Oyono, Hamidou Kane, Aquin, Roy, Wright and Himes with French or American literature? This, of course, raises the whole question of "what makes the nationality of literature?" Political statehood? Language? Geographical emplacement? As fine a literary mind as René Wellek had to confess that, theoretically, this is a moot point. (11)

The literatures of Quebec and Black America, in fact, appear as epigones in a movement which starts with the Renaissance breakaway from the unitary tie between the Church and the State; with the rise of scientific inquiry which not only questions the validity of certain hitherto accepted values and beliefs, but, in the Baconian call for the "advancement of learning", argues for the total revamping of a classical legacy of culture. Hence, the eschewing of rhetoric as the favoured mode of communication, the rejection of Platonic Idealism and Scholastic deductive methodology in

10

philosophy and science, and the adoption of empiricism as groundwork for the new theories of knowledge. Preceding the breakthroughs of Hobbes, Descartes, Locke and Newton, the impact of the Reformation cannot be overlooked. R.H. Tawney and Max Weber point out that the rise of the Calvinist ethic is as radical and fruitful a departure from the medieval world view as the substitution of fact for faith. But how did such a total cultural reordering affect the imagination?

Specifically, the replacement of Latin by the vernacular as the "language of culture", the substitution of a national point of view for a continental, the ascent of the middle class as patron and consumer of the arts, and the stress placed on milieu, character and the avowedly secular in literature represent four seminal points of departure which help explain the imagination at work in Black American and French-Canadian literature.

The empiricist outlook, articulated throughout the seventeenth century and calling, in Descartes, for systematic doubting, testing and rejecting of pre-conceived notions (innate ideas) in all fields and particularly with regard to artistic and cultural matters, allows for the historical perspective behind the existence of such literatures. Just as the middle-class novels of Deloney, Defoe and Richardson convey the effects of a radical shift whereby the aristocratic ethos could not survive in a society where the bourgeoisie held economic control, it would seem that the vision expressed in the literatures of Quebec and Black America comes as the culmination of a process of secularization. If milieu, character, plot are enlisted for the creation, in the eighteenth century novel, of an emergent moral value congruent with the confidence of the middle class it appears likely that the twentieth-century affirmation of ethnicity may inject in the novel a set of attributes as significant for the understanding of a singular cultural phenomenon as the features of Deloney's, Defoe's and Richardson's novels.

Since the 'novel' (as distinguished from Northrop Frye's three other forms of fiction: Romance, Confession and Satire) is the creation of a total economic, philosophic, politic and religious overhaul, molding as well as translating the values of the middle class, two chief characteristics stand out: the modernity and the 'openness' of the genre. The publicness of the novel's forum makes it imperative, I believe, to approach the literatures of Quebec and Black America as cultural barometers. In my discussion of the novel, I am less interested in a Lubbockian-Jamesian "craft of fiction", in Boothian "rhetoric" and other formalisms than in fiction's debts to the society in which it is rooted, or the outlooks that helped create it. The approach at work, accordingly, is much indebted to Lucien Goldmann, Georg Lukacs, Jean-Paul Sartre, Erich Auerbach, and to the invaluable Ian Watt.

What is the 'world' under discussion? It is, it can be said, the product of a second genesis: that of the nineteenth-century belief in national characteristics when not the beneficiary of Enlightenment theories of progress. It is no coincidence if the literatures of Quebec and Black America are born in the period when, historically, colonies make way for nations, when the pan-European dream is shattered by the rise of nationality which culminates, a century later, in the celebration of multiple ethnicity. We examine the Rousseau-like figure of Caliban, born in insularity, in exile, away from tradition-bound concepts of 'culture' and 'models'.

In Shakespeare's last play, *The Tempest*, there is an altercation between Prospero, the Duke of Milan, and Caliban, the "savage and deformed slave" whom the Duke has reduced to servitude. The gist of it is Prospero's anger at Caliban's persistence in foul-mouthedness and ingratitude, considering the civilized virtues — of which the power of language is uppermost — bestowed upon him. Caliban replies with accusations of usurpation, false representation and trickery in Prospero's take-over of an island rightfully belonging to him and his mother. To cap things off, he adds that the use he has for Prospero's prized gift, language, is to curse him better! (12)

A number of critics, ignoring the brevity of this scene in the structure of the play, have analyzed its rich symbolic texture and seen in this confrontation an almost step-by-step summary of modern colonialism. The French scholar, O. Mannoni, in *Psychologie de la Colonisation*, the Barbadian novelist, George Lamming, in *The Pleasures of Exile*, and the German Africanist, Janheinz Jahn, in *Neo-African Literature*, have all seen in this altercation a parable for our times, while the Martinican poet, Aimé Césaire, has gone further in his *Une Tempête*: reordering Shakespeare's play in the polarization of the Fanonian "wretched of the earth".

Mannoni's interpretation, in seeming to erect a pattern of justification for the colonial policies of Europe, has earned him the full wrath of Frantz Fanon. (13) George Lamming's approach, articulated in cultural elitist terms, seems too open-ended to Jahn. (14) Jahn's own point of view, for that matter, is perhaps a speculative and systematized attempt to suit his thesis of a "Geist", unifying, culturally, peoples of African extraction, irrespective of geographical location and historical conditionings. (15) Nevertheless, Jahn comes closest to respecting Shakespeare's meaning.

Shakespeare's *The Tempest* is a Masque, an art form strongly dependent on symbolism. It presents figures that are suggestive, evocative and allusive; and it often relies on mythopoeic references for full effect. If we accept this, and recognize with Browning (16) that the power of the symbolism carried by Prospero and Caliban overcomes by far the meager externalized relationship between the two, we may explore the meaning of each figure and, while respecting the essential half-tones, come out with applications appropriate for a present cultural dilemma.

Prospero, as the name itself implies, is the sophisticated product of an urban, metropolitan, culture. A man of the Renaissance, of the "revival of learning", his culture or outlook is derived from his reading of the best that has been thought and expressed. It is because he chose to spend his time

12

"bettering his mind" through constant reading, rather than tend to the administrative affairs of his dukedom, that his more pragmatic brother succeeded in driving him from Milan, into exile. Caliban, on the other hand, is a mysterious, almost preternatural figure, at ease with a non-verbal sensory world of feelings and moods. His only meaning, before he meets Prospero, is to be part of Nature's continuum, to feel rather than think, to dream rather than talk, to be sensual rather than rational. He is a definite figure of darkness to Prospero's lightness, "A devil, a born devil,... this thing of darkness... whose mother was a witch,..." says Prospero. (p.29) Both figures are antithetic, prototypical for Shakespeare's dramatization of illusion and reality, the known and the unknown, the conscious and the unconscious; themes that recur in his early and late comedies and obsessed many of his tragic heroes. Significantly, there are echoes of King Lear, Macbeth, Hamlet, not to mention all the Benedicks and Malvolios of the comedies, when Prospero reflects:

> *We are such stuff*
> *As dreams are made on, and our little life*
> *Is rounded with a sleep.* (p.25)

The Prospero-Caliban antithesis is ultimately the division each individual carries within himself. At the end of the play Prospero's contrapuntal benignity vis-à-vis Caliban (who tried to have him killed) implies Prospero's recognition that the "poisonous slave", son of the devil and of a witch, is really the dark side of his self, denied so long as he was a metropolitan man but accepted during his sojourn in insular darkness through the practice of witchcraft. Thus the prayer uttered in the Epilogue is that of a repentant Christian man, fully aware of the views of the society he is about to re-enter on the subject of the black arts (Prospero also knows very well that Caliban's mother, Sycocrax, was deported to the island because she dealt in magic):

> ...my ending is despair,
> Unless I be relieved by prayer,
> Which pierces so, that it assaults
> Mercy itself, and frees all faults.
> As you from crimes could pardon'd be,
> Let your indulgence set me free. (p.30)

In the structure of the play, however, Prospero's experiences in regions of the unknown have furnished him with the necessary means to regain Milan. He has gone through an education.

But the crucial point for our discussion is that, initially, in the first Act, Prospero is an ill-educated man. When we first meet him, stranded on an

13

island, faced with creatures of the dark and the mysterious, Prospero must shed light or else he is ill at ease. This need for light explains his lack of scruples in his dealings with Ariel, and his self-righteousness regarding Caliban. Any means seems to be appropriate for Prospero, so long as it is to restore the kind of milieu or outlook he is used to. The key to this restoration is language, books. Yet, Caliban, for all his alleged stupidity, sees through Prospero's shallowness; when he counsels Stephano and Trinculo to make sure before assaulting Prospero "to possess his books: for without them/ He's but a sot" (p.22), we have the implied motive behind his surliness and abusiveness toward Prospero. Caliban is revolting against the sham, the pretenses, of the metropolitan man's alleged superior brand of experience, and sees mainly deceit ("...I am subject to a tyrant; a sorcerer, that by his cunning hath cheated me of the island" p.21). There is an added poignancy to this revolt since Caliban knows he did not need Prospero's help to feel and to dream, to have a humane sensitive rapport with his milieu and to build images as reflectors of these feelings. This is made evident in Act III when, in order to reassure Stephano in the dark, he says:

> Be not afeard; the isle is full of noises,
> Sounds, and sweet airs, that give delight, and
>         hurt not.
> Sometimes a thousand twangling instruments
> Will hum about mine ears; and sometimes voices,
> That, if I then had waked after long sleep,
> Will make me sleep again: and then, in dreaming,
> The clouds, methought, would open, and show
>         riches
> Ready to drop upon me, that, when I waked,
> I cried to dream again.    (p.22)

It can be argued, however, that this passage only proves Caliban's indebtedness to Prospero, for it is through Prospero's gift of language that Caliban is able to articulate what was hitherto non-verbal. Notwithstanding the fact that Caliban may very well have had a language of his own in the first place, incomprehensible to Prospero, it can conversely be argued, as Jahn does, that in his choice of images and sounds, Caliban has subverted the metropolitan man's language, subordinating it as a medium for the end expression of *his* sensitivity. Caliban partakes of two cultures, but they are integrated into *his* view of the world:

> So he captures, in his own and Prospero's language a culture
> Prospero did not create and cannot control, which he, Caliban,
> has recognized as his own. But in the process the language is
> transformed, acquiring different meanings which Prospero never

expected. Caliban becomes "bilingual". (17)

Now, one does not have to go beyond Shakespearean meaning to find in the Prospero-Caliban set of symbols an appropriate metaphorical application for the dilemma brought about by the sprouting of a number of minor, regional, national or ethnic literatures. African, Antillean, French-Canadian and Black American writers need not hurl abuse at their French or English/American Prosperos, but they do claim a metaphorical or actual land of their own, and an experience of the world differentiating them from linguistic or geographical congeners. As such, they adopt Caliban's stance and their novels offer the singular view of a world Prospero did not make.

What are, consequently, the *specificities* of Calibanic literature? I should like to focus on the novels of Black America and Quebec and discuss the themes ordering them. While respecting each culture's historicity, I hope to demonstrate that the stages reflected in the 'open' form of the novel lead to a possible *descriptive* theory embracing a host of literatures which evolved from a common 'post-European' genesis. Emerging in the nineteenth century, in the historic context of Europe's dream of aggrandizement, post-European literature comes, paradoxically, as a logical continuation in a process of miniaturization of the concept of culture that started with the late Renaissance in Europe.

One suspects that often the discussion will have to deal with statements of uneasiness and discontent. Yet all this should be interpreted as a logical unravelling. For, given the fact that one is indebted to an Other's language which, at least to a certain degree, implies a certain conditioning in outlook, view of the world and of self, (18) the post-European writer's dominant temper reflects the archetypal Shakespearean predicament. If Prospero is as much a part of Caliban as Caliban is of Prospero—and Prospero, at least, does not realize this until he has battled with Caliban—the same is true of the post-European writer vis-à-vis the European icon. But he has to shatter it first in coming to terms with his dilemma.

Admittedly, the *specificities* which preoccupy the Black American and the French-Canadian writer stem neither from a common political fate nor from a common racial or ethnic background. Perhaps one could not find a better point of departure than these immediate polarities, for an analysis that aims through diachronic argumentation to show how the Black American and the French-Canadian writers nonetheless share a common aesthetic programme.

Because the world of Maria Chapdelaine, or that of Bigger Thomas, is specific, and self-sufficient for dramatization and evaluation, I aim, first, to identify and describe this world as closely as possible. Thus it is imperative that each literature be discussed separately, in its organic progression, before attempting any comparison. Second, the conclusions reached state what empirically must have been evident all along: the echoing and

15

parallelism of the two literatures. From the initial premise of a European 'organic whole', we come to a resolution with another organic whole which is that of post-European literature within which Black American and French-Canadian literature's rapport is explained.

Richard Wright's concluding insight —"The Negro, like everybody else in America, came originally from a simple, organic way of life, such as I saw in French Québec." (19) — may well motivate the discussion that follows; since it tries to articulate what Wright hinted at: the definite relationships between Quebec and Black American culture and literature.

1 Robin W. Winks, *The Blacks in Canada*, p.462.
2 Richard Wright, *White Man, Listen!*, p.69.
3 Winks, pp.414-415.
4 Marcel Trudel, *L'Esclavage au Canada Français*, especially chap. i, iv, and v.
5 Everett C. Hughes, *American Assembly, The United States and Canada*, p.22; see also James B. Eayrs, *Ibid.*, p.91.
6 Paul Chamberland, *l'Afficheur Hurle*, p.59.
7 A comparative approach also underlies two recent books, but with respect to the rapport between Quebec and English-Canadian literature, and Quebec and Haitian literature. See Ronald Sutherland, *Second Image*; Maximilien Laroche, *Le Miracle et la Métamorphose*.
8 Ian Watt, *The Rise of the Novel*, pp.9-34.
9 René Wellek and Austin Warren, *Theory of Literature*, p.49.
10 Self-conscious Haitian literature dates further back, of course; at least to the Indigenist movement during the twenties and thirties. French-Canadian literature, though it has its roots around the middle of the nineteenth cintury, became self-conscious or self-assertive only with the last World War. Black American literature goes back to the nineteenth and even eighteenth century, yet assertiveness definitely comes late, with Wright in the forties.
11 Wellek and Warren, pp.52-53.
12 William Shakespeare, "The Tempest", in *Complete Works*, p.13. All subsequent references are to this edition and included in the text.
13 Frantz Fanon, *Peau Noire, Masques Blancs*, pp.87-107.
14 Janheinz Jahn, *Neo-African Literature*, p.240.
15 Jahn, p.242.
16 Robert Browning, "Caliban Upon Setebos", *Selected Poetry*, introd. Horace Gregory, pp.120-128.
17 Jahn, p.242.
18 cf. the misunderstanding surrounding the term Négritude between French and English-speaking African writers. See Gerald Moore's

"The Politics of Negritude", *Protest and Conflict in African Literature*, pp.26-42.

19 Richard Wright, Ibid., p.71.

# BLACK CULTURE

# AND THE NOVEL

Black culture in the United States is the product of a communal experience achieved through an homogeneous historical tradition in a distinct geographical milieu. It is a culture indigenously elaborated and articulated upon American ground. The removal from Africa having annihilated all direct links with that continent and obliterated whatever historical tribal heritage the Blacks had, Black American culture offers a rich field for an analysis of forms of survival and quest for identity that are unique as well as complementary to other modes of cultural formation in the New World.

Throughout the course of the slavery period, from the seventeenth to the nineteenth century, the uprooted Blacks slowly constructed their new culture. As is common with all incipient, emerging nationalities, when a diversity of peoples or tribes grasp the extent of their collective identity, the new culture is an oral one rooted in folklore. Enslaved on the plantations, the Blacks invented musical forms and gave expression to an oral literature indicative of their plight. There is sadness and resiliency in the Blues; in Gospel music, an unshakable hope in divine salvation, for which atonement is reached in slavery's valley of tears; yet there is gaiety in the dances and in the tales, for through despair, grows an understanding of fortitude and strength which twentieth-century Existentialists think they have discovered.

Robert Bone, in *The Negro Novel in America*, asserts that until the Negro Renaissance, in the 1920's, the group experience produces an essentially non-literary folk art. Which is a bit misleading. Black literature first manifests itself in the nineteenth century through the "Slave narratives", stories of escape from servitude by Blacks which fed the Abolitionist movement. Within the ranks of that movement we find, in the years preceding and following the Civil War, writers depicting the Black condition.

19

Brer Rabbit

These writers were for the main part White. Thus the didactic fiction they produced is epitomized in Harriet Beecher Stowe's *Uncle Tom's Cabin* (1852). Not surprisingly, the first known novel by a Black author, William Wells Brown's *Clotel* (1853), is a mixture of slave narrative and Abolitionist faith.

Arising in the North, the Abolitionist school of writing gave impetus to a Southern reaction during the Reconstruction period. The plantation writings of Joel Chandler Harris, Thomas Nelson Page, Thomas Dixon, antithetically celebrate the glory of the 'good old days' of the slavery period when the Whites and the Blacks allegedly lived in harmony, since, as master and slave, each knew his 'place'. To prove their point, these writers oppose to Uncle Tom the likes of Brer Rabbit and Uncle Remus, types closer to what the Southerners believe to be the truth about the Blacks. It is within the framework of a Romantic idealization of the South's way of living that the second generation of Black writers appears. Paul Laurence Dunbar, Charles Waddell Chesnutt, to name the most important, do not indulge in outright racial expostulations, glorifying one so-called Master race. But in one's predilection for dialect and a particular form of folk humor (Dunbar), and the other's fascination with the courtly manners of the genteel South (Chesnutt), they share the Harris-Page-Dixon outlook.

Thus literature *about*, and not so much *of* and *by*, Black people was born. It is no coincidence if upon figures such as Uncle Tom, Brer Rabbit, Uncle Remus, various stereotypes will rest. How could it be otherwise? Since whether we are dealing with William Wells Brown or Harriet Beecher Stowe, Joel Chandler Harris or Charles Waddell Chesnutt, we are really faced with a moral dilemma, the confrontation of a Northern and a Southern American ethos, within which the Black condition is but a footnote. Even with the addition of Mark Twain's Jim, the image of the Black male remains that of a patient, good-humoured, common-sensical, obedient, inoffensive, shuffling and head-scratching subordinate. (1) How the conscious and deliberate correction of this image will take place, starting with Jean Toomer, will be discussed later. I should like now to take an overview of standard critical approaches to Black literature — the Black novel and its major critic, Robert Bone, in particular — in order to indicate their limitations.

In the face of his traditional typecast, Bone points out that the Black man, in *life* and in *literature*, is alternately attracted by the two polar opposites of Assimilationism and Nationalism. On the one hand, he is tempted to accept wholeheartedly his stereotype and wants to conform to the image the White man has of him; indeed he models himself on White standards, and becomes "White" if the colour of his skin is light enough (the phenomenon of "passing"), and if it is not, he exhibits the alleged Caucasian contempt for his race. On the other hand, he rebels against his "image", knowing it is not of his own articulation. As the Black man denies his

21

stereotype, his reliance on self and collective identity is, in Bone's words, nothing but "defensive in character", and constitutes an essentially reverse form of racism. (2) Bone feels that these two concepts are essential for the understanding of the Black American's cultural history. So much so that they furnish him with a pendulum motif for his chronology of the Negro novel up to 1952.

Four periods, according to Bone, would encompass the evolution of the Negro novel:

From 1890 to 1920, the war between Assimilationism and Nationalism, the mulatto middle class versus the black "common folks", is a favoured theme. In addition to Chesnutt and Dunbar, writers of the period include W.E.B. DuBois, James W. Johnson, and Sutton Griggs.

The Negro Renaissance, 1920-1930, characterizes the second period. It is the era of Jazz, the "Roaring Twenties", a time when the overall society in America and Europe was enthralled by an uninhibited lifestyle and indulged in wild drinking and dancing. In such a climate of liberated mores and manners, where the primitivism of African art and the dancing of Josephine Baker are celebrated, blackness became the symbol of whatever it was that made the epoch so exciting. The Black man, Bone argues, accepted this new stereotype and actively cultivated what it implied: Black culture has something that the White does not have. The accent, accordingly, fell on celebrating the differences between the Whites and the Blacks. In literature, the two traditional concepts are again opposed. Nationalism is embodied in the "Harlem School" grouping writers such as Langston Hughes, Claude McKay, Countee Cullen. Assimilationism, or opposition to the stressing of Black culture, is maintained by the "Old Guard", the people, says Bone, who in the preceding period tried to assimilate and now feel that in affirming his distinctness the Black man is setting back the movement toward integration. DuBois and Brawley felt that "unassimilable elements in the race should be hidden and not exposed to public view in sordid novels." (3)

The third period, 1930-1940, is that of social realism in American letters. Black literature partook of that movement. The Great Depression had come and in its wake the migration from the rural South to the industrial North created an urban proletariat. The novel is decidedly rooted in the city which, swelling with the ranks of malcontents, becomes the center of turmoils of various kinds. The predominance of Marxism as social doctrine is not the least of these turmoils; it is ardently affirmed by intellectuals and artists. The Black man, of course the hardest hit by the Depression, has more than ever grounds for protest. During this period, Nationalism is actively exploited, albeit without the exoticism of the twenties; Assimilationism is almost non-existent. The radicalism of the day, geared to social issues, translates itself in Richard Wright's classic *Native Son*.

Lastly, Bone divides the period 1940-1952 in two. First, there is the Wright School of protest which is belatedly carrying on the social-realistic vein, and second, the revolt against it. Against the likes of William Gardner Smith, Chester Himes, Ann Petry (the vanguard of the Wright School) three kinds of writers are going to rebel: those who write an "escapist" type of literature, like Frank Yerby; those who are writing what Bone calls "the assimilationist novel proper", which does not deal at all with race material (Willard Motley, and the 'reformed' Himes and Petry); and finally, those who are dealing with Negro life but who approach "the Negro concretely as a human being", and do not use him in a "conflicting racial pattern" (William Demby and Ralph Ellison). With such systematization, Bone can then oppose the Nationalist (here the Wright School) and Assimilationist (Yerby, Motley) strains he has been pursuing all along. As they dialectically eliminate each other, there is only one logical conclusion. That is the kind of novel, Bone says, Ellison writes: the novel of "aesthetic" pursuit. A novel, Bone implies, which does not deal with (racial) conflicts. (4)

I have dwelled purposely on Bone's approach and treatment in order to show the limitations of his historical and sociological criteria applied to literary criticism. Bone's historicism, to be sure, is interesting and valuable, but only as far as it goes, 1952. But, given the fact that he chose to interweave a distinct, even if mild, sociological viewpoint in his approach the result is unsatisfactory. Can we really believe that notions such as Assimilationism and Nationalism, which Bone himself admits straddle *life* and *literature*, have been put to rest in 1952 with Ellison's *Invisible Man*? Indeed, in the social arena, the landmark 1954 Supreme Court decision had not even taken place, let alone the claims of Black Power, Black studies, Community Control, and what not. Can we believe, moreover, that what we have since 1952, with James Baldwin, LeRoi Jones, William Melvin Kelley, Paule Marshall, and Ishmael Reed, is the novel of "aesthetic" pursuit?

Bone is but the most obvious example of an uncritically accepted standard. (5) Such criticism is unfortunately within the time-honoured tradition that sees an inevitable correlation between art and the nature of the society in which it grows. The better sociological critics (Leslie Fiedler, Edmund Wilson, Ian Watt, Raymond Williams and others) have indeed illuminated our reading of literature with a sophisticated and subtle approach in showing the structural relationships linking art and socio-economic conditions at various stages in history. Unfortunately, for Black literature, the sociological approach has meant an indifference to the text and a working-out of personal anxieties borne by the critic, which Ralph Ellison, for one, acutely resented. (6) It should be possible to attempt an analysis of Black culture, as expressed in the genre of the novel, by taking an opposite approach, which does not ignore social polarities but insists on exploring the deeper realms of the American psyche, its myths and symbols.

Relying on the extended metaphor of Caliban and Prospero for a descriptive analysis of the dominant features of some twenty novels published between 1853 and 1969, what do we find? That the polarization between As-

23

similationism and Nationalism, for instance, is the expression of the divided self of the American Black man, the tensions of a hybrid personality. There is no need for a social explication of this fact when the Caliban-Prospero symbolism is so appropriate. For what is Caliban if not Prospero's son? Nowhere in the play does Shakespeare state that Prospero begot Caliban. The devil did it. Yet if there is this central meaning that Sycorax's dabbling in the black arts made her the bride of Lucifer (a notion which a tradition going back to the early Middle Ages would warrant), (7) it follows that Prospero, in becoming the devil's disciple through his own indulgence in witchcraft, is wedded to Sycorax. He is, then, as much as Lucifer, a paternal figure to Caliban. This is not stretching things too far, considering the hostility existing between the two when we first meet them. Is it just because of Prospero's usurpation, or Caliban's foul-mouthedness? If so, how can we explain this somewhat belated hostility, for Caliban did trust Prospero? One may reply that this is exactly the point: Caliban, as he himself indicates, naively confided in Prospero who, consequently, took over the island. The troubling question remains. Prospero did not always view Caliban as an object of disgust. For why go through the pains of teaching him language, educating him, in a manner similar to Prospero's attentions toward his legitimate daughter, Miranda? It is possible to surmise that some change of attitude, similar to that manifested so explicitly in the Epilogue, took place. This change would be in keeping with the fundamental duality, Prospero's own ambivalence discussed earlier. What we have in the hostile confrontation, in one of the first scenes of the play, is Prospero's sensing of himself, of *his* sin in Caliban. In the dark, mysterious figure, the metropolitan man sees the result of his illegitimate practice in the forbidden arts. Prospero being what he is early in the play, a man infatuated with a partial view of himself, such an explanation does not seem invalid. Neither is it in the light of his pure and chaste daughter, Miranda. Is not the thought of possible compounding of *his* own sin, now through incest, behind his charge that Caliban tried to seduce Miranda?

If Prospero is Caliban's father, and Caliban Prospero's son, one can interpret Shakespeare's meaning in quite a different light. In a deep sense the playwright is showing the inter-relationship between beings, through his favourite family complex. No matter how denied, refused, or condemned, human kinship is, as in a troubled family, fraught with misunderstanding but ineluctable. Have we been led far afield from the American scene?

In the Black's uprootment from Africa, the severance of tribal and family ties, in the operation of slavery where the plantation owner indulged in a transplanted medieval *droit de seigneur*, enjoying sexual dalliances whose existence (and the existence of the off-spring) he and his society's outlook absolutely denied; in, briefly, the increasing divorce between the conscious and the repressed self, we have, underneath the whole American divorce between Black and White a repetition of the Caliban-Prospero

24

problem. Even the fantasy level germane to Shakespeare's spectacle is appropriate. The misunderstanding between the races in America, as pointed out in the writings of Ellison, Jones, Kelley and others, is steeped in a never-never realm; it is the result of a *will* to fantasy because it is rooted in denial.

It remains to be seen whether the American Prospero will come to a point in his experience where he is willing, like his prototype, to accept himself fully. His initial reaction, nonetheless, when confronted with the reflection of himself in the figure of darkness, is one of recoil and denial. At this juncture appears the first dominant theme in the Black American novel. From Caliban's viewpoint we are offered the 'other' truth of Prospero's culture through the Black man's trials with his self.

1 For the general background of Black American culture and the novel, see Margaret Just Butcher, *The Negro in American Culture*, pp.132-148; Addison Gayle Jr, "Cultural Hegemony: The Southern White Writer and American Letters", *Amistad*, pp.1-24; Robert A. Bone, *The Negro Novel in America*, pp.11-28.

2 Bone, p.5.

3 Bone, pp.95-96. For corroboration of this negative view by the Black bourgeoisie, see Seymour L. Gross, "Stereotype to Archetype", in *Images of the Negro in American Literature*, pp.14-15.

4 Bone, p.171.

5 Herbert Hill, ed., *Anger and Beyond*, p.xv; see also Saunders Redding, "The Negro Writer and his Relationship to his Roots", in *The American Negro Writer and his Roots*. Edward Margolies, *Native Sons, A Critical Study of Twentieth-Century Negro American Authors*. David Littlejohn, *Black on White: A Critical Survey of Writings by American Negroes*.

6 I am referring, of course, to Ellison's debate with Irving Howe, see Howe's "Black Boys and Native Sons", in *Dissent*, reprinted in his collection of essays, *A World More Attractive*; and "The World and the Jug", the product of two separate articles, first published in *The New Leader*, reprinted in Ralph Ellison's book of essays, *Shadow and Act*.

7 And even earlier, see Auguste Viatte, *Les Sources Occultes du Romanticisme*, p.19.

# QUEBEC CULTURE

# AND THE NOVEL

In 1959, Maurice LeNoblèt Duplessis died. The death of this politician who had dominated Quebec's political life for three decades — signaled the end of an era. For Duplessis was the sour incarnation of a long-standing tradition, the alliance between the Church and the State, in terms of which he could brag of having bishops eating from his hands. A bachelor who shunned the claims of the flesh, molded by his rural origins, he held intellectuals, artists and plain educated people in utter contempt. Duplessis clung to quasi-mystical beliefs in the virtues of the past while he conceded the present of industrialization and technology to the American trusts and corporations that owned the economy of his province. When Duplessis died in Quebec's northern wilderness, while visiting the installations of one of those combines whose rights for exploitation of iron ore were obtained for a pittance, his was the ironical death of a King, a *Roi Nègre*. (1)

Knowing his record, intellectuals and artists, who had formulated their dissent throughout Duplessis' rule in the pages of *Le Devoir* and *Cité Libre* did not cry "Vive le Roi" but thought joyfully nonetheless that their fight against obscurantism had been rewarded. (2) Now, it was felt, Quebec would open its windows to the world. But this latter task would befall a new generation and their vision would not be quite the same as their liberal elders'.

The new generation, grouped around little magazines such as *Liberté*, *Parti Pris* and the publishing cooperative Hexagone, (3) informed by the revised Marxism of the Third World decolonization movement and its literature of revolt, explained the Duplessis phenomenon not as a cause but as an effect of a larger cause: the historical French-Canadian state of dispossession and alienation. Inspired by the coming-to-independence of

*from the film* Quebec Duplessis, et Après *by Denys Arcand (N.F.B.)*

former colonies (17 African countries in the span of 1960 alone, as one writer exclaims in wonder), (4) the painful consciousness of a sorry state gave birth to the Separatist movement. Telescoped into the extreme violence of the F.L.Q. terrorists, the post-Duplessis social and intellectual effervescence culminated in the Fall 1970 murder of a Quebec Cabinet member, Pierre Laporte (a man who in the fifties stood as a symbol of rebellion against Duplessis).

Within such a turbulent context contemporary French-Canadian literature arises. The radical social critics of *Parti Pris*, *Liberté* and Hexagone are also the creative writers who self-consciously proclaim the theme of *le pays*, through the imperative of *la parole* of the committed (*engagé*) artist. By *le pays* is meant the actual land to be observed, investigated (lucidly and not mythicized religiously as before), in order to be celebrated and embraced because, in its alienation and tradition, pitifulness and warmth, it *is* Quebec, "Terre-Québec", to use Paul Chamberland's term, binding the artist and his people. *La parole* is the power of the writer's (more often that not the poet's) angry, prophetic and lyrical word whose vitality is to symbolically liberate the land. This program entails a definite attitude on the part of the writer who must find his inspiration not in individual preoccupations and anxieties but in others, in the people, since it is believed no preoccupation or problem can be limited to the individual. Because of the historical perspective at work (Marxist to be sure), it is argued that the collective experience of the French Canadian explains the malaise and psychological unrest that have historically plagued the writer. By opening himself to *le pays*, by committing himself to the investigation and celebration of the land, the artist creates an art that is aesthetically and socially redeeming.

This three-point programme seems to echo another one. Césaire's *Cahier d'un Retour au Pays Natal* effectively articulates the same three points. The *pays* for Césaire is alienated and dispossessed: this is the vision of "home" presented at the outset of the poem while the narrator is in Paris considering a possible return to Martinique: "... les Antilles qui ont faim, les Antilles grêlées de petite vérole, les Antilles dynamitées d'alcool, échouées dans la boue de cette baie, dans la poussière de cette ville sinistrement échouées." (p.26) Because this ambient dispossession is paradigmatic of the poet's own sense of alienation (symbolized namely in the powerful Parisian subway scene: "Un nègre comique et laid et des femmes derrière moi ricanaient en le regardant. ... J'arborai un grand sourire complice ... Ma lâcheté retrouvée" p.65) he comes to the awareness that the land is to be embraced and affirmed as a first step in a journey toward self-understanding. Hence, "Je réclame pour ma face la louange éclatante du crachat." (p.65)

As an existential repossession of self takes place through the recognition of his and his people's actual situation, the poet is now able to use "*la parole*", the liberating power of the word auguring of the liberation of the land. A third dialectical stage of assertion, self-articulation, is reached and it explodes in lyrical expression symbolic of the new-found liberated individual and collective self. Says Césaire:

> que je m'exige bêcheur de cette unique race
> que ce que je veux
> c'est pour
> ..................
> la sommer libre enfin
> de produire de son intimité close
> la succulence des fruits    (p.75)

But the poet in order to reach this third stage has to be committed to his task, to recognize himself through others; for without this engagement the artist is stifled much like the total inertia of land, town, people represented in the first part of *Le Cahier*. The imperative of commitment occurs in the secondary act of consciousness of Césaire's *Cahier*, as the poet effectively resolves to return home:

> "Ma bouche sera la bouche des malheurs qui n'ont point de bouche, ma voix, la liberté de celles qui s'affaissent au cachot du désespoir."
> Et venant je me dirais à moi-même:
> "Et surtout mon corps aussi bien que mon âme, gardez-vous de vous croiser les bras en l'attitude stérile du spectateur, car la vie n'est pas un spectacle, car une mer de douleurs n'est pas un proscenium, car un homme qui crie n'est pas un ours qui danse."
> (p.42)

Admittedly, other poets of the Négritude movement, Jacques Roumain, David Diop, René Dépestre (*not* Senghor, since his is a deeply religious poetry of reconciliation and harmony with the dead and the ancestors) echo in the strident note of revolt one finds in the poetry of Gaston Miron, Paul Chamberland and Jacques Brault. (5) But the task artfully delineated by Césaire first in 1939 (and revised for the final 1956 version, probably the one read by the Quebec poets) is perhaps the seminal influence at work in the literature of the sixties in Quebec. Notwithstanding the internal evidence in his poetry, Paul Chamberland has in an essay paid homage to this influence:

> J'accomplis ce que Césaire appelle un "retour au pays natal".
> C'est alors que s'inaugure une étrange mais vitale conjugaison: celle qui enferme le *je* et le *nous* en un seul mouvement. Le retour

au pays natal, à l'homme réel, au pays réel, impose deux attitudes rigoureusement liées: 1- *je* me reconnais tel que je suis, tel que la *situation* m'a fait,.... 2- je *nous* reconnais tels que nous sommes, je prends acte de notre vie, de notre misère, de notre malheur.... (6)

Moreover, like Négritude, the literature of Quebec is one of "exile". (7) Before the sixties' claim to *le pays*, a number of literary and cultural movements had tried to come to grips with this consciousness of exile. The ambiguities, paradoxes and ironies that emerged as a result are worth surveying.

In the 1860's, the foremost poet of the *Mouvement Littéraire de Québec*, Octave Crémazie, had bemoaned the plight of writers having to live in a society of grocers and consequently took his leave for France where he died. (8) But the movement's stalwart, l'Abbé Casgrain, prevailed, assigning to religion and mystical concepts of the land, language and family (all of which will be later called the Messianic mystique) the mode for survival the French-Canadian writer must celebrate. *L'Ecole du Terroir* is thus given birth and dominates the literary output up to the Second World War. In the 1900's a counterpart to the Quebec City movement is founded, *L'Ecole Littéraire de Montréal*, an outgrowth of the nineteenth-century Institut Canadien, a free-thinking, anti-clerical group attuned to the heritage of the French Encyclopédistes (and whose membership include some of the leaders of the ill-fated Patriots' Rebellion). (9) Inasmuch as the Institut was composed of an élite, with no real ties with the people, and certainly fought by the dominant clergy, its influence was not deeply felt. The *Ecole Littéraire de Montréal* knows a similar fate. One great poet emerges from its fold of *beaux parleurs*, Emile Nelligan, who, writing from a tortured romantic vision, succumbs at the age of twenty to the dangers of insanity, as already suggested in the imagery and symbolism of his most famous poem, "Le Vaisseau d'Or". From Nelligan on to St-Denys Garneau, Paul Morin, René Chopin, Alain Grandbois and Anne Hébert there are basically two poles in French-Canadian poetry: dark solitary ruminations and escape from the land. (10) Garneau and Hébert, first cousins, and descendants of colonial *seigneurs*, extend Nelligan's painful vision and retreat in a closed private world where the joys and innocence of lost childhood are contrasted with an anguishing present. Garneau ends up by more or less killing himself; Hébert seems to have resolved her anxieties by claiming *le pays* and *la parole* (one of the first Quebec poets to do so) but like Grandbois, Morin, Chopin and other poets, the solution for her seems to lie in departing from the land of exile and returning to France.

From the late 1930's to the early 1950's a movement grouping for the first time novelists and essayists is organized: *La Relève* named after a review, and its successor, *La Nouvelle Relève*, both put out by Roger Charbonneau, Jean Le Moyne and Robert Elie. Whatever were the preoc-

31

cupations of that group (with which St-Denys Garneau collaborated and from whose ranks are to be found his most ardent admirers, e.g. Jean Le Moyne), they really had little to do with Quebec. Theirs were attuned to the philosophy of Emmanuel Mounier (whose review *Esprit* was the bible of the group) and Jacques Maritain, which emphasized the supremacy of Christian humanism and the cult of the person, oblivious, of course, to the larger issues of the tribe. As could be expected, this movement's influence will only extend to its limited group of members. Living at a time when the land was bankrupted by the likes of Duplessis and an omnipotent Jansenistic clergy (in 1954 the movie *Luther* was banned from showing in Montreal; in 1959 an interview with Jean-Paul Sartre and Simone de Beauvoir was not shown on the state television network, Radio-Canada, because of Cardinal Léger's disapproval, etc.), these intellectuals were contemplating the spiritual wealth of the individual soul.

Yet, at least one known significant pre-1960 artistic movement tried to confront the actual cultural situation of Quebec society: the *Mouvement des Automatistes* comprised mainly of painters and sculptors such as J.P. Riopelle, J.P. Mousseau, M. Ferron and led by Paul-Emile Borduas. This movement is famous for its 1948 Manifesto, *Refus Global*: a piece of writing which amounted to the principal signatories' dismissal from their positions at state-supported art schools in Montreal, and little else. But in retrospect, the *Refus* seems to foreshadow at time contemporary radicalism. Attacking the traditional shibboleths of fear of the English-speaking world, of modern technology, of avant-gardism whether in the arts or in ideologies, decrying what was felt to be a regressive view of man and society due to extreme clericalization ("Petit peuple serré de près aux soutanes restées les seules dépositaires de la foi, du savoir, de la vérité et de la richesse nationale. Tenu à l'écart de l'évolution universelle de la pensée..."), (11) the manifesto went on to call for:

> Rompre définitivement avec toutes les habitudes de la société, se désolidariser de son esprit utilitaire. Refus d'être sciemment au-dessus de nos possibilités psychiques et physiques. Refus de fermer les yeux sur les vices, les duperies perpétrées sous le couvert du savoir, du service rendu, de la reconnaissance due.
> ...Refus de se taire... ...Refus de toute INTENTION, arme néfaste de la RAISON, ...
> PLACE A LA MAGIE! PLACE AUX MYSTERES OB-JECTIFS! (12)

And it is at this level of affirmation, particularly in the last sentence, that the Automatistes show their true colours, or their limitations. After a courageous denunciation of their society's ills, the only alternative proposed is that of Surrealism. (Indeed, *Automatisme* for the one poet of the group,

32

Claude Gauvreau, means literally the experience in poetic form and unmediated spontaneous verbilization led by Desnos, Breton and others in the twenties and thirties in France.) Further, there is a contempt for Reason, and one suspects the material order which is not far from the one historically borne by the Church. Magic, whether it is the Roman Church's or Breton's, specifically with respect to French-Canadian society, is still an opiate. So, the one pre-1960 literary and artistic movement that correctly diagnosed the problems of French-Canadian society petered out on the altar of another form of cultism instead of articulating an aesthetic relevant to the society. Borduas died in Paris in 1960, a heartbroken man in exile. The most renowned of the original signatories, Jean-Paul Riopelle, has been living in France for a number of decades and rarely comes back to his native land.

The purpose of this introductory overview is to point out how indeed the fact of exile—as a pervasive sense of spiritual malaise—is a dominant experience against which French-Canadian culture and literature have to be tested. In the discussion that follows, it is therefore imperative to start with the historic cause of this situation, to analyze the consequent cultural conditioning and to observe its reflection in the novel, before resuming the general theoretical discussion regarding the significance of Calibanic culture.

The basic historic trauma in the French-Canadian experience in North America is the termination, in 1760, of French rule in a country that had been named New France. Two resultant attitudes are usually assigned to this termination: one is that the French Canadian feels he was defeated, and that he is part of a "conquered people"; and the second is a sense of abandonment by the mother-country, France. As Mason Wade, the foremost American authority on Quebec history, says:

> An important part of the French Canadian's special outlook
> arises from his consciousness of belonging to a conquered, or at
> least a minority people. He may deny this, and is sure to protest
> that his ancestors were abandoned by the French rather than con-
> quered by the English, whenever some arrogant "Anglo-Saxon"
> prefaces a denial of French-Canadian claims with: "After all, we
> conquered you." But the state of mind, conscious or unconscious,
> is still there, for the French Canadian is encircled by an English-
> speaking world which clashes with his own in many respects, and
> he is constantly reminded that it was not ever thus. (13)

Although Edmund Wilson emphasizes the first of the two ingrained attitudes ("French Canada has never got over the battle of the Plains of Abraham — in which, one French Canadian said to me, 'we are told that we

33

were defeated' "), (14) both are primal for understanding the French Canadian psyche. They motivate the post-Conquest Messianic ethos the French Canadian felt he had to proclaim in order to survive on a continent where he was now left to himself. From 1760 until well into the twentieth century, the land, the family, religion, language, all the traditional values left by the Ancien Régime were clung to as defenses. They became so entrenched as to constitute a particular ethos through which the defensive attitude of the post-Conquest culture is proclaimed as a necessary atonement for these, the "chosen people" who were by dint of the example of their spiritual superiority to serve as a beacon in the Anglo-Saxon materialist wilderness of North America. L'Abbé Casgrain, one of the first clerical celebrants of the Messianic mystique, writes:

> Quelle action la Providence nous réserve-t-elle en Amérique? Quel rôle nous appelle-t-elle à y exercer? Représentants de la race latine en face de l'élément anglo-saxon, dont l'expansion excessive, l'influence anormale doivent être balancées, de même qu'en Europe, pour le progrès de la civilisation, notre mission et celle des sociétés de même origine que nous, éparses sur ce continent, est d'y mettre un contrepoids en réunissant nos forces, d'opposer au positivisme anglo-américain, à ses instincts matérialistes, à son égoisme grossier, les tendances les plus élevées, qui sont l'apanage des races latines, une supériorité incontestée dans l'ordre moral et dans le domaine de la pensée. (15)

To l'Abbé Groulx, a student of Gobineau, Le Bon, and other racialist thinkers of the late nineteenth century and, perhaps, the most influential historiographer of French Canada until his death in 1968, this mystique is "la race". (16)

Skeptics who had benefited otherwise from their studies abroad took a different view of this lifestyle, particularly since, as early as World War I, heresy was on the rise in the face of the non-productivity of farm life and the urban call of new values. Michel Brunet, the historian, sees *le messianisme* as: "Un faux spiritualisme... On confondit pauvreté et esprit de pauvreté, renoncement volontaire et privations imposées par les circonstances. Au lieu d'apprendre à dominer les biens matériels afin de les mettre au service d'un idéal, la jeunesse reçut l'ordre de mépriser la richesse." (17) More denunciatory, Pierre Elliott Trudeau considers that ethos to be a misanthropic defense mechanism built as a result of fear to protect and comfort a people, who, after 1760, could not or would not face up to the secular order now identified with foreigners of a different language and religion:

> Pour un peuple vaincu, occupé, décapité, évincé du domaine commercial, refoulé hors des villes, réduit peu à peu en minorité,

*from* Québec-Presse *Archives*

et diminué en influence dans un pays qu'il avait pourtant découvert, exploré et colonisé, il n'existait pas plusieurs attitudes d'esprit qui puissent lui permettre de préserver ce par quoi il était lui-même. Ce peuple se créa un système de sécurité, mais qui en s'hypertrophiant lui fit attacher un prix parfois démesuré à tout ce qui le distinguait d'autrui, et considérer avec hostilité tout changement (fût-ce un progrès) qui lui était proposé de l'extérieur. (18)

How has such a trauma affected literature, particularly the genre of the novel? Jean-Charles Falardeau, a sociological critic, considers that French-Canadian novelists: "Consciemment ou inconsciemment — sont des redresseurs de torts. Soit qu'ils acceptent ou qu'ils rejettent leur société, soit qu'ils la condamnent ou qu'ils ambitionnent de la transformer, ils expriment à son sujet un voeu global." (19) This redress of wrongs takes place in three stages. The first, and most inconsequential, from 1860 to 1900, is the period of the historical novel, which follows in the wake of the impetus given to the budding French-Canadian literature by the publication of François-Xavier Garneau's *Histoire du Canada*. The disciples of Garneau, grouped around the poet Octave Crémazie and l'abbé Casgrain in the *Mouvement Littéraire de Québec*, saw in that *Histoire* a reservoir for protest (the *Histoire* itself was initially conceived as a protest against Lord Durham's assertion in his famous Report that the French Canadians had no history) from which they would draw themes and concerns essential to the indigenous literature. Thereafter Joseph Marmette, Phillippe Aubert de Gaspé, even Robert de Roquebrune (who chronologically is not of that period but writes in that genre in the 1920's) wrote historical novels, where in fact they rewrote history, emphasizing and aggrandizing noble exploits of the colonial period while generally omitting the unhappy events leading to the Conquest.

Gilles Marcotte has pointed out the typical ploy of the genre. In de Boucherville's *Une de perdue, deux de trouvées* (1864) and Aubert de Gaspé's *Les Anciens Canadiens* (1864), the indignities of the Conquest are melodramatically avenged by a French-Canadian girl who refuses to marry an 'Anglo-Saxon' on the grounds, as Gaspé's heroine points out, that the blood which was shed fighting the man's compatriots cannot be violated by contracting marriage with the "oppressor", lest everything be in vain! (20)

The second stage, from 1900 to 1940, is that of the rise and fall of the Messianic mystique. It is characterized by the affirmation of a rural-based way of life conveyed in the *romans du terroir* of Louis Hémon, Félix-Antoine Savard, Harry Bernard, Claude-Henri Grignon and Damase Potvin, as well as by its decline and fall, such as in *Trente Arpents*. The third stage, from 1940 to present day, expresses the process of revolt and self-articulation resulting from the shift in values occasioned by modern urban-industrial contingencies.

These divisions follow closely enough those enunciated by a variety of critics. Marcel Rioux, a University of Montreal sociologist, calls the first stage, from 1760 to 1935, "idéologies de survivance nationale"; the second, from 1935 to 1950, "rejet des premières idéologies, tentatives d'objectivation"; and the third, from 1950 to our day, "idéologies de contestation et recherches d'identité". (21) J.S. Tassie is somewhat more pertinent with his concept of the alliance between the development of French Canada and the latter's historical evolution. He sees the first stage as "la période coloniale qui se termine par la conquête anglaise," where there is no indigenous literature to speak of, except the later writings of the 'historical' school reflecting that period. He identifies the second stage as "la période de stabilisation dans une société homogène", reflected in literature by the *Ecole du terroir*. The last stage is that of "la période moderne de transformation", identified with *le roman citadin*. (22) What is lacking here is a chronological division. One has to interpret, rather than read explicitly, that the second period goes from 1760 or thereabouts to the 1920's. And the latter period from the 1920's to present. Gérard Tougas, judging from the divisions of his *Histoire de la Littérature Canadienne-Française,* considers four stages: "L'âge de Garneau (1845-1865)": "Vers la création d'une tradition littéraire (1865-1899)"; "L'Epoque Moderne (1900-1939)"; and "L'Epoque Contemporaine (1939- )." (23) Since Tougas is not primarily concerned with the evolution of the novel (but with that of French-Canadian literature as a whole) one should not take him to task for his second division which includes only one novelist: Laure Conan. Gilles Marcotte, on the other hand, restates the traditional three categories. The first, from the beginnings to 1920, he reviews very fast, unable to see any validity to the novel of that period (the novel is "un enfant malvenu"). In the second category, from 1920 to 1938, in light of the fact that "le roman se rapproche décisivement de la réalité," Marcotte finds that a process of "personalization" occurs wherein as the novel is rooted in the concrete Quebec environment it finds its real beginnings. The third, from 1938 to present day, is characterized by "l'observation". Marcotte believes that in that period a literary revolution is brought about by Lemelin, Ringuet, Roy, who clinically observe and describe the people, the milieu, the man, particular to Quebec. (24)

In the divisions of these critics we find the common cleavage of the rural and the urban scene. The former propounds the traditional values associated with the land, religion, and family. The latter, the urban scene, is a rejection of the Messianic mystique resulting from the break-up of the rural order. This break-up begins in the 1920's after the First World War, gains momentum during the Second, and comes to full emergence in the late fifties and continues to this day. As the industrialization process takes place, the migration to the cities accelerates. So that by the early 1940's, during the War (which more than anything else undermined the "Old Order" as the

37

war industries compelled a significant migration to urban centres), with the emergence of novelists such as Lemelin, Roy, and Guèvremont, the French-Canadian outlook can no longer be situated in a bucolic set-up. This fundamental cleavage between the rural and the urban scene constitutes the two essential poles in our analysis of this Calibanic literature.

1 For a view of Duplessis, the man and the populist, demagogic politician, see Pierre Laporte's *Le Vrai Visage de Duplessis*; for a caustic courageous denunciation of the quagmire in which his alliance with the Church kept public education and intellectual life for decades, by a Christian Brother who will then be exiled in Europe by his superiors, see Jean-Paul Desbiens' *Les Insolences du Frère Untel*; for the story of Duplessis' collusion with the reactionary segment of the Church, in particular his successful engineering of the Archbishop of Montreal's resignation, in the early fifties because Mgr Charbonneau had dared to defend the rights of asbestos mine workers in their 1949 epoch-making strike, see Renaude Lapointe's *L'Histoire Bouleversante de Mgr Charbonneau,* particularly pp.11-34, 60-70; finally, for an analysis of the intellectual and economic implications, not to say the social, of that 1949 strike, when Duplessis' decision to use the Quebec State Police (the infamous "Police Provinciale") as his personal goon squad to break up the strike forced a number of intellectuals and public figures to take sides and to actively manifest an anti-Duplessis commitment, see Pierre Elliott Trudeau's *La Grève de l'Amiante,* particularly Trudeau's chapter dealing with the socio-intellectual implications, "La Province de Québec au Moment de la Grève", pp.3-90.

2 *Le Devoir* is a small-circulation but very influential daily newspaper founded around 1910 by Henri Bourassa, a fiery nationalist politician. From its beginnings as more or less an organ for a certain historical school of politicians, it has over the years, and particularly under Duplessis, stood as the conscience of the liberal intellectual community in Quebec. Pierre Laporte, the assassinated Minister of Labour, before going into politics, served as its Quebec City and parliamentary correspondent for a number of years. Indeed his aforementioned book (see previous footnote) relates how Duplessis, in the mid-fifties, unable to contain his anger at *Le Devoir* and its correspondent's damaging reports on his feudal tactics, had Laporte banished from his presence; see the chapter "Maurice Duplessis et les Journalistes", pp.125-138. *Cité Libre* was a monthly intellectual review founded by Pierre Elliott Trudeau, Jacques Hébert, Pierre Dansereau and other committed lawyers, doctors, professors, et al. in 1950 to maintain an outlet

for the fight against Duplessis, dramatically spurred by the Asbestos (an Eastern Townships' town named after the main natural resource of the region) strike. One cannot emphasize enough how *Le Devoir* and *Cité Libre* by being the only voices for the anti-Duplessis forces during the years of "la grande peur" (see Desbiens' book, pp.66-67) when everyone else trembled under the yoke of "Le Cheuf ", deserved their characterization as symbols of resistance which could rightly claim victory when Duplessis died and a sorry era disappeared along with him. *Cité Libre*, in the post-Duplessis years, having lost its initial avocation, found a new one in focusing against the rise of separatism. This new quest is illustrated by such doom-sounding articles as Trudeau's "La Nouvelle Trahison des Clercs," or "Les Séparatistes: Des Contre-Révolutionnaires". The attack is, of course, directed against a younger intellectual generation and its outlets, *Liberté, Parti Pris.* After protracted internecine fights (Pierre Vallières [the would-be Fanon of Quebec if we are to believe some reviews of his autobiography, *Nègres Blancs d'Amèrique*], an avowed separatist "revolutionary", had, in 1964-65, managed to take over *Cité Libre's* editorship, much to the later dismay of Trudeau and others when they read his articles), and Trudeau's and Gérard Pelletier's entry into federal politics, in 1965, the review folded.

3  *Liberté*, a review more concerned with the arts than political engagement, grouped young novelists, poets and film-makers such as Jacques Godbout, Jean-Guy Pilon, P.M. Lapointe, Hubert Aquin, Yves Préfontaine, in 1958. In the mid-sixties, following some of its leaders' involvement in Third World literature (Godbout, Aquin, Préfontaine) and separatist effervescence in Quebec, it along with *Parti Pris*' ideological bent, gave impetus to "le Pays" celebration. *Parti Pris*, founded in 1963 by a number of students at the University of Montreal doing graduate studies in philosophy and political science — some of whom had started publishing creatively (Paul Chamberland, Jean-Marc Piotte, Pierre Maheu, André Major, Laurent Girouard and others) — proclaimed the need of Third World-like revolution, along the lines articulated by Frantz Fanon, Albert Memmi and the earlier writings of Marx and Lenin, so as to create a "Free, Secular and Socialist" Quebec. It folded in 1968 when the social climate forced a commitment in revolutionary deeds rather than words. Interestingly, none of *Parti Pris*' writers followed up, leaving what they had sown to be reaped by proletarian types such as Vallières, the Rose brothers and others who had a somewhat better perception, stemming from their lower-class origins, of the reality the writers — all issued from the bourgeoisie, as Vallières says in his autobiography —

had been trying to change through verbal commitment ("la parole"). Hexagone, a publishing cooperative founded in 1958 by the poet Gaston Miron, Louis Portugais, Gilles Carle (the last two film-makers) and others is important for its publication of a type of poetry, particularly Miron's, that depicts the sense of alienation and dispossession which is the poet's because it is "le pays", giving birth thus to a cultural movement increasingly investigated in the little magazines of the mid-sixties, and creative literature as well.

4 Marcel Chaput, *Pourquoi je Suis Séparatiste*, p.18.

5 This is discussed in an article of mine, "Pays, Parole et Négritude", *Canadian Literature*, pp.58-63.

6 Paul Chamberland, "Dire ce que je Suis", *Parti Pris*, pp38-39. See also Pierre Vallières' *Nègres Blancs d'Amérique*, p.202, where he mentions his introduction to Césaire's work by Gaston Miron. Césaire's resounding speech at the 1956 Congress of Negro Writers and Artists (the very speech which so antagonized James Baldwin, see pp. 145-146, n. 9), "Culture et Colonisation" was reprinted in a 1963 issue of *Liberté*, pp.15-35. Yves Préfontaine, one of *Liberté*'s early editors, and a poet in his own right, is the author of a study of Négritude, *Quatre Figures Martiniquaises* [A. Césaire, E. Glissant, E. Yoyo, J. Sudelor].

7 A term which first appears critically, it would seem, in Gilles Marcotte's article, "Une Poésie d'Exil", *Canadian Literature*, pp.32-36.

8 See Michel Dassonville, pp.54-55.

9 The whole period of liberal intellectual thinking which rejected the Church and called for a revolution, and culminated in the 1837 rebellion, as well as its consequences for the rest of the nineteenth century is the subject of an important study by Joseph Costisella, *L'Esprit Révolutionnaire dans la Littérature Canadienne-Française de 1837 à la fin du XIX Siècle*.

10 See Gilles Marcotte's *Une Littérature qui se Fait*, pp.79-84.

11 Paul-Emile Borduas, *Refus Global*, p.1.

12 *Ibid.*, p.7.

13 Mason Wade, *The French Canadian Outlook*, p.14.

14 Edmund Wilson, *O Canada, An American's Notes on Canadian Culture*, p.69.

15 H.D. Casgrain, *Oeuvres Complètes*, p.370.

16 As shall be seen in the analysis of his novel, *L'Appel de la Race*.

17 Michel Brunet, *La Présence Anglaise et les Canadiens*, p.163.

18 Pierre Elliott Trudeau, *La Grève de l'Amiante*, pp.11-12.

19 Jean-Charles Falardeau, *Notre Société et son Roman*, p.11.

20 Marcotte, *Une Littérature qui se Fait*, p.15; see also Philippe Aubert de Gaspé, *Les Anciens Canadiens*, p.233. Says the

heroine: "Vous m'offensez, capitaine Archibald Cameron de Locheill! ... Est-ce lorsque la fumée s'élève encore de nos masures en ruine que vous m'offrez la main d'un des incendiaires? Ce serait une ironie bien cruelle que d'allumer le flambeau de l'hyménée aux cendres fumantes de ma malheureuse patrie! ... jamais une d'Haberville ne consentira à une telle humiliation."

21 Marcel Rioux, "Aliénation Culturelle et Roman Canadien", *Recherches Sociographiques*, p.145.
22 J.S. Tassie, "La Société à travers le Roman Canadien-Français", *Archives des Lettres Canadiennes*, pp.154-157.
23 Gérard Tougas, *Histoire de la Littérature Canadienne-Française*, pp.311-312.
24 Marcotte, *Ibid.*, pp.12-34.

THE

# HYBRID BLACK

In the first three novels of this analysis, *Clotel, House Behind the Cedars,* and *The Autobiography of an Ex-Coloured Man,* we have the depiction of a dilemma with which an American of African ancestry has to live. How to reconcile one's Americanness, fully a participant in the American Dream of pursuit of happiness through material success, with one's Africanness, which has to do with one's colour that is objected to? How to live with one's sense of self when this sense is in constant danger of being thwarted by the Other's surface view? This dilemma has been caught in a nutshell by Frantz Fanon: "Quand on m'aime, on me dit que c'est malgré ma couleur. Quand on me déteste, on ajoute que ce n'est pas à cause de ma couleur... Ici ou là, je suis prisonnier du cercle infernal." (1)

Because in the early novel, up to the 1920's, we are dealing with mixed-blood Americans, called mulattos, quarteroons, octoroons and quadroons who are the writers as well as the characters of Black fiction, this "infernal circle" takes the form of tragedy. In *Clotel,* and others, the tragedy stems from the characters' (preferably women) proximity to Caucasian physical criteria and the consequent rejection they suffer upon discovery of Black blood in their ancestry. Thus appears the theme of the "tragic mulatto" in American letters, which is really, and literally, romantic melodrama complete with recourse to heartbreaks and tears.

*Clotel* (1853), is hardly a classic novel; evidently, it cannot be evaluated against the formal standards used when dealing with the work of an Henry James or a Gustave Flaubert. It owes its form, rather, to the tradition of the slave narratives, and its intent to the Abolitionist movement. Written by a man who really did escape from slavery, and later earned a living lecturing to abolitionist audiences in the northern United States and Europe, this novel is important from an historical point of view.

43

Central to the slight fictional drama is the recourse to the reader's emotions better to render the horror of slavery. This pathos, which Brown uses after a tradition popularized by Harriet Beecher Stowe's *Uncle Tom's Cabin*, relies on the device of presenting characters, preferably interrelated, that are seemingly Caucasians but who, because of their partial African ancestry, find themselves put into bondage or relegated to the level of the Blacks. It has to do with a fundamental ambiguity, both on the part of the characters and on that of the overall society which rejects them. But the authors of such melodramas are not interested, at this early stage, in investigating the metaphysical and psychological depths of such a situation. Unable to accept their ostracization — especially when it is alleged, as in *Clotel*, that the heroine of the same name has been fathered by no less a person than Thomas Jefferson, slave master and former President of the U.S. — the mulatto characters suffer a tragic end, bitterly lamenting the vagaries of Fortune and the ways of men. Death by unnatural cause, suicide to be specific, is common fare.

Here is the prototypical description of the mixed-blood female, the very unrestraint in authorial presence (the author being, more often than not, himself of mixed-blood) serving as harbinger of woes to come:

> There she stood, with a complexion as white as most of those who were waiting with a wish to become her purchasers; her features as finely defined as any of her sex of pure Anglo-Saxon; her long black wavy hair done up in the neatest manner; her form tall and graceful, and her whole appearance indicating one superior to her position. (p.42)

It is significant to note the emphasis on colour, features, hair texture, demeanour, all that can be *seen*, and that which should count, supposedly, as opposed to the genetic factor, the *unseen*, which tips the scale against the visual evidence.

The same technique is used in Charles Waddell Chesnutt's *The House Behind the Cedars* (1900), a romance set during Reconstruction in the South. The plot is about a girl's attempt at following in her brother's footsteps, that is, in successfully "passing" for Caucasian. She succeeds for a while under her brother's guidance. However, her Southern gentleman lover of the upper class is informed of her antecedents on the eve of their marriage. He breaks off their engagement and she, unable to withstand the pressures of both Black and White worlds, dies of pneumonia, incurred, oddly enough, while hiding under a rainstorm in the forest at night from White and Black suitors.

The tragic, or melodramatic, temper is sustained by comments on the lady's physical beauty (a character is speaking):

But as I was saying, this girl is a beauty; I reckon we might guess where she got some of it, eh Judge? Human nature is human nature, but it's a d-d shame that a man should beget a child like that and leave it to live the life open for a Negro. If she had been born white, the young fellows would be tumbling over one another to get her. ...She has a very striking figure something on the Greek order, stately and slow-moving. She has the manners of a lady, too — a beautiful woman, if she is a nigger! (pp.102-103)

Obviously, such comments do not speak enough for themselves. The author does not hesitate, accordingly, to intervene, to dictate, as it were to the reader's sentiments:

The taint of black blood was the unpardonable sin, from the unmerited penalty of which there was no escape except by concealment. If there be a dainty reader of this tale who scorns a lie, and who writes the story of his life upon his sleeve for all the world to read, let him uncurl his scornful lip and come down from the pedestal of superior morality, to which assured position and wide opportunity have lifted him, and put himself in the place of Rena, and her brother, upon whom God had lavished his best gifts, and from whom society would have withheld all that made these gifts valuable. (p.116)

Another novel that pursues the dichotomy between the kinetic and the genetic is James Weldon Johnson's *Autobiography of an Ex-Coloured Man* (1912). It is an improvement in form and technique. (Certainly the apparent unconcern with form on the part of the early novelists must be correlated with the didacticism involved, the urgency to express their discontent.) Johnson's narrative concerns the growing years of a young mulatto in the North and in the South, his piano-playing as an adult in Harlem, his world-travelling with a rich Dorian Gray-like white decadent, his disenchantment with the Black world upon his return to America, and his subsequent "passing" and marriage with a White lady. This seems to be quite an order, but Johnson succeeds in making of this first-person narrative a convincing account of moral ambivalence, mainly because he is a much better writer than either Brown or Chesnutt, and much more sophisticated in his approach to the tragic theme.

The opening description of the central character (this time it is a boy) tells us we are in familiar territory:

I was accustomed to hear remarks about my beauty; but now for the first time, I became conscious of it and recognized it. I noticed the ivory whiteness of my skin, the beauty of my mouth,

45

the size and liquid darkness of my eyes, and how the long black
lashes that fringed and shaded them produced an effect that was
strangely fascinating even to me. I noticed the softness and glos-
siness of my dark hair that fell in waves over my temples, .... (p.17)

We do have to remind ourselves this is a boy speaking, and not Brown's
Clotel or Chesnutt's Rena; for the attitude toward colour, features, hair
texture is the same as in the preceding novels though, if not more extreme.
Yet, by invoking economic necessity and a humanistic legacy, by denouncing human absurdity, Johnson makes a good case for the right-to-be, the
authenticity, of a self-sufficient mulatto bourgeoisie. He even foreshadows
Ralph Ellison's "invisibility" concept when the disillusioned hero, back
from his European peregrinations, reflects:

> I argued that to forsake one's race to better one's condition
> was no less worthy an action than to forsake one's country for the
> same purpose. I finally made up my mind that I would neither dis-
> claim the black race nor claim the white race; but that I would
> change my name, raise a moustache, and let the world take me for
> what it would .... (p.190)

Tragedy, in the form of the mixed-blood's fatal attraction toward the
White world at the expense of negating his other heritage, has not been
forsaken, however. The rest of the book shows that Johnson's journey has
yet to be mapped out by Ellison. For, while Johnson carefully avoids to
state, in the above quotation, that the Narrator's opting out of all race is
indeed an opting into the White world, the Narrator's subsequent material
success, social standing, and his marriage take place within such a world. So
the conclusion of the narrative reveals the cost that had to be paid. Instead
of the melodramatic suicide favoured in the earlier novels, death here takes
its toll in the soul. Here is the remembered picture of connubial bliss: "I was
in constant fear that she [the wife] would discover in me some shortcoming
which she would unconsciously attribute to my blood rather than to a fail-
ing of human nature." (p.210) And there is the psychological sense of
security that "passing" should have assured:

> Sometimes it seems to me that I have never really been a
> Negro, that I have been only a privileged spectator of their inner
> life; at other times I feel that I have been a coward, a deserter, and I
> am possessed by a strange longing for my mother's people. ..., I
> cannot repress the thought that, after all, I have chosen the lesser
> part; that I have sold my birthright for a mess of pottage. (pp.210-
> 211)

In contrast to the preceding novelists, Johnson does not rely exclusively on pathos for effect; his technique is more subtle, allusive; it is even tainted with irony, as the two above quotations indicate when compared to other "tragic mulatto" endings. Ironically, again, the authorial presence that intrudes on the story, or the characters' motivation, is less felt here, and this undoubtedly shows Johnson's mastery over his material. But in the end, while Johnson's sensitive portrait of the alienated character of a mixed-blood indicates an undeniable mastery of form and intellectual maturity and sophistication, his novel is nonetheless webbed-in by a similar final sense of futility, as in *Clotel* and *The House Behind the Cedars*.

The "tragic mulatto" theme is the subject of numerous novels in the twenties and thirties. Nella Larsen, Jessie Fausset, Walter White, Wallace Thurman, to mention just a few, carry on the melodramatic tradition of the earlier period. (2) It would be innacurate, consequently, to say that this theme is exhausted at a particular moment considering the variations it undergoes. I have indicated some of the changes that could already be seen in Johnson's novel. Nowhere are their portents so well elaborated upon, both stylistically and intellectually, than in Jean Toomer's *Cane*, the best literary work produced by the Negro Renaissance.

*Cane* (1923), seems at first glance, to be an odd collection of short lyrical poems and stories. However, because of the lead story, "Kabnis", whose dominant concern orders the whole book, and because Toomer was also experimenting with form, *Cane*, like *Winesburg Ohio*, can be considered an experimental novel. "Kabnis" is predicated, like the works seen earlier, on the dilemma facing a number of mixed-blood characters at odds with their divided self, the biological form of the social division of the land. The story opens as they are brought back together in the South of their origins. The leading character is Kabnis, a schoolteacher, who returns home after experiencing the effects of "passing" in the North. He is introduced as an alienated person, a schizophrenic (from his very premises, we can already see how Toomer breaks with tradition: he starts with the mulatto's tragic state in order to go beyond.) Kabnis' divided self is referred to by another character, Lewis, and Toomer's highly poetic language depicts the "tragic mulatto's" predicament: "can't hold them, can you? Master; slave. Soil; and the over-arching heavens. Dusk; dawn. They fight and bastardize you. The sun tint of you cheeks, flame of the great season's multi-coloured leaves, tarnished, burned." (p.218)

Kabnis is alienated and a misfit not only because of the denial of blackness adopted in order to "pass" in the North, but mainly because of his education and outlook (he is a man of words, as opposed to senses, in the favourite Negro Renaissance antithesis). In the contrasting set of images and symbols used by Toomer, Kabnis emerges as a victim passively conscious of contradictions only a return to the native soil of the South can possibly solve:

47

*from the Schomburg Collection, N.Y.P.L.*

The form thats burned into my soul is some twisted awful thing that crept in from a dream, a godam nightmare, an wont stay
still unless I feed it. An it lives on words. Not beautiful words. God
Almighty no. Misshapen, split-gut, tortured, twisted words.
Layman was feedin it back then that day you thought I ran out
fearing things. White folks feed it cause their looks are words.
Niggers, black niggers feed it cause theyre evil an their looks are
words. Yaller niggers feed it. This whole damn bloated purple
country feeds it cause its goin down t hell in a holy avalanche of
words. (p.224)

Contrary to previous tragic mulattos, Kabnis senses the need for reconciliation with his Calibanness, with the dark, primitive, non-verbal world
materialized in the Southern landscape. An organic world which evokes
self-sufficiency and an elemental vitality whose sexual symbolism is the
sugar cane thrust in the feminine embrace of the earth:

Houses are shy girls whose eyes shine reticently upon the
dusk body of the street. Upon the gleaming limbs and asphalt
torso of a dreaming nigger. Shake your curled wool blossoms,
nigger. Open your liver lips to the lean, white spring. Stir the rootlife of a withered people. Call them from their houses and teach
them to dream. (p.104)

This passage reveals how the vitality of the dark world is stressed in the
arrangement of symbols (houses and street, civilization and the natural
world) that signals the relationship that must exist between Prospero's and
Caliban's world. The dark world of sensual nature, the unconscious, the
repressed self is the foundation for the light world of the conscious self. The
senses must be reunited with the spirit. Kabnis must reclaim his roots to escape from alienation incurred by claiming the house at the expense of the
street.

The traditional "tragic-mulatto" writers would rest their melodramas
precisely on this point, that the mixed-blood, by definition, cannot claim
roots of his own. Toomer momentously indicates the end of such ambivalence by assigning Kabnis' rootlife, indeed all rootlife, to the world of
nature or that of the dark self. This reconciliation takes place at the end of
the story in a highly allegorical scene where Kabnis descends into a hole, a
somewhat nether world of unknown forces, where Father John, an old blind
Black preacher, resides. Since this encounter relates directly to religious
beliefs, its detailed discussion will take place later in our analysis. Suffice it
to say now that the symbolic reunion between the mixed-blood and the
Black preacher is striking in its innovative aspect. Kabnis' final recognition
and acceptance in Father John of himself, his 'id', takes its dramatic im-

portance in the contrast which opposes such a stance to that of the preceding alienated mulattos: where this 'id', or the African ancestry used to be a negative source of denial upon which rested melodrama, now it is the end point of a journey toward consciousness, spiritual fulfillment. (That this journey antedates the Orphic quest central to the aesthetics of Négritude, and that we can already see with Toomer that the Black American experience and Négritude are symbiotically wedded — will become evident in a later chapter of this essay.)

The theme of the "tragic mulatto" insofar as it presents a profound historical ambiguity in Calibanic culture, ends with Toomer's resolution. Though, as mentioned earlier, a number of writers will continue to exploit this theme, the dilemma itself, defined as a situation begging for an affirmative choice, has ended. That is why exploitation is the word for works such as *Quicksand* and *Passing*. Contemporaneous with Toomer's resolution we have with W.E.B. DuBois, Claude McKay, Langston Hughes and others furthering the articulation of Calibanic values and mores not preoccupied with Prospero's acceptance or rejection. This cultural movement of self-assertion is obviously contrapuntal to the theme of hybridity: it is, in addition, a mature stance.

Significantly, starting with Ellison's *Invisible Man* and moving on to the later novels of Chester Himes and William Melvin Kelley, the early tragic tempo is subverted and turned into a comic or consummate ironic mode relying on the same preoccupations with biology and social structure as in the early works. In the three novels that shall be discussed presently the authorial presence is equally strongly felt; even if in Ellison's case it is by means of a first-person narrative, in Himes' by using the device of the omniscient author, and in Kelley's through fabulation. Yet the intent and purpose of such presence is totally different from that of the early novelists. Undoubtedly, all three authors are indebted to historical changes and to their literary precursors for the detachment that enables them to satirize so successfully. It is interesting, however, to note this shift in attitudes toward interracial sex which along with other themes constitutes an eloquent answer to the oft-heard question whether or not relations between Blacks and Whites in America, or their perceptions of each other, have improved since the Emancipation Act.

Chester Himes' *Pinktoes*, published in 1962, is, in setting, tempo, atmosphere and plot, rooted in the Harlem of the Negro Rennaissance. As such, the novel would be disturbingly anachronistic were it not for the fact that this turning to the past is contrived for satirical comment. It is quite sure that Himes, a young man in his teens at the height of the Negro Renaissance, could not have participated in it. But he has read on the period and, though an expatriate in Europe for a good number of years, he can recall with great gusto the festival that Harlem life was when the cake walk, rent parties, and primitivism were actively pursued.

50

*Pinktoes* is a comic novel that uses sex in a manner that in some quarters has been called Rabelaisian. (3) In dealing particularly with sex between the races, Himes conveys his understanding of hybridity in American culture. The figure of Mamie Mason, Harlem Madame, and her house, where a number of interracial parties are held, serve as nerve centres for the satire. Himes' humour, to be sure, is not refined nor subtle. But seen as a vehicle for authorial comment and, principally, in conjunction with the theme we have been pursuing, it is highly effective. The following passage gives the clue to Himes' intent:

> Joe's [Mamie's husband] big job, however was that of consultant on interracial relations for the national committee of a major political party. Mamie claimed this was the only reason she gave so many parties. Where could one consult better on interracial relations than at interracial parties where interracial relations became even more related, she contended. (p.73)

Parties where males and females of both races pair off in every conceivable combination (and the gallery of characters that come and go boggles the mind) fulfill that design. Satirizing the societal set-up where the cultures of Prospero and Caliban are kept apart, supposedly because they have nothing in common, Himes uses the historical fact, stemming from the Plantation system, of racial admixture to drive his point home. Perhaps in the antebellum era interracial sex was the sole privilege of the Plantation master. Now, with zest, and detachment, Himes shows how neither Prospero nor Caliban is right in claiming exclusivity or purity. Whites and Blacks in America have never been so together (and by extension their cultures) as in bed.

With Ralph Ellison and William Melvin Kelley there is the sobering and refining of slapstick into cultivated irony. Ellison's *Invisible Man* (1952) is, of course, a journey toward self-awareness, taking the nameless protagonist from the South to the North, from the main currents of the American Dream into the fold of the Communist party of the thirties, and finally into a conscious acceptance of invisibility. (Prospero will not acknowledge Caliban's existence. We see already in Ellison's key conceit, invisibility, the presence of irony: highly visible blackness that yet remains unseen: Prospero's conception of undifferentiated blackness which prevents the recognition of individuality.) This journey operates on two levels, the realistic and the surrealistic, as it represents a form of descent into hell. The hero's fate is meant to be, by accretion, both allegorical and symbolic. Allegorical, because the collective lot of the Black is embodied in the hero. The whole of the racial nightmare is experienced—in the South and in the North—in the rural set-up and in the ghetto of Harlem, in the hope that the Communist party represented for a time in the thirties, and in that of the

51

capitalist system with philanthropists of the Abolitionist tradition — within the industrial system as well as outside of it. In short, the allegory is meant to be total, so much so that the hero's journey into the world of invisibility parallels very much Christ's own journey into the world of man. Both voluntarily let themselves be destroyed, both overcome their physical destruction with a spiritual belief (religious for Christ, existential morality for the invisible man), and, finally, both promise to be reborn and to come back into the world of the living at the opportune moment. The journey, second, is symbolic because it is in fact Caliban's destiny. The unfolding of events in the story is almost a systematic recapitulation of Caliban's striving to penetrate Prospero's culture, only to be rebuffed or deceived, in Shakespeare's play. But there is more, the ending in the conscious acceptance of self reiterates Kabnis' quest in terms of human universality, in a humanism which undoubtedly places Ellison next to Camus, Beckett, Sartre and other great existential writers.

Upon graduation from high school, Ellison's hero and some of his classmates are subjected to a ritual designed to instill in them the sense of their 'place' in society. The ritual is presided over by the town's businessmen. It is varied. The boys are made to fight each other blindfolded, then are thrown coins on an electrically-wired carpet which, naturally, gives them an electric shock every time they reach for the money. Then there is the prime feature of the ritual pertaining to the sexual code. A white naked female is brought to dance in front of the naked boys. If they express either signs of desire or repulsion they are exposed to brutalization (there is an obvious allegorical overtone to this scene, recalling Christ's dilemma about the coin). Sex, thus, is used also for satirical intent. Ellison aims at deflating, from a very authorial point of view, Prospero's idolization of Miranda's innocence and virginity and to indicate, in no uncertain terms, that a chief reason for Prospero's ostracization of Caliban is the irrational fear that translates itself in the belief that Caliban is a beastly lecher bent on ravishing Miranda. How Ellison succeeds is in the use of contrast, ambiguity of situation, where pretense, deceit, is shown for what it is, especially when it is the reflection of a dominant cultural attitude. For instance there is the desciption of the naked female in the dramatic scene early in the novel: "The hair was yellow like that of a circus kewpie doll, the face heavily powdered and rouged, as though to form an abstract mask, the eyes hollow and smeared a cool blue, the color of a baboon's butt." (p.23)

In the North, the hero encounters other White women, in somewhat more genteel surroundings. The resultant meaning, in line with the constant contrapuntal dynamics of the novel, is that Miranda cannot be made to play the role of a disincarnated symbol forever. She cannot be told, or be made to feel, that Caliban is an inhuman animal that she should keep away from without wanting to find out the truth for herself. And she does. And she has been doing so for a longer period of time than one might presume, Ellison

52

says, when the hero reflects after his first sexual experience in New York: "And my mind swirled with forgotten stories of male servants summoned to wash the mistress's back; chauffeurs sharing the masters' wives; Pullman porters invited into the drawing rooms of rich wives headed for Reno." (p.360)

A long pathetically funny scene comes immediately after the final riot that eventually brings the hero to a conscious appraisal of his invisibility. In the pitiable character of Sybil, Ellison explodes once and for all the Miranda-like cultural pretense. Sybil herein craves for her sado-masochistic pleasures:

> 'But I need it,' she said, uncrossing her thighs and sitting up eagerly. 'You can do it, it'll be easy for YOU beautiful. Threaten to kill me if I don't give in. You know, talk rough to me, beautiful. A friend of mine said the fellow said, 'Drop your drawers... and ......'. A really filthy man,' she said. Oh, he was a brute, huge, with white teeth, what they call a 'buck'. And he said, 'Bitch, drop your drawers,' and then he did it. (p.448)

The pathetic, and even tragic, character of Sybil emerges in the ambiguity that she is indeed a victim of Prospero's outlook, or education. How else explain her present insanity, if not through the early inculcation of certain sexual traumas? Indeed: " 'Well, ever since I first heard about it, even when I was a very little girl, I've wanted it to happen to me.' 'You mean what happened to your friend?' 'Uh Huh!' ". (p.449) Prospero's victimization of Caliban, it is clear, has boomeranged and destroys that which he so cherished, his symbol of purity. Ellison's belief that Prospero's denial of Caliban results in *his* own destruction as well has seldom been so well illustrated as in the character of Sybil who finds sexual gratification only by means of perversion: " 'Come on, beat me, daddy -you-you big black bruiser. What's taking you so long?' she said. 'Hurry up, knock me down! Don't you want me?' " (p.452)

Thus we have Ellison's dramatization of hybridity in American culture. William Melvin Kelley does not have Ellison's creative range, nor does he have his depth of vision. Nonetheless he succeeds in the ironic mode of his second, perhaps overly contrived, novel *Dem* (1967). It is the story of a junior executive's astonishment when informed that his wife, due to a very rare physiological occurrence (superfecundation), has given birth to twins, one black and one white. It is explained that:

> Superfecundation is the fertilization of those two eggs within a short period of time by sperm cells from two separate intercourses. Now obviously, if you had fertilized both eggs, no one would be able to distinguish it from usual two-egg twinning.

But if your wife had... relations with another man, who is very different physically from you, and each of you fertilized one egg, each of you would pass his traits on to the particular twin he had fathered. (p.83)

This conceit roots Kelley's treatment of hybridity. When it is learned that a Black man is in fact the father of the dark twin the subsequent search for Cooley, through the back alleys and cellars of Harlem, represents Pierce's exposure to Caliban's culture; it is a carry-over of the womb metaphor where, symbiotically, Caliban and Prospero are linked. In the second half of this fabulistic novel Pierce encounters people such as Carlyle who "conks" (uncurls with a hot comb) his hair, Gloria who wears a bright red wig, and Calvin an Ellisonian Rinehart figure of invisibility whom Pierce fails to recognize as Cooley (in the end he does, when it too late). All these characters are grotesque figures representing the dark side of Pierce's consciousness. Unfortunately, though, given the nature of fabulation, Kelley does not come to a successful resolution with the plot. He has Pierce lapsing, for instance, into a dream sequence which bears the unmistakable Joycean stamp, if not Himes' type of humour, as white and black males and females cavort in bed. Finally, the novel falls off into witless humour of the "what-people-will-say" variety, now that the doorman of Pierce's apartment building knows about the twins.

Yet, if only because of one scene that pits Pierce against a huge black figure of a woman, Kelley's work is a minor masterpiece for what he attempts and succeeds in doing. The black woman is everything that is antithetical to Pierce's outlook and lifestyle. Confronted with her, Pierce can only stare in a stupefied state. To the black woman, Pierce, who is being "passed" off as a light-skinned Black from Canada, increasingly comes to represent what is wrong with educated young Blacks (ironically reversing the "tragic mulatto" theme). More than anything else, the connotative, the suggestive aspect stands out. In this long scene, we get an externalized picture of absolute contrast in colour, style, speech, tone and attitude, in short the Caliban-Prospero initial polarization; but, symbolically, the two extremes complement each other and are one:

It was only a few steps to the kitchen. Just inside the door, a table blocked the way, a money-filled saucepan in the center. Behind the table, the kitchen was a high-ceilinged room. At one time it had been some bright color. Now it was impossible to tell what color; no one would have chosen the gray which covered the walls.

At the far end was a spattered white stove, crouching hidden behind a Black woman at least as tall and twice as wide as Mitchell [Pierce]. She wore a black dress decorated with large yellow sunflowers, one of which stretched across her broad back, like the picture on a team jacket.

"Is this where I pay?"

"No place else, baby." She turned now, smoke rising from an iron kettle behind her. She was the woman he had seen sitting beside the highway.

"Well?" She moved toward the table. "Ain't you got change?" She stood behind the table, large hands hanging at her sides. "It's in the pan there. Go on, I trust you."

"Didn't I see you a few hours ago on the highway?"

She wrinkled her tiny nose. "Highway?"

Perhaps he was mistaken. But... "You look very familiar to me."

"I ain't never been to Canada."

Mitchell was confused, decided to let the matter drop. "Is this where I pay?"

"That's what I said. Don't you light-skinned niggers never listen to anybody but white folks?"

"Why yes." He took a five-dollar bill from his wallet. "And could I have three drinks. Do you have bourbon?"

"Course I do." She bent into a cabinet, brought out the bottle. "Three?" She squinted at him.

Perhaps three drinks were too many. "Yes." He wanted them all himself; they might relax him. "One's a double."

She poured the drinks, using a jigger glass with a thick bottom. "What's wrong now?"

"Not a thing."

"What's wrong with you boy? You a retard?" She did not wait for his answer, but returned to the stove, picked up a two-pronged fork, began to spear each piece of chicken, bringing it close to her face for inspection.

He choked down a large swallow. "It's just that I think I've seen you before."

Her back to him: "I probably look like your mama."

Mitchell smiled, almost laughed. His mother, dead now eight years, had been small and dry. "No, that's not it." He took another swallow. The alcohol could not possibly be in his arteries yet, but knowing it was on its way made him feel better. "But—"

"I get one of you at every party Gloria gives." She spun around. "You light-skinned, educated boys! Young Black girls scare you, so you come out and talk to mammy."

Mitchell tried to laugh. "Really that's not."

"Well, mammy's a girl too and she ain't got time for scared boys. Unless you want to come on in the kitchen with me." She shook her head. "No you don't want that. Go on away from here. Mammy ain't got no time no more for scared boys. Mammy wants men!"

Mitchell finished the double bourbon. "I'm not afraid."

"Then why you hanging around the kitchen?" She advanced on him, pointing the prongs of her fork at his eyes. "Go on now." (pp.116-117)

On this note of stark contrast dominated by the mythical proportions of the Black mammy dwarfing the fragile figure of Miranda we can conclude our analysis of hybridity, a phenomenon of misalliance and mistaken identity not unlike the dramatic encounter between Pierce and the mammy, but, whose resolution lies in the mammy's embrace. From a tragic stance of Calibanic insistence to be integrated into Prospero's world, we moved to its successful resolution in Toomer's *Cane*; finally we looked at certain variations indicative of a total change of values and outlook whose sources and constituents we will explore in a forthcoming chapter.

1 Frantz Fanon, *Peau Noire, Masques Blancs*, p.114.
2 See Jessie Fausset's *Plum Bun*, Nella Larsen's *Quicksand* and *Passing*; Walter White's *Flight*; Wallace Thurman's *The Blacker the Berry*. Bone examines these novels in detail, see pp.95-106.
3 See dust jacket of the British edition (Arthur Barker Ltd).

# THE HYBRID

# QUEBECER

Abandoned by France and/or conquered by Britain in 1760, the French Canadians thereupon suffered a scission in their collective self. This scission explains the turning for protection to a Messianic mystique whereby the French Canadians root themselves in a rural order revolving around the land, language, family and faith. Notwithstanding the fact that the land was truly not the great purveyor and maternal protector it was purported to be, and that the woman could not be construed as a source of endless fertility, the French Canadian, armed with spiritual fervour, willingly turned his back on the secular environment and sought comfort and sublimation for his frustrations, anguishes and anxieties. Hence the painful hybridity: the towering image of a small self-enclosed people confident in its mission of being a divinely-inspired and divinely-protected people at odds against a majority of materialistic "foreigners" for whom it will function as a god-ordained exemplum (for Quebec was the Augustinian divine commonwealth!). In fact, as the following novels demonstrate, the contingencies of existence were becoming more pressing.

*Maria Chapdelaine* (1915), the classic novel by Louis Hémon celebrating the rural set-up and its ethos, contains, as in a microco m, all the attitudes that we have discussed in general. This novel, about a turn-of-the-century French-Canadian family living in the village of Peribonka, in the Lac Saint-Jean region, focuses its dramatization of Maria Chapdelaine's thwarted love for François Paradis on the fundamental myths elaborated since the Conquest: fidelity to the land, the family, *la race*, the faith, that are held to be sacred virtues that the French Canadian must uphold, lest he perish. Nothing has changed and nothing must change if Quebec is to go on existing.

Let us examine the attitudes towards three of these fundamental

59

values, the land, the woman, the faith, before discussing how they come to bear on the central character, Maria Chapdelaine. The land is early introduced as abundant, fertile. The general picture is one of light, of happiness, and more importantly, of stability, of assurance, as when Maria's mother, Mme Chapdelaine, is described:

> Les poings sur les hanches, dédaignant de s'attabler à son tour, elle célébra la beauté placide et vraie de la campagne au sol riche, de la campagne plate qui n'a pour pittoresque que l'ordre des longs sillons parallèles et la douceur des eaux courantes, de la campagne qui s'offre nue aux baisers du soleil avec un abandon d'épouse. (p.60)

The land is later presented as part of an alliance grouping the family, love and spirituality. The significance, of course, is that all the earthly attributes are at one with divinity; they are part and reflection of the divine order. One feels that the description of thé Chapdelaines looking back on their early life applies to a whole people and a whole way of life:

> La vie avait toujours été unie et simple pour eux: le dur travail nécessaire, le bon accord entre époux, la soumission aux lois de la nature et de l'Eglise. Toutes ces choses s'étaient fondues dans la même trame, les rites du culte et les détails de l'existence journalière tassés ensemble, de sorte qu'ils eussent été incapables de séparer l'exaltation religieuse qui les possédait d'avec leur tendresse inexprimée. (p.113)

Yet an ominous note is introduced: the land is not as abundant and felicitous as Mme Chapdelaine would think. M. Chapdelaine is talking to his helper and both are working in the fields. Work on the land is hard, not quite as rewarding in material terms as the spiritual vision these farmers have: "La terre est bonne; mais il faut se battre avec le bois pour l'avoir; et pour vivre il faut économiser sur tout et besogner du matin au soir, et tout faire soi-même, parce que les autres maisons sont si loin."(p.38) Hémon introduces Lorenzo Surprenant, a French Canadian who left Peribonka, to make a living in a New England industrial town. Coming from the outside and no longer a part of the prevalent ethos, he sees clearly the kind of life the rural folks are living. What he replies to the overall celebration is again quite ominous. To the freedom, the abundance, the fertility, and the implied feeling of assurance, he says: "Il n'y a pas d'homme au monde qui soit moins libre qu'un habitant.... Vous êtes les serviteurs de vos animaux: voilà ce que vous êtes. Vous les soignez, vous les nettoyez; vous ramassez leur fumier comme les pauvres ramassent les miettes des riches." (pp.149-150)

The attitude towards the woman is not one where she is seen as a mistress, or as a symbol of sensuality. Always in these rural novels she is portrayed a source of fertility and abundance, a procreator. François Paradis, Maria's tragic lover, envisions her not as a possible mistress but in the realm of maternal possibilities: "Il sentait qu'elle était de ces femmes qui, lorsqu'elles se donnent, donnent tout sans compter: l'amour de leur corps et de leur coeur, la force de leurs bras dans la besogne de chaque jour, la dévotion complète d'un esprit sans détours." (pp.82-83) The maternal image of the woman is likewise referred to when the village curate has a talk with Maria following her lover's tragic death in the woods. (1) It is quite significant that the curate ignores the sensual female in Maria who is mourning as he tells her to look towards her still unfulfilled maternal role as a source of hope, if not as a *raison d'être*. In other words, Maria has no cause for grief since she is not married and has yet to fulfill her role as mother and wife: "Une fille comme toi, plaisante à voir, de bonne santé et avec ça vaillante et ménagère, c'est fait pour encourager ses vieux parents, d'abord, et puis après se marier et fonder une famille chrétienne." (p.140)

Religion, as has been said, is the great spiritual force that galvanizes the rural folks in their fight for survival. Consequently, the novel opens with the people of the village coming out of mass on Sunday morning: "La porte de l'église de Péribonka s'ouvrit et les hommes commencèrent à sortir." (p.11) The *messianisme* bemoaned by Brunet, this abnegation towards necessities of the material order, the negation of womanhood in her sensuality, the fundamental sublimation of all matters of the secular order in spiritualism, is better understood when one knows the far-reaching role that the priest played in the rural parishes, for as Hémon says: "... le prêtre canadien n'est pas seulement le directeur de conscience de ses ouailles, mais aussi leur conseiller en toutes matières, l'arbitre de leurs querelles, et en vérité la seule personne différente d'eux-mêmes à laquelle ils puissent avoir recours dans le doute " (p.137)

All these attitudes take a momentous dimension in the characterization of Maria Chapdelaine and her story. Maria is a young woman, a dutiful daughter, living with her parents on the farm, doing her share of work and destined to marry François Paradis, a dashing young man in the tradition of the *coureurs de bois*. As François unfortunately dies, all the possibilities that he symbolized for Maria vanish: happiness, sensuality, a life different from that led at home. She finds therefore consolation in her faith, in what the curate tells her; she is willing to resign herself to Fate, not unlike the Corneillian heroine whose example of abnegation will be proposed to generations of French-Canadian girls. However, temptation enters. She is courted by two young men, symbolizing two opposite ways of life: that of the city and all its material advantages, and that of the country that she knows. Maria is decidedly tempted to embrace the opportunities offered by Lorenzo Surprenant: "... la vie magnifique des grandes cités, de la vie plaisante, sûre, et des belles rues droites, inondées de lumière le soir,

61

pareilles à des merveilleux spectacles sans fin." (p.153) By contrast, Eutrope Gagnon, the local boy, gauche and timid, promises only: "Faire le ménage et l'ordinaire, tirer les vaches, nettoyer l'étable quand l'homme serait absent, travailler dans les champs peut-être, parce qu'ils ne seraient que deux et qu'elle était forte. Passer les veillées au rouet ou à redoubler de vieux vêtements." (p.163)

While Maria is courted by these polar opposites she confronts the world of the material present (and the future) and that of the past: the scintillating world beyond Peribonka she would like to enjoy and the traditional world of obedience and duty, unrelieved by secular pleasure which is her mother's lot and the villagers'. Her first reaction clearly shows her choice: she wants to renounce her mother's way of life in her initial rejection of Eutrope Gagnon: "Non, elle ne voulait pas vivre comme cela." (p.164) Her renunciation stems not only from the fact that she is fascinated with Lorenzo's world but, also, because she agrees with Lorenzo's denunciation of the rural way of life. She too believes that its celebration is a myth-making process, a systematic, conscious and unconscious construction of the mind carried by people who could not do otherwise lest they succumb to despair. Lucidly, Maria is ready to renounce her mother's world in agreeing with Lorenzo's observations: "C'est vrai ce que disait là Lorenzo Surprenant; c'était un pays sans pitié et sans douceur." (p.152)

Yet, whereas the stage is set for a momentous negation, Mme Chapdelaine dies. Maria has to reconsider her decision. Two main factors will be brought to bear on her conscience: what her father tells her, the not-so-subtle pressure of his celebration of his dead wife's inspirational qualities, and the 'voices' that Maria (like a latter-day Joan of Arc) hears, the voices of the past, those of the collective unconscious.

At first, Maria's reaction to her father's narration of abnegation, endurance, selflessness, and other heroic and supra-heroic qualities that the French-Canadian rural mother possesses (the association through her between land and divine order) is one of obedience: "Vivre ainsi, dans ce pays, comme sa mère avait vécu, et puis mourir et laisser derrière soi un homme chagriné et le souvenir des vertus essentielles de sa race, elle sentait qu'elle serait capable de cela."(p.206) But she remains doubtful. Then she hears the voices of the collective unconscious. In fact she hears three voices, and the third is the decisive one. Quite significantly, in it there is the alliance of the land, the maternal role and divine order: "... la voix du pays de Québec, qui était à moitié un chant de femme et à moitié un sermon de prêtre." (p.211) The content of the message conveys the messianic trait, the global alliance of man-land-and-God, but, furthermore, it reveals the repertoire of myths and legends the traditional nationalist school in French Canada utilizes (even up to present day) to galvanize the energies of the French-Canadians: "Car en vérité tout ce qui fait l'âme de la province tenait dans cette voix: la solennité chère du vieux culte, la douceur de la vieille langue jalousement gardée, la splendeur et la force barbare du pays neuf où une racine ancienne a retrouvé son adolescence." (p.211) Maria heeds what the voices say to her. Despite her initial impulse she now embraces what she knows consciously to be a superannuated vision of life: she will marry Eutrope. Her justification is not only that she has to carry on her mother's role, but, on a deeper level, she accepts the Messianic myth for what it symbolizes: the survival of her people. This is impressed upon her when the voices tell her that the French Canadian, in order to endure, must forsake any individualism and uphold the common values and beliefs legated by tradition through the lifestyle of simple folks such as Peribonka's and, more importantly, in the symbol of continuity and fidelity contained in motherhood: "Rien ne changera, parce que nous sommes un témoignage. De nous-mêmes et de nos destinées, nous n'avons compris clairement que ce devoir-là: persister... nous maintenir...." (p.212) And her story closes on the apotheosized glorification of the past, a society's resiliency to change:

> C'est pourquoi il faut rester dans la province où nos pères sont restés, et vivre comme ils ont vécu, pour obéir au commandement inexprimé qui s'est formé dans leurs coeurs, qui a passé dans les nôtres et que nous devrons transmettre à notre tour à de nombreux enfants: Au pays de Québec rien ne doit mourir et rien ne doit changer.... (pp.212-213)

The past also is the essential backdrop to Lionel Groulx's *L'Appel de la Race* (1922), set in Ottawa and centred on a marriage between a French-Canadian and an English-Canadian woman that has resulted in the assimilation of their off-springs into Anglo-Saxon culture. The theme of assimilation is extended however to include a larger historical frame which Groulx is interested in (to the extent of using art as propaganda): the 1920 issue of separate schools for French Canadians in Ontario. As a member of the Canadian House of Commons, the protagonist, Jules de Lantagnac, is brought to confront this issue. The threat of assimilation is, therefore, both private and public, familial and historical; that it comes as no surprise when the novel's climactic point, de Lantagnac's momentous speech in the Commons denouncing the English, is paralleled by the dissolution of his marriage.

Thus, this first novel by one of French Canada's dominant nationalist leaders deals with the same theme with which Hémon was concerned: the necessity for Quebec to present an homogeneous front against an outside threatening environment. The attitudes towards religion, land, and language are similar in both books; except that in Groulx's novel these values are lumped into a racialist frame of reference evolved from Groulx's reading of Gobineau, Le Bon and Barrès. Religion is introduced in the conventional pattern. In the early part of the novel, Père Fabien impresses upon de Lan-

63

tagnac, uneasy about his French heritage, that the Church is the "key" to the understanding of the Québécois:

> Et de là, M. le philosophe, continua plus ému le religieux, de là, pour chercher la clé du mystère, vos yeux s'en sont allés d'eux-mêmes, n'est-ce pas, vers l'église prochaine, vers son clocher d'argent? ... En même temps qu'il est resté le signe loyal d'une latinité authentique, il se dresse comme la plus haute fleur d'une terre où le travail n'est jamais triste, emblême d'une race où l'esprit est toujours le plus haut. (p.27)

The land is similarly identified as depository of the ancestors' heritage. As in *Maria Chapdelaine*, it is celebrated in a mystique from which, it is alleged, no French Canadian can withhold recognition. That the land is more a spiritual image tied to a subconscious archetype rather than a concrete environment can be seen in de Lantagnac's reply: "J'avais là, devant moi, le champ de bataille de mes ancêtres, les vieux défricheurs, les vainqueurs des forêts vierges. Je voyais le reliquaire de leurs sueurs et de leur dure peine. Ce sol, me rappelais-je, a été conquis, pied par pied, pouce par pouce sur la forêt millénaire." (p.26) This invisible partnership of man and land is restated at the end of the novel when de Lantagnac makes his speech in the Commons. Because it is assumed this partnership rests on a fundamental divine plan, it is felt that a denial of the French Canadian, an injustice directed at him, is tantamount to being a sacrilegious act. Groulx seems to imply as much in rhetorically asking: "... est-il au pouvoir de quelques milliers de persécuteurs d'écraser une race qui plonge ses racines au plus profond du sol canadien, comme l'érable, son symbole immortel?". (p.224) Language, finally, is another indivisible element; any threat posed to it is as sacrilegious as when directed against some of the other values. At one point there is a reference to the type of French de Lantagnac's daughters are being taught at school, the upshot being its questionable value since it is Parisian and not the particular Quebec variety:

> Nellie et Virginia articulaient, ô ciel! le vrai français d'essence ontarienne, le pur et authentique Parisian french. Non seulement leur père devait leur apprendre une langue nouvelle, ignorée; force lui était de nettoyer d'abord leur esprit, du jargon prétentieux et barbare dont un faux enseignement l'avait encombré. (p.50)

Yet it seems, in Groulx' mind, that all these traditional values need a more dramatic centre of reference. Hence *la race*, as an all-encompassing doctrine, is directly emphasized: under its banner are all the battles of the French Canadian to be fought, all his problems to be explained, indeed all of life's complexity summarized. As de Lantagnac explains to Père Fabien, who suggested a trip to the province of Quebec of his boyhood, as a means of renewing with his heritage, *la race* finally motivates him to recapture his lost identity: "la tombe des Lantagnac que je me suis accordé à mes ancêtres, à ma race. Je l'ai éprouvé, je l'ai touché avec une réalité sensible: le Lantagnac que j'étais allait devenir une force anarchique, perdue." (p.29) The reference here to the world of the dead, the heritage of the ancestors, indicates Canon Groulx's nationalist affiliations. Later on he demonstrates fully that this notion of *la race* stems indeed from a certain nineteenth-century European school. In a discussion between de Lantagnac and the priest regarding the effects and consequences of his marriage, the latter reveals the reasons for his disapproval of such alliances. First, he denounces the miscegenation that went on between Europeans and Indians back in the pioneer days, and which may account for the 1760 defeat: "Qui sait, avait dit le Père, avec une franchise plutôt rude, qui sait si notre ancienne noblesse canadienne n'a pas dû sa déchéance au mélange des sangs qu'elle a trop facilement accepté, trop souvent recherché?" (p.65) Next, the priest tries to scientifically prove his understanding of miscegenation by quoting LeBon's long since discredited *Lois Psychologiques de l'Evolution des Peuples*: "Les croisements peuvent être un élément de progrès entre des races supérieures, assez voisines telles que les Anglais et les Allemands d'Amérique. Ils constituent toujours un élément de dégénérescence quand ces races même supérieures, sont trop différentes." (pp.165-166) However, such statements coming from a priest cannot but demonstrate the towering influence the clergy enjoyed: de Lantagnac is, of course, led to believe that his marriage is an aberration that must be destroyed if he is to re-enter *la race*. For here is the question debated in his conscience: "... ai-je le droit de démolir mon foyer, d'opérer la dispersion de mes enfants? J'irai plus loin: mon devoir de député, le dévouement que je dois à ma race m'obligent-ils jusqu'à de si terribles sacrifices?" (p.179) The answer is a foregone conclusion.

De Lantagnac's sacrificial ritual is ultimately similar to Maria's: the individual's personal claim to happiness is stifled by the weight of collective impositions. What makes it particularly appalling, though, is the fact that the priest has caused the dissolution of an institution that the Church (of which the priest is God's servant) considers as an indissoluble sacrament in canonical law.

Another important novel in the Messianic period of French-Canadian culture is Mgr Félix-Antoine Savard's *Menaud Maître-Draveur* (1937). It tells the story of a woodsman's growing sense of dispossession of his forests, his family, culminating in insanity. Throughout, enhancing Menaud's tragedy, the message the 'third voice' communicates to Maria Chapdelaine is repeated as a leitmotiv: "nothing must die, and nothing must change in the province of Quebec." Against the backdrop of men at work in the woods, this prose poem celebrates the myth of the land, the bravery of the people, the courage and heroism of the ancestors, the necessity to remain faithful to

65

Traditional rural scene          *courtesy of Cinemathèque Québecoise*

their legacy, and warns against the presence of an undefined "enemy". But the reality of the day (which Harvey, for instance, tries to communicate in *Les Demi-Civilisés*), its increasing urbanization and industrialization, Menaud cannot accept. He immerses himself into the world of the past and of *Maria Chapdelaine* which he does not cease to read and enjoy. He projects, over his disintegrating environment, images of an inner landscape more and more divorced from the outer. Nowhere in French-Canadian literature, it would seem, has the anguish brought about by the passing of the traditional order and the coming of the new one, the conflict between the world of the past and that of the present and the future, been so passionately portrayed. Menaud and what he symbolizes are defeated but it is the failure of a whole way of life that takes place.

In Menaud's defeat is pointed out the necessity to embrace the secular order, with the required concrete stance, tools and courage, the movement of revolt, starting in the forties, will articulate from the standpoint of the city. But let us analyze the components of Menaud's tragedy.

As in the novels previously discussed, land, language, faith and family, individually or lumped together in the Messianic mystique, are celebrated and clung to by the old woodsman, the more desperately so as he withdraws into a mythical world. Menaud, his son Joson, and Alexis, a young woodsman, are introduced as part of the same mold as François Paradis, in the *coureurs de bois* tradition: "Menaud, Joson, Alexis, eux n'avaient point bronché, étant d'une autre race, de celle que la terre mesurée, avec ses labours et ses moissons, ses rigueurs et ses tendresses, n'avaient pas encore apprivoisée. Pour eux, la vie c'était le bois où l'on est chez soi partout...." (p.28) If there seems to be an attempt to create an opposition between the *"coureur de bois"* and the farmer, the nomad and the sedentary, it is better to emphasize and celebrate the majesty of the land Menaud and Alexis almost physically possess as they roam through its vastness. The symbolic significance of a land-based Chapdelaine is magnified in the land-roving Menaud who sees God's ample designs everywhere: "Lui, du clan des loups de bois, jamais il n'avait tant aimé la terre, toute la terre de son pays, mais surtout cet âpre rang de Mainsal, décrié par tous les laboureurs de glaise... ce sol jaune ou il avait pris souche, libre parmi tous les sols." (pp.114-115)

Menaud's vision of the environment around him parallels the third voice's in *Maria Chapdelaine*. There seems to be a symbiosis between the past Menaud reads about and the present he ideally conceives, so that the imaginary and the actual, dream and reality, idealization and concreteness are all one: "En somme, tout cela, tout autour, dans les champs et sur la montagne, assurait qu'une race fidèle entre dans la durée de la terre elle-même... C'était là le sens des paroles: 'Ces gens sont d'une race qui ne sait pas mourir'..."(p.117).The old man's spiritual involvement with the land is so passionate that he too, it is implied, hears a "voice" commanding him to go

67

further. The legacy is no longer that Quebec must not change, but that it must aggrandize itself, repossess its lost spaces: "Posséder, s'agrandir! Voilà le mot d'ordre venu du sang, l'appel monté de la terre, la terre qui toute, dans la grande nuit de printemps, clamait: 'Je t'appartiens!' " (p.119) Faith is, likewise, the same deeply-rooted attachment found in *Maria* Chapdelaine. Indeed it is that particular view of faith which roots the Messianic mission of the descendants of French settlers in North America: "Nous avions apporté d'outre-mer nos prières et nose chansons: elles sont toujours les mêmes." (p.2) Another part of the sacred heritage to be upheld is language: "...notre langue, nos vertus et jusqu'à nos faiblesses deviennent des choses sacrées." (p.2) And, beyond specific celebrations, there is the general global ethos.

Mgr Savard's concept of *la race* arises from the 'voice's' in *Maria*: it is the collective, the organic, sense of the French-Canadian experience in North America. But his concept differs from Groulx's: insofar as it is not overtly associated with any racialist nineteenth-century European doctrine. Here it means the fidelity of the French Canadian to his origins, a sense of personal and collective identity that has allegedly insured historical survival. It is not accidental therefore that Menaud's reflections on the subject are predicated on the initial passage in Hémon's book: "Nous avions apporté dans nos poitrines le coeur des hommes de notre pays vaillant et vif, aussi prompt à la pitié qu'au rire, le coeur le plus humain de tous les coeurs humains: il n'a pas changé." (p.2) The present is informed by the perspective of the past, the legacy of the ancestors Menaud is wont to look for in his son, Joson: " 'Une race qui ne meurt pas!' Menaud la voyait là, vivante, non dans les livres, mais dans sa chair dressée devant lui." (p.18) But this is the extent of the correspondence. Not only are Menaud's hopes destroyed when Joson accidently dies, but more important, the old man does not see the reflection of the past either in the actual world or in his daughter's, Maria's, behaviour. Thwarted in his dreams, the old man lives in a state of painful desperation. Whether it concerns his family or the woods, Menaud's strident consciousness of his legacy keeps him in a state of revolt, the more hopeless because it cannot find any channel to exteriorize itself. For instance, as the woods are being sold to foreign interests, Menaud finds release only in a dream sequence whereby the collective unconscious tells him to find his freedom. He is told this freedom is in himself; but the woodsman cannot apprehend it, he is a captive. One may surmise, a captive much like his generation and the ones before which imprisoned themselves in a spiritually-sustaining mystique that nevertheless locked them out of the material world:

—Tu sais maintenant, lui dit quelqu'un de cette foule; délivre
la liberté!
—Où est-elle?

—Dans ton sang.
—Qu'est-ce qui la retient captive?
—Toi-même. (p.67)

Menaud's tragic bout with existence is, in addition, more forcefully portrayed in his attitude towards his daughter, with whom he is as overpossessive as he is with the land, and with the same results. When he hears that Délié (a young man working for the "foreigners" who are now acquiring the forest) is courting his daughter Maria, he flies into a rage as blind and irrational as it is ill-founded, since the girl has no interest in the man. It would seem, however, that Délié serves but as a pretext for Menaud to discharge his overflow of frustration at a world, a present, a reality completely alien to his vision:

> Car tu le comprendras un jour, transmettre son nom, son sang, ce n'est pas cela qui contente le coeur; mais, dans la chair qui vient de soi, sentir battre les mêmes amours et brûler les mêmes haines, mais voir des pas s'orienter pour être le relèvement de ses gestes, voilà le désir qui fait vivre quand on regarde ses enfants. Né d'une race qui bataille ici depuis trois siècles, j'avais le droit d'espérer que le pacte fait avec la terre de mes aïeux ne se briserait pas dans ma maison.... J'avais le droit de compter que la fille à Menaud ne trahirait pas en épousant un bâtard de déchu. (pp.161-162)

The term *bâtard* signals that a concern with bastardization as symbolic of the degeneration of the present generations (giving birth to a contrast with the greatness of the ancestors, the past) is equally dominant in this novel. It is as if the line read in *Maria Chapdelaine* ("Rien ne changera parce que nous sommes un témoignage"), as it comes to haunt Menaud, instills in him an irreconcilable sense of guilt. The heart of Menaud's attitude, it would seem, lies in his belief that it is because the legacy of the ancestors has been betrayed through bastardization that he is being deprived of his woods by "foreigners". If the fidelity and security assured in the Messianic ethos have failed the descendants it is not because the ethos itself could not protect indefinitely from the outside world, but rather because the descendants were not faithful. Délié, thus, in Menaud's eyes stands as the living symbol of degeneration, although he is the one character in the book willing to listen to the winds of change and espouse progress. All of Menaud's frustrations find nonetheless, momentarily, an object for focus; Délié is the necessary 'nemesis' in Menaud's tragedy: "Non, Menaud n'aimait point ce gars-là! De tout son instinct d'homme libre et jaloux du sol. Il était pour lui, de ces esclaves dont les épaules ont les gales du bât, qui livrent, pour de l'argent, la montagne et les chemins à l'étranger." (p.14)
However, in spite of Menaud's rantings against Délié, his daughter,

69

Maria, the "foreigners" or the implacable fate that ravished his son, he never ascribes the collapse of his world to any single visible cause. Befitting his tragic stature, Menaud's 'hubris' lies in that which gives him spiritual sustenance: the mystical celebration of the land which he never allows his mind to rest from, much less to question. Every event builds up his incapacity to cope with the secular world and inexorably weaves his life up to the climactic point of enmeshment in a total schizoid web. Has catharsis been reached when, in the technique of ancient tragedy, the reader is indirectly told of the off-stage resolution of the conflict: "On entendait son père battre de ses appels le grand désert de la folie?" (p.264) A painful one indeed.

But the definitive *roman du terroir* both for the glorification of the rural order and its decadence is Ringuet's *Trente Arpents* (1938), another novel built like a classical tragedy with its constitutive four divisions, its larger-than-life protagonist, Euchariste Moisan, its rise-and-fall progression and, lastly, its cathartic effect which cannot but impress on the reader the fact that the rural order is undeniably dead, for its symbolic incarnation is left a prey to quiet desperation, exiled in a New England factory town. Ringuet, using the broad canvas of three generations of the Moisan family, tells the story of the patriarch, Euchariste, from his early manhood in the region of Saint-Jacques l'Ermite, as he is about to get married, work his own farm and raise a family, and right to his old age as a night watchman in a factory. Moisan successfully manages his farm and he begets thirteen children to bear witness to his prosperity; or, mythically, to fulfil the covenant of land-family-divinity at work in the traditional culture. In the fullness of life, thus, Euchariste is silhouetted against the fertility of the land to which corresponds the fertility of his wife. God's plan, which is never doubted since it roots the very notion of life, is next consecrated when the eldest of the children hears the Lord's call and becomes a priest. Having reached in the second part of the book, Summer (for the four parts correspond to the seasonal cycle), the highest degree of fulfillment, the Moisan family, and particularly Euchariste, are henceforth doomed.

Ominous signs appear, as is wont to happen in classical tragedy, as success radiates. A relative who has emigrated to a New England factory town, like Lorenzo Surprenant in *Maria Chapdelaine*, comes for a visit with his American-born wife and the tinsel and glitter of city life reverberate from his gold teeth and loud talk. The seeds of the flowers of evil are planted in his wife's seduction of one of her awed country nephews, the third of Euchariste's boys, Ephrem (significantly, the first to leave the farm and embrace the city life; the one in whose home, in New England, Euchariste is exiled; and. lastly, the one whose American-born wife is also adulterous). Second omen, Oguinase, the priest in the family, is of a weak constitution and soon dies of consumption in the Autumn division of the book. Third, Lucinda, one of the girls, follows in Ephrem's footsteps and leaves for the city where (in the Winter division) she turns to prostitution. Fourth, the post-World War I course of modern life erupts in the village when automobiles appear and industrialization starts taking place. But, fifth, and more dramatically, the mother Alphonsine dies giving birth to her thirteenth child. Nowhere is the profound tragic irony of the omen more evident than in the placidity, contiguous with the organic process of life, with which the mother's death is accepted:

> Et, avant qu'Euchariste ait pu pleinement se rendre compte de ce qui se passait, il se trouva dans la grand-chambre, au pied du lit où une forme vague et un masque cireux et exsangue étaient tout ce qui restait de son Alphonsine. Les enfants se tassaient dans la porte, les aînés sanglotant, les petits cherchant à comprendre pourquoi on les retenait là, tandis qu'un soleil doux les appelait au dehors. Dans un coin de la cuisine, l'aînée, Malvina, berçait une petite fille en qui la vie de la mère était passée pour toujours.
>
> Pendant trois jours et deux nuits, la maison fut envahie par la parenté et le voisinage. Cela, heureusement, était survenue pendant la période relativement inactive d'entre semailles et moisson; il n'en fallait pas moins, le jour, soigner les bêtes à l'accoutumée et faire l'ordinaire des travaux. (p.119)

However impervious to the meaning of these omens, and congenitally drawn to espouse life as a process of determined destruction and creation, the Moisan family is from then on led to a likewise implacably determined course, that of their fall, principally in the figure of the patriarch.

Euchariste, crafty and shrewd, keeps tons of hay in store with the hope of capitalizing on the rise in prices consequent to increased war demands. One night a fire burns his barn completely to the ground. Euchariste is responsible for that mishap since, preoccupied with his discovery that a neighbour has outsmarted him in a land deal, he left a lighted pipe in the barn. The first signs of character flaw appear in the greediness and excessive pride which explain the unfortunate fire. Euchariste, heretofore the richest and shrewdest among the farmers, is doomed when the qualities that insured his success turn into the excesses of avarice and pride. These crucial flaws soon accumulate when Euchariste next loses two legal suits, lodged against the neighbour who outsmarted him, and further, loses all his savings when the local notary absconds with his clients' deposits. At this stage, the end of the third division (Autumn), the climactic point has been reached.

Although some time elapses between Euchariste's bequeathing of the land to his eldest surviving son, Etienne, and his exile in New England, these three main setbacks, each connected to flaws in the protagonist's character, have sealed his fate. The rest of the novel, the fourth division (Winter), is the anticlimactic, implacable disintegration, not only of Euchariste but of the world he symbolized in the earlier image of fertility and abundance. Successively, the sons and daughters of Saint-Jacques l'Ermite's farmers leave for the cities in greater numbers. The land cannot sustain them. The Moisan family falls apart; another child dies of consumption; the youngest son cannot find work and has to be supported, with his family by Etienne, the beneficiary of Euchariste's land, who in turn, beleaguered by his own mounting problems resorts to the Darwinian principle of "survival of the fittest" by unemotionally sending his father for a visit to Ephrem, a journey which is to be of no return. Pictures of degradation (from the perspective of the traditional culture, to be sure) abound in Euchariste's journey to and sojourn in exile: in Montreal he gets lost in the streets adjoining the train station, but he finds his way back after rude sarcasms from prostitutes among whom, unbeknownst to him, is his daughter Lucinda; in White Falls, he finds his daughter-in-law one afternoon with a man in his undershirt and innocently believes her statement that he came to offer him a job. These scenes, pregnant with bittersweet if not bitter irony, serve well a technique that is evidently to the point: the old man's inability to grasp the truth in these situations is a dramatic parallel to a more fundamental blindness which existed already in the more glorious days of Summer, of fertility and abundance, as the earlier ignorance of the omens demonstrates. Such is the power of the Messianic myth.

We can now turn to an analysis of the myth's constituents which give this novel its particular tragic power: that of French-Canadian society at a cultural if not historic crossroads. First must be pointed out the references to the land, the mother, the faith and the family common to the tradition of the *terroir*. The land, as in *Maria Chapdelaine*, is portrayed in a maternal imagery, a central organic universe against which everything is measured:

> La terre, impassible et exigeante, suzeraine impérieuse dont ils étaient les serfs, payant aux intempéries l'avenage des moissons gâtées, assujettis aux corvées de drainage et de défrichement, soumis tout l'année longue au cens de la sueur. Ils s'étaient regroupés sur et presque contre la dure glèbe dont on ne tire rien qui ne lui soit arraché à force de bras. Par sa volonté muette, ils avaient reconstitué la trinité humaine: homme, femme, enfant, père, mère, fils. (p.18)

The woman, seen only as mother, is naturally envisaged as a paradigm for the land: like the land, the woman-as-mother is to be fertile, abundant and the symbol of the Biblical call to work. Here is Euchariste's notion of love as he contemplates marrying Alphonsine:

> Certes, il aimait Alphonsine. ... Certes, il ne la parait point

d'irréel et ne lui tissait pas une robe de madone; l'idée qu'il s'en faisait n'avait rien de romanesque. Au contraire, il savait fort bien ce qu'elle pourrait lui donner: forte et râblée, pas regardante à l'ouvrage, elle saurait à la fois conduire la maison et l'aider aux champs à l'époque de la moisson. De visage avenant, bien tournée de sa personne, elle lui donnerait des gars solides après des plaisirs auxquels il pensait parfois sans honte ni hâte exagérée. C'est pourquoi d'un coeur consentant il s'était laissé aller à l'aimer ou plus justement à la vouloir avant même l'habitude de la voir chaque dimanche. (p.11)

If the man is reluctant to celebrate sexual passion, happiness to him is that his relationship with the woman be consecrated by a higher calling which is the Biblical exhortation to multiply and propagate God's design: the more the land and the woman are abundant the better the Christian. Religion, therefore, is the principle of order that governs everything. The priest, in particular, inasmuch as he is the centre of power, the dominant figure whose counsel and guidance are sought, appears as the 'real' man in the community. Any analysis of the family or societal structure must understand his very vital role as a 'father' in the rural environment. That such a role entails the emasculation of the legitimate father and husband in the traditional culture certainly accounts for the castration complex against which many 'sons' in the urban modern period revolt, as shall be seen in a subsequent chapter. (2) But here is the masculine principle long wedded in Quebec to the feminine principle of the land, or Alphonsine's real 'husband':

Paysan il était certes, et marqué pour toujours du signe de la terre malgré les années de collège, en dépit des quatre ans de séminaire et des onze ans de prêtrise pendant lesquels il avait été chef de paroisse, à la fois pasteur, juge et conseiller de tous, arbitre de toutes les disputes, intercesseur auprès du ciel qui dispense les pluies et accorde les beaux temps, âme véritable de cette communauté étroite et hermétique qu'est la paroisse canadienne-française. (p.37)

Bordering on sacrilege, the following question nonetheless can be asked: If the priest is the real 'husband' and progenitor, is it surprising that the Church in Quebec long proclaimed the existence of the large family (such as the Moisans) as one essential duty to be fulfilled (what historically is called "revenge of the cradle") lest the French Canadian perish? At any rate, it appears clearly that the woman's fertility stood as barometer for success in the Messianic ethos. (3)
    After carefully dwelling in the representation of tradition, Ringuet clinically (in real life the author was a medical man) paints its decadence. At

73

the end of the book, old Euchariste, aware of the ruins of his family and of the land, has to realize: "La terre faillait aux siens, la terre éternelle et maternelle ne nourrissait plus ses fils." (p.287) (True to type, though, like Menaud he muses that industrialization and failed descendants are to blame for this.) Religion is not the center of stability and security it once was: the two Moisan children who have joined religious orders have both died of consumption. God's design has failed in the disintegration of the family. One of the avowed aims of Messianism, that redemption of "pagan" Anglo-Saxon North America Quebec has to accomplish, is portrayed in the end, in its ironic subversion as Euchariste, the fallen symbol, reflects about what he had been taught now that he is in New England:

> Les rares fois, que, chez lui, Euchariste Moisan avait évoqué les "Etats", il avait imaginé des villes et des campagnes lointaines, mais semblables à celles qu'il connaissait. Et il les avait vues lentement envahies par le Québec. Tant de familles de sa connaissance avaient émigré que cette coulée vivante et prolifique ne pouvait ne pas avoir prolongé là-bas la patrie laurentienne et formé un nouveau Québec américain. ... Un million et demi de "Français" dans le seul Est des Etats-Unis, dans la seule Nouvelle-Angleterre!
>
> Et voilà que venu au foyer de son fils, en une ville où lui disait-on, près d'un tiers de la population était de sang français, il ne retrouvait rien qui lui fût prochain. (p.251)

Indeed, it is no doubt such a painful awareness of failed, misguided hopes which gave birth to the "Beat" sense of void, articulated in the late fifties by a descendant of these French-Canadian immigrants, Jack Kerouac.

So, as the book closes on the bleakness of exile, the darkness of the soot and grime of White Falls, U.S.A., in jarring contrast to the golden open fields and sunny days of the first half of the novel, these two poles coalesce in Euchariste's decrepitude:

> A table, au déjeûner du midi, il mangea le nez dans son assiette, levant les yeux de temps à autre pour voir si ses petits-enfants l'observaient. Mais ils causaient entre eux et en anglais, apparemment insensibles à la présence de ce paysan qu'ils ne connaissaient point, dont apparemment ils ne savaient rien sinon que c'était un de leurs grands-pères; non pas celui de Washington Street, un bon vieil Irlandais aux dents et à lunettes d'or, ...; mais bien l'autre grand-père, sorti du fond du lointain, et nordique Québec, du Québec rustre et arriéré, ... Un grand-père qui ne sentait point la boutique de barbier, mais l'étable. (pp.249-250)

A powerful if sad resolution takes place: the death of a family, a way of life, a culture. One must admit that the seeds of destruction were present all along in the composition of the Messianic myth, in the very outlook so brilliantly introduced in the opening pages (when young Euchariste is sitting on a veranda with his uncle, whiling away the "eternal moment" of a late sunny sunday afternoon, presenting an arresting image of imperviousness and obliviousness to the world outside their immediate environment). Yet, one cannot help wishing Fate had been more lenient.

1 On the mythology of the French-Canadian mother which, in some respects, corresponds to that of the Jewish mother and, perhaps, to that of other ethnic groups who in the experience of hardship benefited from the maternal role of woman, albeit to excess, see Jean LeMoyne's essay, "La Femme dans la Civilisation Canadienne-Française", *Convergences*, pp.69-100.

2 On this theme of the French Canadian's emasculation due to the type of religion that evolved in Quebec, see Jean LeMoyne's essay, "L'Atmosphère Religieuse au Canada Français", *Convergences*, pp.46-66. (It was first published in a *Cité Libre* issue of 1951, creating quite a stir.) Upon reading LeMoyne's well-argued essay, one can, no doubt, see in the aberrations brought about by a Jansenistic clergy (particularly through its tutelage in the field of education, a monopoly that was unquestioned until 1960) significant factors explaining the violence of the sixties among the young: "Notre morale est naïve comme un symptôme: la hantise sexuelle et l'obsession compensatrice de l'autorité que nous rencontrons ici nous situent en pleine psychopathologie. Nous ne mourons pas tous, mais nous sommes tous frappés. Des malades paissent des malades. Des victimes engendrent des victimes." (p.57)

3 LeMoyne, pp.71-72; again on the subject of castration, see pp.69-70, where LeMoyne finds significant that Saint John the Baptist who, in the New Testament, is a man of virility and strength, is made into the image of a curly-headed pre-pubescent as the patron saint of Quebec. Interestingly, on the night of June 24, 1968, in the presence of Prime Minister Trudeau, the traditional parade on the patron saint's feast day was wrecked by violent demonstrations, not unconnected, one may surmise, with an affirmation of virility denied for so long by the symbolism of the little angelic figure. (The "boy" Saint-John the Baptist had actually been replaced in the 1968 parade by a stylized, less offensive emblem. That resentment still rankled at the very mention of "la Saint-Jean" forced, in the summer of 1970, the indefinite cancellation of the annual parade.)

# THE REVOLTED

# BLACK

The second major theme of the Black American novel is dialectically linked to the theme of hybridity. Germane to the melodrama or the tragedy of the mulatto is the mood of discontent with an overall culture that will not absorb an independent class of mixed-blood (cf. Johnson) or, as was more often the case, will not differentiate between someone that "is known to be a Negro"(to use Himes' phrase), though he does not *appear* to be, and one who is recognizably Black (cf. Chesnutt and Brown).(1) Though this discontent is one of the chief features an ante- and post-bellum Black literature, the protest articulated never blends the moans and groans into a loud shout of revolt.

Nowhere is there the kind of sweeping indictment that Richard Wright brings to the scene with *Native Son*. The novelists in the Brown and Chesnutt tradition, and even the writers of Slave narratives, work rather in the framework of Christian morality, when not appealing to pathos, to inveigh against the "evil" (a term that recurs) of slavery or of the caste system. In other words, the early writers are at bottom optimists, dyed-in-the-wool believers, as it were, in the American Dream ethos. They believe in an evolutionary process strongly reliant on a Puritan sense of destiny; if consciences are appealed to in a proper way then the barriers of slavery and caste will come down. Underlying the tragic ending of Chesnutt's and Brown's novels is the notion that if people really knew what it is to be a Clotel or a Rena Warwick, as the reader does get to know them, then acceptance would come, Prospero would recognize Caliban's humanity.

But is really with the Negro Renaissance that, as in many other things, revolt takes roots. The discovery of self-conceived and articulated values, emphatically Calibanic rather than Prospero-oriented, which takes place in the Jazz age — with Harlem becoming, literally, the cultural centre of the

77

Black world — and the stressing of Caliban's tentative self-sufficiency, establishes the groundwork upon which Wright's thoroughly disillusioned generation will vent its revolt with fury. In a way, it seems odd to consider a time suited to dancing, singing, hedonism, sensuality, and general festivity in the framework of revolt. There are two reasons which encourage such a perspective. First, starting with a writer such as Toomer, there is a radical break with the Reconstruction outlook. Continuing with DuBois, McKay, Hughes, and a number of other writers, the new attitude is one of self-discovery, a Calibanic search for indigenous roots. Contrary to the previous writers' plea for acceptance in the "other's" culture, we have a departure from tragic alienation towards a reconciliation rooted in self-recognized and assumed experience. Whether this reconciliation is celebrated in wild rag-time music, cake-walk dancing, the verbal witticism of a Langston Hughes or the explorations of a Toomer, a central fact emerges: there is an undeniable *joie de vivre*, a lyrical celebration of what it means to be alive and truly at ease with oneself. Second, Black nationalism, described simply as group self-consciousness, takes its roots in this period. In the acceptance of Africanity, whether it is in the rhythms of the new songs and dances, or in the imagery that bursts through a book such as *Cane*, or, again, the lyrical primitivism of a McKay, writers find the breeding ground for that radicalism so magnificently embodied in Ellison's character, Ras the Exhorter, the prototypical Harlemian nationalist. At any rate, Harlem, as the urban centre representative of the new outlook, is the symbolic nexus of reference for the understanding of the violence, despair, and hope which follow in the wake of Richard Wright's Bigger.

The Negro Renaissance is the base from whence we shall begin the exploration of our second theme. Next, we shall consider the stance of revolt in the writer's depiction of the Blacks' social milieu (the ghetto and the concept of alienation), and finally, we shall deal with the violence in the characters' lives wherein rests the notion of the Black novelist's revolt. We will move from a strictly Calibanic viewpoint to one where Caliban hurls his full defiance at Prospero's experience.

In a speech given at Howard University in 1966, Léopold Sédar Senghor, the poet-President and chief theoretician of Négritude, acknowledged that the writers and artists of the Negro Renaissance were the first and true originators of this movement:

> Without overlooking the role played by Haiti, the fact remains that you were the ones, who between the years 1920-1925, started the Negro Renaissance, and gave birth to the New Negro, conscious of his Négritude, determined *to live it*: to defend it and make it famous ... . For you were not only talking about Négritude, you were living it, you were Négritude. (2)

Omitting Senghor's customary rhetorical flourish, one must note the significance of this recognition. How could it be otherwise? For the imagery, the symbolism, the call for rhythmic verse, notwithstanding the appeal to indigenous cultural roots dear to Senghor, Césaire, *et al.* were all being expressed in the Harlem of the twenties. There, an unselfconscious négritude was being created in a lifestyle spiritually abundant and fertile, stemming from a throbbing sense of harmony with the rediscovered self. A passage from one of *Cane*'s stories, "Theatre", expresses this: "Girls dance and sing. Men clap. The walls sing and press inward. They press the men and girls, they press John towards a center of physical ecstasy. Go to it Baby! Fan yourself, and feed your papa!" (p.93) Here, to a great extent, Senghor and Césaire will find the aesthetics of Négritude. Black stands for beauty, and fecundity, so does dusk or night, whereas White (Prospero's culture), dawn or day stands for desiccation, sterility. The previously quoted passage in "Box Seat" conveys this contrasting imagery:

> Houses are shy girls whose eyes shine reticently upon the dusk body of the street. Upon the gleaming limbs and asphalt torso of a dreaming nigger. Shake your curled wool-blossoms, nigger. Open your liver lips to the lean, white spring. Stir the root-life of a withered people. Call them from their houses and teach them to dream. (p.104)

W.E.B. DuBois's *Dark Princess* (1928), an innocuous and naive novel about an alliance between the coloured peoples of the world designed to overthrow "white supremacy", although marred by a dubious story line, nonetheless expresses in one passage a similar play of images:

> First and above all came that sense of color: into this world of pale yellowish and pinkish parchment, that absence or negation of color, came, suddenly, a glow of golden brown skin. It was darker than sunlight and gold; it was lighter and livelier than brown. It was a living, glowing crimson, veiled beneath brown flesh. It called for no light and suffered no shadow, but glowed softly of its own inner radiance. (p.8)

But it is McKay's *Home to Harlem* (1928) that epitomizes the celebration of négritude. In a novel that focuses on the festive atmosphere of Harlem, oblivious to plot and character, the message borne in the successive tableaux-like scenes is to enjoy whatever comes naturally, to lead an uninhibited kind of life. It is McKay's intimate belief that, upheld by this vitality and abundance of life, the Black man is in a far better position than the White, who is looking for an intellectual meaning to the universe.

McKay feels that Blacks *know*, understand life's meaning in their very being because they are part, and an active one, of the natural process. (Such belief, of course, corresponded to the overall primitivist craze of the day. The "slumming" Jay Gatsby crowd certainly agreed with McKay's views; just as Sartre will regarding Senghor's similar statements.) (3) Jake coming 'home', after living in Europe, anticipates on the boat the luxuriance and richness that awaits him in Harlem. The picture that emerges is a lyrical celebration of the gratification of the senses: sounds, sights and feelings mingle and mean Harlem:

> Oh, to be in Harlem again after two years away. The deep-dyed color, the thickness, the closeness of it. The noises of Harlem. The sugared laughter. The honey-talk on its streets. And all night long, ragtime and "blues" playing somewhere... sighing somewhere, dancing somewhere! Oh, the contagious fever of Harlem. (p.9)

Another significant feature of McKay's novel is the use of contrasting imagery similar to Toomer's and DuBois's. The multiple colour variations found among Black people — instead of rooting melodrama — are celebrated as indicative of abundance and richness, and a source of pride in oneself. Black is sensed to be beautiful:

> Ancient black life rooted upon its base with all its fascinating new layers of brown, low-brown, high-brown, nut-brown, lemon, maroon, olive, mauve, gold. Yellow balancing between black and white. Black reaching out beyond yellow. Almost white on the brink of a change. Sucked back down into the current of black by the terribly sweet rhythm of black blood.... (p.29)

Yet it is in the nucleus of the Negro's animalism, his primitive vitality, that resides the heart of McKay's affirmation of Black culture. In the following, long but highly pertinent, passage one can observe the implications behind the use of contrapuntal symbolism: animalism *v.* intellectualism; sensuality *v.* coldness; primitivism *v.* gentility. Again pride in self, in one's blackness or Africanity, is lyrically conveyed:

> Haunting rhythm, mingling of naive wistfulness and charming gayety, now sheering over into riotous joy, now, like a jungle mask, strange, unfamiliar, disturbing, now plunging headlong into the far, dim depths of profundity and rising out as suddenly with a simple, childish grin. And the white visitors laugh. They see the grin only. Here are none of the well-patterned, well-made

80

emotions of the respectable world. A laugh might finish in a sob. A moan end in hilarity. That gorilla type wriggling there with his hands so strangely hugging his mate, may strangle her tonight. But he has no thought of that now. He loves the warm wriggle and is lost in it. Simple, raw emotions and real. They may frighten and repel refined souls, because they are too intensely real, just as a simple savage stands dismayed before nice emotions that he instantly perceives as false. (p.156)

A faint false note can be heard, however, in these novels of the Renaissance, not loud enough to jar the festivities but sufficient to indicate that the seeds of the coming revolt are planted in the very urban environment where the Negro rediscovers himself. Harlem may be a place of "sugared laughter" and its streets may "honey-talk", yet McKay cannot help but admit there is another reality after the music fades — that of the foul smells of the ghetto. Jake and a friend witness a street fight, and the friend muses: "We're all just lumped together without a chanst to choose and so we nacherally hate one another. It's nothing to wonder that you' buddy Ray done ran away from it. ...We're too close and thick in Harlem. Need some moh fresh air between us...." (pp.131-132) DuBois also is aware of these realities when Perigua, one of the leaders of the would-be revolution, asserts: "We're tame tabbies; we're fawning dogs; we lick and growl and wag our tails; we're so glad to have a white man fling us swill that we wriggle on our bellies and crawl. We slave that they may loll; we hand over our daughters to be their prostitutes." (p.60)

Another important characteristic appears which, added to the preceding, constitutes the ingredients for Wright's revolt: the Black man's alienation, induced by the very realities the ghetto so well represents. (4) These realities often are the scourge of racial discrimination. As Halsey, in Toomer's Cane, succinctly puts it: "Prejudice is everywheres about this country. An a nigger aint much standin anywheres." (p.221) DuBois' Matt experiences it when his application for internship in medical school is turned down: "Well — what did you expect? Juniors must have obstetrical work. Do you think white women patients are going to have a nigger doctor delivering their babies?" (p.4) Ray, a bookish Haitian, works on a train with Jake in Mckay's novel, unable to continue his education for lack of resources. The significance of Ray resides in his identification by the other characters as a doomed man. He is destined to a tragic end because he is preoccupied with ideas and not senses. But, beyond serving as a foil in McKay's structural opposition of Black and White worlds, we are led to believe that Ray's tragedy lies in that awareness, through consciousness, of the despair of the Negro's condition and his inability to do anything about it. This same attitude is expressed in Wright's *Native Son* and Ellison's *Invisible Man*. The cook on the train summarizes: "Better leave that theah

81

Richard Wright                from the Schomburg Collection, N.Y.P.L.

nigger professor alone and come on 'long to the dining-car with us. That theah nigger is dopey from them books o' hish. I done told befoh them books would git him yet." (p.75) Alienation here, then, takes a modern form of existential malaise; the character strives for an identity that escapes him because he is rootless. Eventually Ray suffers a mental breakdown. Yet he indicates an awareness of his fate when he admits to Jake:

> The fact is, Jake, Ray said, I don't know what I'll do with my little education. I wonder sometimes if I could get rid of it and go and lose myself in some savage culture in the jungles of Africa. I am a misfit — as the doctors who dole out newspaper advice to the well-fit might say — a misfit with my little education and constant dreaming, when I should be getting the nightmare habit to hog in a whole lot of dough like everybody else in this country. (p.127)

The unbearable socio-economic conditions of the ghetto, and the equally unbearable sense of malaise and meaninglessness in oneself, stemming from racial discrimination, are the motives behind the flood of violent revolt that follows the pattern of Wright's Bigger Thomas. Starting with Wright there is, in the Negro novel, a hard-eyed, systematic appraisal of the socio-economic plight of the urban Black. *Native Son* (1940) presents an analytical picture of the conditions which serve as natural breeding grounds for the likes of Bigger. Promiscuity, shabbiness, and economic and political exploitation are interrelated facets of ghetto life, once the rose-coloured glasses of the twenties have been taken off. Promiscuity is conveyed in such a scene as the following, witnessed by Bigger, hiding from the police and looking at what is taking place in an apartment of a tenement building facing him: "In one bed sat three naked black children looking across the room to the other bed on which lay a man and a woman, both naked and black in the sunlight. There were quick, jerky movements on the bed where the man and the woman lay, and the three children were watching." (p.231) The shabbiness of the dwellings is expressed in the depiction of dwellers running after rats or other vermins: " 'Bigger, he's behind the trunk'! the girl; whimpered." (p.8) Economic exploitation is in the rents paid for rat-infested quarters: "And he had heard it said that black people, even though they could get good jobs, paid twice as much rent as whites for the same kind of flats." (p.233) It is also in the price paid for consumer items: "Bread sold here for five cents a loaf, but across the 'line' where white folks lived it sold for four." (p.234) And the form of business-ownership in the ghetto adds to the overall exploitation: "Almost all businesses in the Black Belt were owned by Jews, Italians, and Greeks. Most Negro businesses were funeral parlors; white undertakers refused to bother with dead black bodies." (pp.233-234) Finally, there is political exploitation, that of the Black politicians who have learned their techniques from the White bosses. At the end of *Native Son*, Max, Bigger's lawyer, queries him about his "leaders": " 'Didn't you trust them?' " To which Bigger replies: " 'I don't reckon they wanted anybody to trust 'em. They wanted to get elected to office. They paid you to vote.' " (p.331)

Similarly, Ann Petry's *The Street* (1946), (116th street in Harlem), contains a relentless picture of ghetto depravity. The story centres on a young Negro woman's efforts during World War II to succeed in life when she is living in Harlem, has a jobless husband who later deserts the home, and a son who, left most of the time by himself, wanders among derelicts and prostitutes and consequently gets into trouble with the law. Lutie toils at various jobs but, like so many other characters of the Negro novel, she is defeated in the long run and so is her family. The individual's feeling of "asphyxiation" is extended to the physical environment that he inhabits. This is readily evidenced in the association that Lutie makes in connection with her apartment: "All through Harlem there were apartments just like this one, she thought, and they're nothing but traps. Dirty, dark, filthy traps. Upstairs. Downstairs. In my lady's chamber. Click goes the trap when you pay the first month's rent. Walk right in. It's a free country. Dark little hallways. Stinking toilets." (p.50) The feeling of being webbed-in is furthermore experienced when witnessing the exploitation of consumer goods: "All of them — the butcher shops, the notion stores, the vegetable stands — all of them sold the leavings, the sweepings, the impossible unsalable merchandise, the dregs and dross that were reserved especially for Harlem." (p.99)

Jim, the husband, also has little conviction that he can control his destiny. He cannot find a job to support his family and the reason for this is in the very process of a system that dehumanizes human beings who are born black. The male's loss of self-respect becomes evident: "Waiting, waiting, waiting to be called up for a job. He would come home shivering from the cold, saying, 'God damn white people anyway. I don't want favors. All I want is a job. Just a job. Don't they know if I knew how I'd change the color of my skin." (p.24) Lutie experiences parallel constant assaults on her dignity. At one point she works for a white family in Connecticut and overhears conversations that reveal to her a jarring conception of the Negro, and specifically the Negro woman. In their eyes she cannot be granted the basic dignity cognate with femininity: "Apparently it was an automatic reaction of white people — if a girl was colored and fairly young, why, it stood to reason she had to be a prostitute." (p.33)

A notable sociological fact, the break-up of the Negro family unit, is dealt with, and in Lutie's case it is tied to the socio-economic pattern. Racial prejudice has a direct bearing on social productivity (or the lack of it). In eroding a man's self-respect, it dispossesses him of his potential for work. Since Jim cannot find a job, he becomes more and more demoralized and turns to idle pursuits, such as philandering and drinking, to fill the time:

"This street was full of broken homes, and she thought the men must have been like Jim — unable to stand the day after day of drab living with nothing to look forward to but just enough to eat and a shelter overhead. And the women working as she had worked and the men getting fed up and getting other women." (p.52)

Ellison describes the shabbiness of the ghetto dweller's habitat, in Wright's manner, when the hero has to exterminate some vermins: " 'The filthy, stinking things', Mary cried. 'Git that one under the table! Yon' he goes, don't let him git away! The nasty rascal! (p.283) Living in such conditions, victims of various forms of economic exploitation, it comes as no surprise (or it should not, as Ellison for one implies) when the inhabitants riot. And as riots erupt they are accompanied by looting, the most festive occasion, it would seem, in the life of the slum-dwellers: "All the street's signs were dead, all the day sounds had lost their stable meaning. Somewhere a burglar alarm went off, a meaningless blangy sound, followed by the joyful shouts of looters." (p.465) And as one character puts it, upon being asked how the riot (the last one) started: " 'Damn *who* started it' Dupre said, 'All I want is for it to last a while.' " (p.468)

Consequent to the depiction of ghetto life, it is the experience of alienation which comes to dominate and hinges the Black novelist's revolt, starting with Wright. *Native Son* epitomizes in every respect the existential protest of the Negro (or the existential fate of modern man, as European intellectuals, namely Sartre, were quick to point out). (5) In this story, the plot in its linear form concerns the killing of a white girl in Chicago by a Negro and the comeuppance with the forces of the law that follows. The 'detective' aspect of the novel is only a pretext for a highly dramatic portrayal of the Negro's condition in America: in Bigger is symbolized the hopelessness of his being. The concept of alienation is introduced early in the book, as Bigger, speaking to his buddies, reflects: "Goddamnit, look! We live here and they live there. We black and they white. They got things and we ain't. They do things and we can't. It's just like living in jail. Half the time I feel I'm like on the outside of the world peeping in through a knothole in the fence...." (p.23) The dividing wall symbolism, with the accompanying sense of "asphyxiation" for those behind it, is introduced and will recur in other novels of revolt. Wright, in this seminal work, shows that alienation is not just Bigger's problem. He carries its philosophico-sociological ramifications into the psychological one of mental imbalance. (An attitude that was foreshadowed, of course, in the character of Ray in McKay's *Home to Harlem*, and which will be repeated in that of the Vet in *Invisible Man*.) Here, in the character of an inmate that Bigger meets in jail, as elsewhere, the root cause of this extreme form of alienation is the Negro's consciousness of his plight and his incapacity to live with it; as is explained to Bigger:

He went off his nut from studying too much at the university. He was writing a book on how colored people live and he says somebody stole all the facts he'd found. He says he's got to the bottom of why colored folks are treated bad and he's going to tell the President and have things changed, see? He's *nuts!* (p.318)

Alienation more often takes the form of a sense of dispossession in the "have-not" facing the "have", a sense where the individual feels drained of all material and spiritual resources. Such is the case when Bigger meets Mary Dalton, his eventual victim, the rich blonde and beautiful daughter of his employers. She is a Miranda figure, full of candid sympathy and good-will towards the Negro, whom she sees as an object to be pitied and patronized. The contrast is too much for Bigger: "The guarded feeling of freedom that he had while listening to her was tangled with the hard fact that she was white and rich, a part of the world of people who told him what he could and could not do." (p.66) Bigger's feeling of not belonging to himself, of being deprived of an elemental sense of identity, is explicated when Bigger ruminates about the "have" (the White) so different from him: " ... he felt that they ruled him, even when they were far away and not thinking of him, ruled him by conditioning him to his relations to his own people." (p.110) Lastly, Wright goes on to associate the Negro's state of segregation with one of dehumanization that, on a collective level, takes the form of colonization; the same, it would seem, as that the former African colonies experienced. This is presented in the unfortunate rhetorical last part that fouls up the structure of the novel: Max, Bigger's lawyer, says to the tribunal: "Taken collectively, they [the Negroes] are not simply twelve million people; in reality they constitute a separate nation, stunted, stripped, and held captive *within* this nation, devoid of political, social, economic, and property rights." (p.364)

The Negro's loss of identity is a major theme of Attaway's *Blood on the Forge* (1941), a tale about three brothers, Big Mat, Chinatown and Melody, who are sharecroppers in the South of the thirties, until Big Mat's murder of a "riding boss" forces them to migrate to the North. They find work in the Pennsylvania steel mines, where their fellow-workers are newly-arrived European immigrants, Ukrainians and Italians, constituting with the Blacks a pool of "cheap labour". The Negro's dehumanized state is again here depicted both in the South and in the North, in the mask of happiness he has to wear in the presence of Whites: "The stranger rode near. Chinatown began to grin. He wasn't tickled. He always bent his back and grinned a little for white folks." (p.35) Where such a mask is set aside, suicidal recourse to violence takes place. For here is the bottomless despair it aims to hide when, upon being named "deputy", Big Mat reflects about the sense of nothingness he will hurl into violence:

He had been called "nigger" since childhood. "Nigger, nigger never die..." was the chant. The name that they gave him had become a badge signifying poverty and filth. He had not been allowed to walk like a man. His food had been like the dog slops, and he had eaten. In the fields he had gone to the branch and gotten down on his belly. He had drunk his water like a dog left too long in the heat. They had taken his money and his women. They had made him run for his life. They would have run him with dogs through the swamps. They would have lynched him. (p.231)

The similitude between Bob's, the protagonist, and Bigger Thomas' condition is revealed in Chester Himes' *If He Hollers Let Him Go* (1945). The story is set in a West Coast naval yard during World War II; Bob Jones feels crushed by the various racial experiences he encounters. Eventually he is destroyed by a society of which he has never felt part, and, more immediately, because of his involvement with a white woman. He is accused on the basis of the woman's trumped-up charges of sexual assault and sentenced to enrollment into the army for a somewhat delayed death. The "dividing wall" of alienation serves, as in *Native Son*, as dramatic core for the tragic irony of the end defeat:

Living every day scared, walled in, locked up. I didn't feel like fighting any more; I'd take a second thought before I hit a paddy [white] now. I was tired of keeping ready to die every minute; it was too much strain. I had to fight hard enough each day just to keep on living. All I wanted was for the white folks to let me alone; not say anything to me; not even look at me. They could take the goddamned world and go to hell with it. (p.5)

At one point, Bob goes to a cinema where a film is shown portraying stereotypes of the Stepin Fetchit variety. Its dehumanized import is intensely felt and resented: "I was down to a low ebb, I needed some help. I had to know that Negroes weren't the lowest people on the face of God's green earth. I had to talk it over with somebody, had to build myself back up. The sons of bitches were grinding me to the nub, to the meatless bone." (p.95) As racial discrimination increasingly destroys Bob, he comes to feel what most characters experience in the Black novel — the feeling of dispossession that becomes part of the Negro's soul. So that, as shall be seen later in the analysis of violence (and as Wright himself will say), one of the first impulses of the Negro in wanting to assert his humanity will be that of smashing his state of degradation and those he feels responsible for it: "I knew with the white folks sitting on my brain, controlling my every thought, action, and emotion, making life one crisis after another, day and night, asleep and awake, conscious and unconscious, I couldn't make it." (pp.181-

182) Again and again, Bob harps on this notion of "making it", his exacerbation compounded by the fact that he has been conditioned by the ethos of the overall society which proclaims the rewards and virtues of honest work and good morality in terms of material benefit. The bitter awareness that the American Dream cannot be his drives him to despair, and to a prophetic statement about his fate, when he says to his girlfriend (a mulatto buoyed up by the Dream): "But please don't tell me I can control my destiny, because I know I can't. In any incident that might come up a white person can use his color on me and turn it into a catastrophe and I won't have any protection, any out, nothing I can do about it but die." (p.205)

Alienation likewise dominates Ann Petry's *The Street*. The "dividing wall" symbolism is again brought to bear when at one point Lutie reflects about the evils of ghetto life foisted by racial prejudice. 116th Street is a metaphor for the ghetto, and Harlem is the symbol of the Negro's collective state of alienation:

> It was any city where they set up a line and say black folks stay
> on this side and white folks on this side, so that the black folks
> were crammed on top of each other — jammed and packed and
> forced into the smallest possible space until they were completely
> cut off from light and air. (p.130)

Foreshadowing Ellison, the parallel feeling of non-identity is conveyed in a scene where a character, Boots, alludes to his "invisibility" to the white man:

> Porter! Porter this and Porter that. Boy, George. Nameless.
> He got a handful of silver at the end of each run, and a mountain of
> silver couldn't pay a man to stay nameless like that. No name,
> black my shoes. No name, hold my coat. No name, brush me off.
> No name, take my bags. No name. No name. (p.165)

The sense of asphyxiation accompanies also the overall pattern of alienation. Lutie indeed experiences what Bigger, Ray, Bob, Matt and Big Mat experience: "From the time she was born, she had been hemmed into an ever-narrowing space, until now she was very nearly walled-in and the wall had been built up brick by brick by eager white hands." (pp.200-201)

William Gardner Smith's *Last of the Conquerors* (1948), an expatriate novel written in Europe when the author was twenty (presumably as a result of his experiences with the American army in postwar Germany), tells of Negro soldiers trying to lead the same life as their White counterparts on the continent; but they run into the same barriers that they would confront back home. The caste system is more than a geographical institution, it is something that the individuals carry within themselves. Life in Germany is good for the soldiers, however, when they do not run into the prejudices of their White colleagues, as they experience living in a society devoid, so it seems, of the racial disease. So much so that when his tour of duty is ended, the prospect of returning home for the soldier is the dread of once more going back to hell. Murdoch, for instance, confronts that dilemma and he fears the ambient feeling of dispossession that awaits him: "What the hell am I gonna do when I get back to the States? What kinda goddam job you think I can get in Georgia? Diggin' ditches? I don't want to go back there. I don't want to go anyplace in the States. Can you understand that?" (p.67) Another time, the reminder of home brings back the experience of alienation that the Negro suffers anywhere in America, North as well as South:

> There ain't no difference between the South and the North.
> Only thing the South is more honest with its prejudice. That's all.
> In the South they got signs up that say, 'No colored allowed', and you just go someplace else. In the North they don't have no signs, but you go to a big hotel and they say, 'Sorry, the position is already taken'. (p.69)

Hayes, the main character, attends an American movie in the local theatre and he witnesses the same portrayal of stereotypes that Himes' character does. The same negation of basic humanity, the same degradation, is perceived: "The Negro said "yassah" very often and, when mysterious noises came from upstairs, the white actors were very brave but the Negro's eyes opened very wide like spotted gold balls and his mouth opened wide into a wide cavern with white borders." (p.169)

Wiliam Demby's so-called Existential novel, *Beetlecreek* (1950), purports to show, through the contrapuntal pattern of White and Black racial prejudices, that the basic problem involved is irrespective of race; that of man at odds with an incomprehensible universe and with a consequent sense of general futility. (6) The dramatization takes place in a southern town where the Blacks live on one side of the tracks, the Whites on the other. An old white man serves as symbol and chief character of the tale: he lives in the middle, leaning on the Negro side, and becomes eventually the tragic victim of man's "despair".

In the context of our essay, it suffices to observe that the author deals mostly with life among the town's Negroes and dramatizes attitudes and feelings that parallel those seen so far. Even the characterization of the old white man, Bill, validly serves in the realm of alienation. He identifies with the Negroes to such an extent that indeed he *becomes* a Negro, only the colour of his skin makes it otherwise (and as he is destroyed one may see the dreadful irony implied, which certainly adds credibility to the existential aura of the novel). This is introduced when we are told: "He had understood immediately what they felt, though it surprised him to know that even with them there could be the same childhood terror he had known, the same feeling of shame to be in the world, the same need for shadows and dark places to hide." (p.139)

In one of the Negro characters of the ook, David — who is meant to be the outward counterpart of the dual symbolism borne in the figure of Bill (Black Soul, White Skin) — we have attitudes reminiscent of Bigger's, and Lutie's. There is the similar references to the "dividing wall", and the specific feeling of asphyxiation. David experiences both while he is attending college in the North (this again relates to the destruction syndrome that too much consciousness of the Negro's plight brings, as David never does finish college):

> But when he went to that Negro college, he began to feel it, and along with it, the feeling of being suffocated and unable to move. This had nothing to do with his not having opportunities or "civil rights", but it was a strange feeling, very difficult for him to explain to himself, which had to do with feeling Death, feeling frozen, suffocated, unable to breathe, knowing there was little to be done about it. (p.79)

Feelings of asphyxiation, dispossession, alienation are lumped together in the concept of "invisibility" central to Ellison's novel. "Invisibility" is the state in which the Negro is kept by the 'system'. In fact, in ordinary life the Black man is dead as a human being, Ellison says. Only through a *conscious* understanding of his state is the Negro able to survive and maintain a valid sense of reality. Through consciousness he becomes *aware* of his invisibility, of his death-in-life condition. As he becomes *aware*, the Negro manages to be reborn and visible to *himself*. But he must still maintain a tactical pretense of invisibility for *others* (here is the meaning of Rinehart, I believe, and the reason for the narrator's fascination with him) until the timely moment when he will reappear among the living. This is the final message, uttered only at the very end of the novel, almost surreptitiously, but by its very conciseness portentous of dire warnings, it seems, for those still bent on maintaining and enforcing the Negro's invisibility ("The hibernation is over. I must shake off the old skin and come up for breath." (p.502) This is the warning that Baldwin much later will articulate as *The Fire Next Time*, in more direct and explicit rhetoric.

But let us take a closer look and see the variegated shades thrown by this concept. Early in the book is a scene where the hero remembers the dying words of his grandfather, a former slave. They are words of wisdom, the wisdom of one who went through the 'system', and if he managed to survive its dehumanizing process, it is, as the grandfather says, only because he knew how to go along with it, until he could do something, which never materialized, and that perhaps the grandson might bring about: "Live with your head in the lion's mouth. I want you to overcome 'em with yes, undermine 'em with grins, agree 'em to death and destruction, let 'em swoller you till they vomit or bust wide open." (pp.19-20)

Equally important, both in its realistic and symbolic impact, is the scene with Norton, the White trustee of the Negro school attended by the hero, who is accidentally brought into contact with a sharecropping Negro family, where some of the children are the off-spring of incestuous relations between the father and his daughter. The context makes it clear that this is the nadir state of inhumanity in which the system has been working to maintain the Negro. The father says, to a much-shaken and troubled Norton (the Great White father symbolic on a psychological level of the *ego* now confronting his repressed *id*), that he has been, and constantly is, visited by rabidly interested white folks: "Some of 'em was big white folks, too, from the big school cross the state. Asked me lots 'bout what I thought 'bout things, and 'bout my folks and kids, and wrote it all down in a book. But best of all, suh, I got more work now that I ever did have before...." (p.52)

Dr. Bledsoe, the Negro principal of the college, confronts the hero upon learning of his driving Norton to see the incestuous father. Bledsoe thereafter makes sure that "the boy keeps running" (as he says in a reference letter intended to secure the narrator employment up North upon his expulsion from school). The author shows that this man, obedient and subservient to the White trustees who finance the school, is in fact partner (the 'twin' of the incestuous father) in a same state of dehumanization. Ellison describes him as the picture of the bourgeois "Uncle Tom": "Influential with wealthy men all over the country; consulted in matters concerning the race; a leader of his people; the possessor of not one, but *two* cadillacs, a good salary and a soft, good-looking and creamy-complexioned wife." (p.92)

Another central character in the first portion of the book is the mental asylum inmate called "The Vet", whom the hero and Norton meet again by accident. He embodies the expression, also developed in some of the novels seen so far, of the educated Negro who has seen too clearly into the despair of the Negro's condition. The Vet is a highly literate person, and terrifyingly sane (one sees the implication), as Norton witnesses. He mentions that he was a medic in the Army during the First World War, and he follows up with an understatement carrying the same meaning as that conveyed by Ray in *Home to Harlem*, Bigger's fellow inmate in *Native Son*, or David in *Beetlecreek*: " 'Oh yes, and how long were you in France?' Mr. Norton asked. 'Long enough,' he said. 'Long enough to forget some fundamentals which I should never have forgotten.' " (p.83) The "insane" Vet is imbued with a power of lucidity that calls to mind the Shakespearean characterization of the Fool, or the Jester, who sees the truth to which the so-called sane ones are blind. At one point he addresses himself to Norton and the protagonist, and he tells them the facts about the alienation that both are victims of: "Poor stumblers, neither of you can see the other. To you he is a mask on the scorecard of your achievement, a thing and not a man; a child, or even less — a black amorphous thing. And you, for all your power, are not a man to him, but a God, a force —." (p.87)

Living in the North, a new zealot of the "Brotherhood" (as the Communist Party is euphemistically called), the hero confronts soon enough the same pattern of alienation that he thought he had left in the South. At a party, in the Party that proclaims its immaculate intentions towards Black people, he is accosted by a drunken comrade who stereotypes the Negro in a manner not unlike Mary Dalton's when she sees Bigger, in *Native Son*; and here as elsewhere this has the effect of jolting the interlocutor: "How about a spiritual, Brother? Or one of those real good ole Negro work songs? Like this: *Ah Went to Atlanta — Nevah Been there befor*" (p.270) After other incidents — such as a lady-comrade's remark: "But don't you think he should be a little blacker?" (p.263) — the hero perceives how he is seen by the comrades, and this does not correspond to *his* sense of identity. Yet he decides to go along, thinking it is just a small matter, and ironically observes: "And yet I am what they think I am." (p.329)

The Negro's sense of not controlling his own destiny, his sense of not belonging to himself, which is covert or overt in all of the novels seen so far, is expressed by the Vet, who, upon being asked what the "they" is that the other inmates keep talking about, gives this identification of dispossession: "The Vet looked annoyed. 'They?' he said. 'They? Why, the same they we always mean, the white folks, authority, the gods, fate, circumstances — the force that pulls your string until you refuse to be pulled any more.' " (p.137) The significance of dispossession is carried, though, just like everything else practically, in the hero's personal experiences, or in the symbols that the author uses in relation to him. When he is in the hospital, recovering from the explosion that occurred in the paint factory, he is apparently lobotomized and loses all sense of memory, or identity; thus, though unconsciously, he grasps the first symptoms of his anomie, or his invisibility. At this stage the rest of the journey toward self-identity will be an exploration culminating in the full consciousness of his state: "I could no more escape than I could think of my identity. Perhaps, I thought, the two things are involved with each other. When I discover who I am, I'll be free." (p.212) He does when he consciously embraces his invisibility, his death, thus he is born. The Rinehart episode, if anything, serves as the catalyst for his metamorphosis. As he disembodies the term (Rine and hart: the outside and the inside of a same thing), the hero understands that this Harlem figure for which he came to be mistaken represents in his myriad identities his own myriad experiences, and they all amount to nothing, to non-identity, non-entity: "He's been around all the while, but I have been looking in another direction. He was around and others like him, but I have looked

Martin Luther King                    *Ebony Magazine*

past him.... What on earth was hiding behind the face of things? If dark glasses and a white hat could blot out my identity so quickly, who actually was who?" (p.426) The hero's reflection informs him of the interrelation between his experience and the figure of Rinehart, and they signify the collective experience of the Negro: "I began to accept my past ... images of past humiliation... They were me; they defined me. ... I now recognized my invisibility. So now I'd accept it, I'd explore it, rind and heart." (p.439)

The conclusion is in accord with the existential recognition germane to *Native Son* and *Beetlecreek* and a number of other novels: the acceptance of the absurdity of man's condition, the consciousness of one's guiltlessness while one is held to be guilty because of one's colour, the triumph over absurdity (invisibility) by using the rules of an absurd universe (the Rinehart recognition). Thus despair is turned into hope, pessimism into optimism. All these philosophical stratagems are themes or attitudes that are commonplace in modern fiction yet given vital relevance in the Black American's existential quest fashioned by the racial nightmare of his society: "And I knew that it was better to live out one's own absurdity than to die for that of others, whether for Ras's or Jack's." (p.484)

Before the Negro is able to reach Ellison's philosophical detachment, however, his sense of alienation and dispossession, rooted in no uncertain visible terms (the blight of the ghetto and racial prejudice), turns into despair for which violence is the only outlet. The revolt conveyed up to now by the writers' analytical depiction of social ills is supplemented (and given its more distinctive imprint) by the process of violence in the characters' lives. The natural explosion of pent-up frustrations and anger kept repressed and boiling for too long, violence, in these novels, operates as a necessary catharsis. It is a logical step.

Oftentimes in these works, violence is a reaction to White psychophysical violence or represents a release from the repressions imposed by traditional religious attitudes. In either case it almost achieves the level of ritual, one that the Negro has to undergo to divest himself, it seems, of all the burdens he has traditionally had to carry. If there is a distinct undertone of despair to this ritual, it appears sufficiently compensated by the strong overtones indicating that a form of rebirth is experienced. As the Negro releases himself in violence, often a blind and uncontrolled kind, one senses that he is killing all that which he feels has oppressed him, both in a realistic and symbolic fashion. He is equally killing himself for that matter, the self that has become alienated, disenfranchised. The ritual passes from the death to the rebirth phase, on a literal and/or symbolic level, resulting in the Negro's feeling he has acquired a new identity, a new self: a human dimension.

These attitudes are dramatized not only when they occur as incidents in the novels, but particularly in the descriptions used to bring across these facts: their blood-chilling, terrifying, lavish, naked and crude presentation

94

conveys the sense that a fundamental process tied to some primordial impulse is undergone. The precepts of taste and decorum or restraint are set aside. Violence in its crudity is shown for what it is: a basic animal release of aggression. Both Whites and Blacks are alike in that respect. The only justification, as the authors imply, is the positive rewarding outlet it represents for the Negro who kills in order to survive. The negative, degrading, ritual it represents for the White racist who indulges in violence out of self-induced fear is its own best condemnation.

*Home to Harlem* channels practically all potential violence into dancing, drinking, and the pursuit of an uninhibited way of life. But even among uninhibited people violence takes place. Earlier we noticed one of the characters' admission that crowded and filthy quarters are not appropriate for lyrical celebration. When two Negro women are shown "squaring off", McKay does not relate that to any pent-up, repressed anger, since his people by nature do not know of such things as repressions. McKay uses the incident to illustrate another facet of the primitivist philosophy that animates his book. Somehow he is saying violence is less deadly and in accordance with the natural pulse when kept exteriorized:

> The girls rushed to the window and saw the two black women squaring off at each other down in the back yard. They were both stark naked. After the challenge, the women had decided to fight with their clothes off. An old custom, perhaps a survival of African tribalism, had been imported from some West Indian hillside into a New York backyard. (p.142)

These incidents of violence, though practically innocuous (fist-fights, slaps in the face, etc.) contain in addition to a basic natural process of exteriorization, similar to dancing or sex, some other causes tied to the generic pattern we are observing. But McKay shies away from these other causes. Certainly there is in McKay's Jake or Ray a potential for violence similar to Bigger's. But, befitting the escapist tone that his book takes at times, the festive life of the twenties for the moment fulfills the same role as that historically borne by the Church: diverting the Negro's attention from the precise objects for his aggression.

There is no escapism for Wright, however. At the core of what he is trying to say is the feeling that a society that has deprived an individual of all claims to humanity, reducing him to a subhuman level, has created a being who in wanting to assert his humanity can only do so through a ritualistic process of violence. Since the normal channels of human groupings — the family, the Church, the community, a decent standard of living, a sense of being — are all closed, Bigger's only possible recourse is the instinctive reactions left to an animal. His fight for survival through aggression is the pristine struggle for life. In a world reduced to the primitive formulation of the

95

jungle, such as the urban ghetto of the thirties, the only code possible is indeed that of the jungle: kill or be killed. Society, laws, morality, all the attributes of civilization are nonexistent. This concept is substantiated in the unravelling of Bigger's fate subsequent to the accidental killing of Mary Dalton. Frightened, disoriented, Bigger becomes a predator; the more so since he is convinced he is now a mere prey in a hunt soon to be unleashed, whose outcome is not uncertain. The ritualistic process starts its course when he decides to dispose of the corpse:

> Wistfully, he gazed at the edge of the blade resting on the white skin; the gleaming metal reflected the tremulous fury of the coals. Yes, he *had* to. Gently, he sawed the blade into the flesh and struck a bone. He gritted his teeth and cut harder. As yet there was not blood anywhere on the knife. But the bone made it difficult. (pp.90-91)

Bigger has to go on killing, the moment he feels his survival is threatened. He subsequently kills Bessie, his girlfriend, though he just made love to her; Bessie may be a hazard if she is questioned by the police:

> This was the way it *had* to be. Then he took a deep breath and his hand gripped the brick and shot upward and paused a second and then plunged downward through the darkness to the accompaniment of a deep short grunt from his chest and landed with a thud. Yes! There was a dull gasp of surprise, then a moan. No, that must not be! He lifted the brick again and again, until in falling it struck a sodden mass that gave softly but stoutly to each landing blow. (p.222)

The cathartic import is furthermore indicated when, in jail, Bigger thinks back to the two murders and measures their importance. Clearly their depth of meaning for Bigger finds expression when contrasted to his state of dispossession noted earlier. Somewhat analogous to the "gratuitous act" of Existentialism that embodies meaning and significance for the individual lost in a meaningless world, the killings have given Bigger possession of "something": "In all his life the two murders were the most meaningful things that had ever happened to him. He was living, truly and deeply, no matter what others might think, looking at him with their blind eyes." (p.225)

For all the attitudes previously noted — rebirth, purification, repossession — this by no means implies a satisfaction that quiets down the individual who now can peacefully rest. It seems that the 'new' individual, being a creature of violence, a product of violence, has to keep on repeating similar acts, bound to the ritual; even if it means that having no external object upon which to release his aggression, Bigger may very well turn upon himself. There is a nihilistic, masochistic, impulse implied; but one suspects that the deeper implication is that Wright is saying that the 'system' being not changed as such, although the individual Negro may have, acts of violence, such as those that presided at his birth, have to be maintained until the 'system' itself is destroyed. (This position is certainly corroborated by the contemporary riots that used to take place every summer in American cities at a time — the sixties — after all, when some Negroes were in a far more advantageous position than ever in their history.):

> Out of the mood of renunciation there sprang up in him again the will to kill. But this time it was not directed outward toward people, but inward, upon himself. Why not kill that wayward yearning with him that had led him to this end? He had reached out and killed and had not solved anything, so why not reach inward and kill that which had duped him? (p.255)

Attaway's Big Mat, like Wright's Bigger, is an interesting case for the study of the meaning of violence for the Negro. The correlation between violence and religion, or other channels which traditionally operated as subliminal forms of aggression, is a concrete one. Almost simultaneously, as Big Mat denies the former channels, he is shown to be prone to a naked form of violence that bewilders even him: " 'Sometimes I think I goin' to go wild and kill off some people that ain't done me a harm,' groaned Big Mat." (p.181) The occasion that will precipitate this new drive in Big Mat is his nomination as deputy. The following description shows the tie linking his new-found feeling of power and his experience as a typecast sub-human:

> Always within him was that instinctive knowledge that he was being turned to white men's uses. So always with him was a basic distrust of a white. But now he was a boss. He was the law. After all, what did right or wrong matter in the case? Those thrilling new words were too much to resist. He was a boss, a boss over whites. (p.232)

The ominous note soon enough becomes a vital experience as Big Mat substitutes the ritual of violence for the old one of daily reading the Bible. The rebirth noted in Bigger's case applies here: Big Mat finds a new unknown self in the practice of violence. A creature of violence, he will from now on thrive on it; not in the sense expected by those who nominated him, but along the pattern that the release of aggression signifies for the oppressed Black man: "He had begun to heal his ruptured ego with a new medicine. That medicine was a sense of brutal power.... Like the deputies and troopers, he no longer needed reasons for aggression. Cruelty was a thing desirable in itself." (pp.249-250, p.254)

Like Bigger's, Big Mat's violence will not only be oriented towards Whites but also against somebody that is close to him, his mistress. Ostensibly this occurs as Big Mat learns of her infidelities, but Big Mat's change in behaviour towards her is concomitant with the general change in him, the release of violence against Anna structurally follows the pattern previously noted: "Red curls of skin covered her naked back. Except where her hair made a black covering for her face she might have been sprinkled with beads and rhinestones." (p.263)

At the end of the novel, before Big Mat perishes in the same process that gave him 'birth', as he strangles to death an old striker, Attaway stresses the ultimate sense that violence has for this Southern Negro, the rural brother of Bigger Thomas. In addition to the elements of catharsis, purification, ritual, rebirth, there is the idea of "repossession" in the very act of violence. The dispossessed Negro rejoices in a new-found vitality, a liberation of the self that transcends physical death (as in Big Mat's case who is killed as he is savoring his moment of triumph). There appears a new difference in eternity or salvation: the Preacher's celebration of the hereafter has been relinquished for that which can be achieved here and now:

> There was no riding boss over him now. He turned wildly and gazed at the mill. A great exhilaration almost swept him into the air. The towns were down. He was exalted. A bitterness toward all things white hit him like a hot iron. Then he knew. There was a riding boss — Big Mat. Big Matt Moss from the red hills was the riding boss. For the first time in his life he laughed aloud. Laughing crazily, he held the man by the neck.
>
> The old Slav struggled feebly in Big Mat's great hands. He cried out against the hands of Big Mat, the black riding boss. (pp.271-272)

Bob, Himes' exacerbated hero, tries to release his traumas in violence; to little avail. Not being used as an archetypal hero, like Bigger or Big Mat, Bob is not shown as if his destiny depended on violence. He is too complicated a man, and too much at odds with the meshes of the intricate pattern of the American Dream, to be thoroughly gratified by the recourse to only one channel. Yet it may be suspected that this is his tragedy; were he as 'simple' as a Bigger or a Big Mat, he probably would have found liberation in violence. In wanting too much, he ends up with nothing. The contrast at the end, between his attempt at destroying Madge and its upshot when *she* destroys him, is eloquent.

That Bob is at heart a Bigger or a Big Mat is shown in the cathartic dimension that violence takes for him when he is fighting with a fellow white worker: "I began thinking of how I ought to cut him. Whether I ought to slip up and begin stabbing him in the back, trying to get his heart; or wheel him about to face me and begin slashing him across the face, cutting out his eyes and slashing up his mouth." (p.42) Later in the novel, Bob has an argument with a young White intellectual. And he justifies the use of violence by the Negro; he proclaims an ethos, ritually exploited first by the Whites, and now claimed by the Negroes: " 'I don't know about any other minority group problem,' I said, 'but the only solution to the Negro problem is a revolution. We've got to make white people respect us and the only thing white people have ever respected is force.' " (p.107) In the climactic scene at the end, when Bob is incriminated by Madge, as they are about to be caught alone in a room, he becomes enraged and wants to kill her, on the presumption that he has nothing to lose since the white woman's cries will bequeath the same fate to him:

> I gave one great push, threw her off of me and half way across the room, jumped to my feet, grabbed at the first thing I touched, and leaped at her to beat out her brains. She had landed off balance and when I hit at her she ducked, went sprawling on her back on the deck. I went on to swing again, .... (p.220)

But he fails in his design. The additional failure of his expected lynching is no doubt a reflection of the difference in epoch (war time *v.* Depression), in geography (West Coast *v.* Chicago), characterization (Bob, the skilled worker; Madge, a poor White Southerner *v.* Bigger, domestic; Mary, rich White liberal girl) which explains why Himes' treatment of violence is timid compared to Wright's or Attaway's.

Ann Petry's Lutie Johnson suffers an accumulation of set-backs, resentments and frustrations, in her family life, in trying to raise her son in the ghetto, in her attempts to earn a living. This accumulation attains a point of saturation when she learns of her son's arrest. Trying to raise money to bail him out she goes to see a Negro bandleader, Boots Smith, who tries to take advantage of the situation to obtain the sexual gratification that he has longed for. He attacks her, after first trying to pander her to his White boss. Lutie's reaction is symptomatic of the polarization noticed so far where everything the Negro has suffered and internalized explodes in murderous violence: "This quick surface anger helped to swell and became a part of the deepening stream of rage that had fed on the hate, the frustration, the resentment she had toward the pattern her life had followed." (p.265) Lutie manages to knock down her assailant and proceeds to kill him with a metal rod. The previously seen blind and total expression of violence constitutes here also an elemental psychic release. Aggression is experienced by the reader both in the act itself of the principal and the author's mode of narration, and he is presumably to experience the same feeling of liberation that Lutie feels after so many trials:

A lifetime of pent-up resentment went into the blows. Even after he lay motionless, she kept striking him, not thinking about him, not even seeing him. [There ensues a catalogue of what Lutie is symbolically striking at.]
Finally, and the blows were heavier, faster now, she was striking at the white world which thrust black people into a walled enclosure from which there was no escape. (p.266)

For Gardner Smith's expatriates, violence operates in a cause and effect manner. The violence traditionally suffered by the Negroes in America begets a violence in turn directed against the Whites. It does not function in the same dynamics as in Wright, Attaway, or Petry, for the evident reason that the environment where the Negro soldiers live, in Germany, does not lead to the accumulation of concrete frustrations that explode in the forms seen in the previous novels. As we have seen so far, the American experience is a remembered one by the Negroes in Germany. It is recalled in oft-told stories of soldiers like them who after their overseas tour of duty return back home only to be welcomed in a manner that is dreaded by each of these expatriates, who know they will have to go back some day. The contrast is always between what they are presently enjoying and what presumably awaits them. It is that between a dream and a nightmare. There is the story of Woodard, for example, who went back to his native South, 'forgot' and went into a room marked "White only":

The police chief of the town happened to be in the station, and he saw Woodard go into the room. He went into the room and got Woodard and pulled him out onto the platform. Woodard protested. The chief hit Woodard. Then he drew his gun and rammed the barrel into Woodard's right eye, then into his left. (p.84)

The 'system' is sometimes carried over, though, even in Germany, in the attitudes of the White soldiers. Hayes' girlfriend is taken into custody by the M.P.'s, after Hayes himself is insulted with racist epithets when he is on a date with her. Enraged, Hayes is nonetheless helpless. The potential for violence is there, yet it is not actually indulged. It finds subliminal release in a dream Hayes has in his sleep:

In bed that night I killed the M.P.'s many times. I smeared paint over their faces and pushed my fingers into their eyes. I killed them slowly, pushing their eyes out and then beating them and pouring gasoline over them and lighting the gasoline and then hanging the charred bodies to trees as had been done to many Negroes in the South. (p.192)

*Beetlecreek*'s Negroes, except for the implication of their participation in old Bill's killing at the end, do not indulge in violence either in actuality or in dream. They are sedate folks still adhering to the traditional release of religion, and sublimation of one kind or another. The one character who might have obeyed the pattern followed by Bigger or Big Mat, David, releases himself by fleeing the town.

There is no escape through fleeing for Ellison's characters. They live close to the hell of the 'system' which they cannot escape in the traditional formulae, for they are either nonexistent, or unavailable, or irrelevant. Thus the ghetto dwellers of the North have the violent ritual of riots. Sometimes it may be the effect of provocation, but more often than not, Ellison feels, as he points out in the last apocalyptic riot (the one that brings about the hero's conscious opting for "invisibility"), such ritual needs no immediate cause. The very existence of the ghetto and all that it induces, the very experience of racism, are generic blanket causes. In the description of the hero's early experience in the South there is the scene where the inmates of the insane asylum rebel against the authority of their male nurse, Supercargo. He is beaten to death. Sylvester tells of the "purifying" experience he is undergoing as he is kicking the symbol that in his mind represents the same oppression inflicted by the White Power structure that drove him to the state he is now in: " 'Try it, school-boy, it feels so good. It gives you relief,' Sylvester said. 'Sometimes I get so afraid of him I feel that he's inside my head. There!' he said giving Supercargo another kick." (p.78) The first riot the hero witnesses in the North describes a similar attitude when the White marshals are beaten and trampled to death by the populace. He sees a woman methodically releasing herself in a manner unlike her customary rituals in Church: "I saw a woman striking with the pointed heel of her shoe, her face a blank mask with hollow black eyes as she aimed and struck, aimed and struck, bringing spurts of blood, running along beside the man who was dragged to his feet now as they punched him gauntletwise between them." (p.243)

But Ellison's portrayal of violence, like that of Black nationalism, is epitomized in the figure of Ras the Exhorter (who is now Ras the Destroyer), when he is described in the last riot charging down the streets of Harlem on a horse: a Black knight in shining armour! Beyond the mock-heroic caricature, Ellison restates once more one of his dominant themes: violence is self-destructive for the Blacks as well as for the Whites (though he admits that it is a necessary stage that the Negro must go through). In the description of the woman noted above, and the fate that befalls Ras, who dies as he lived and preached, is the ominous warning that while violence is oftentimes a necessary catharsis (nowhere is that better rendered than in the picture of the fat woman during the last riot, joyfully riding atop a milk wagon and splashing milk in the street as she drops the bottles one by one) the Negro must beware that in exteriorizing his demons he does not turn

101

himself into a demonic and insane figure. Then the hoped-for catharsis becomes an engulfment by the very forces one wishes to expell. Thus one becomes a partner in evil of the White racist, a twin-like figure in "invisibility" where both Black and White are victims of their dark unknown forces.

1 Chester Himes, *Pinktoes*, p.20.
2 Quoted by Charles R. Larson in "African-Afro-American Literary Relations: Basic Parallels", *Negro Digest*, p.39.
3 See "Orphée Noir", in *Anthologie de la Nouvelle Poésie Nègre et Malgache de Langue Française*, ed. Léopold S. Senghor, p.xxxv.
4 My understanding of alienation is sociologically-oriented, as when I discuss its inducement in the ghetto that makes for the Black's sense of dispossession; and, more importantly, I use it also in the modern philosophic sense of spiritual, existential, sense of malaise and meaninglessness. As can be seen in the text, I move from the first stage into the second. This double view of alienation roots Charles I. Glicksberg's own use of the concept in his article "The Alienation of Negro Literature" in *Phylon*, pp.49-58.
5 Jean-Paul Sartre, *Qu'est-ce que la Littérature?*, pp.99-103.
6 See Robert A. Bone, *The Negro Novel in America*, p.191, p.195.

# THE REVOLTED

# QUEBECER

The imperatives of the industrial age came to bear in North America during World War II and gained impetus during the postwar period, both in the dismemberment of the European colonial powers and in the emergence of America as the prototypical new industrial state. The newly-decolonized underdeveloped nations grouped themselves into a Third World rooted in the cleavage point between the economic and ideological divisions of the West and the Socialist countries. Quebec could not escape the process of change.

Willy-nilly, the traditional attachment to the land and the ethos that consecrated it are abandoned as literary themes. As we saw in *Trente Arpents*, in an age of mass-consumption and mass-production, where technological gigantism is the order of the day, bucolic celebration is no longer viable. The insanity of Menaud, or the exile of Euchariste Moisan, conveys the impossibility of the French Canadian refusing to enter the urban secular world, refusing to relinquish his spiritual defenses. But, the rural man moving to the cities, as the early novels of the forties show, is initially at a loss, a misfit in a world he does not comprehend and is ill-equipped to deal with. The immediate results are that, alienated, incapacitated, once more facing defeat, he tries to cling to some of the old values, or that he longs in his despair for the old days, when his self-enclosed world was stable, secure and protected. However much he suspects that the traditional order is no longer viable and that he has to reject its tenets if he wants to survive in the secular world, the full-hearted drive for success in the new environment is not his but his son's.

The predominant theme of revolt articulated in the urban novel by the new city-born generation, emerges as a necessary action to counteract the sense of defeat borne by the Messianic ethos. As the French Canadian in-

105

creasingly comes to grips with the material order, with varying degrees of success or failure, there appears a fresh sense of collective identity. The post-forties writers examine the foundations of the traditional order and find them resting on a fear of the outside world and motivated by an historical trauma that was constantly denied recognition. Paul Chamberland, writing in *Parti Pris*, summarizes: "Notre fuite dans le passé, dans la légende, n'a été qu'un mécanisme d'auto-défense contre l'envahissement du présent anglo-saxon. Incapables de nous faire le sujet de notre propre histoire, nous nous sommes livrés en objet de l'histoire des autres." (1) Whereas they purported to be creative and vital, the traditional values are discovered to have been essentially static, designed to consecrate a world of inflexibility where the primary motto was that "nothing must change".

Grasping the extent of an alienation that was institutionalized, and investigating the Messianic collective sense of mission as escapist solace for trauma, the novelists of the urban set-up take the historical burden upon themselves. They analyze the origins of the fables that eventually thwarted and stifled the life of the collectivity. They subsequently define the new historical perspective. The trauma hitherto denied recognition is said to have stemmed from the loss of sovereignty, of the sense of possession of a land that the French Canadian had "discovered, explored and colonized". (2) The turning to the spiritual is understood to be a subliminal search for compensation for a defeat in the material order that could neither be consciously accepted nor forgotten, since the Messianic ethos constantly recalled how life had been during the Ancien Régime. (3) As a result, it is felt in the sixties that the only cure for this malaise, which equally affects the young urban generation, is to revolt against it and to affirm the land and the people.

Trudeau's position is that instead of seeking a way out of the malaise by looking for a scapegoat (be it the Canadian Confederation, the "Anglo-Saxons" or American imperialism), there should be a movement towards an in-depth understanding which, consequently, would lead to the real task at hand — the rebuilding of a promising Quebec, after years of Duplessis and clerical devastation. (4) Nonetheless, the governing feeling in the sixties, both in art and life, is that the tragedies of the Moisans, Menauds and Maria Chapdelaines are to be understood as stemming from an existential uprootment. There lies the root-motivation for the recapturing of spatial dimensions, not as Menaud expressed in vague yearnings, or Groulx in an asinine racialist frame, but precisely named in the movement for *le pays*.

This movement, in its most strident form, does not shy away from lyrically celebrating violence; but (with the exception of *La Chesnaie*) this comes only in the last stage of revolt, following the initial rejection of the rural order (in the person of the fathers), and filling the void created when, in the face of ghetto conditions, the sons in these novels look for an orien-

106

tation more radical than their parents' sterile idealization of rural life. But before we analyze these components of revolt in French-Canadian fiction from the early forties to the late sixties, a discussion of a novel, published while the Messianic myth was still dominant, is necessary, for it introduces in its conspicuous iconoclasm the present chapter.

Jean-Charles Harvey's *Les Demi-Civilisés*, published in 1933, was deemed a scandal and earned for itself the notoriety of a "cause célèbre" following its publication, inasmuch as it was attacking the tenets of *la race*, the faith, the attitude towards woman-as-mother and clericalism. As a result, Harvey was ostracized by the archbishop of Quebec, expelled from his job as a journalist, banned from the city of Quebec and, some years later, forced to sign a confession repudiating his work before Duplessis would give him an obscure position in the civil service. (5) Quite a hierarchy in penalty for a little novel now aesthetically discredited, (6) whose sole claim to fame is really a somewhat prudish advocation of free love at a time in Quebec's history when such "sin" should not have dared speak its name.

The story, set in Quebec city, revolves around a young intellectual, Max Hubert, who rebels against the conventions of his society for he sees the paralysis that has kept French Canada static to have been caused directly by the Church, and, indirectly, by the élite it educated for its leadership. Harvey, like the post-forties novelists, sees the traumas of French Canada residing essentially within and not without Quebec. The opening lines of the novel introduce the writer's commitment. The first-person narration opens with the hero's description of his origins; these are at the polar opposite of Groulx's mythos of the purity of *la race*: "Je me nomme Max Hubert. Mon sang est un mélange de normand, de highlander, de marseillais et de sauvage. En ce composé hybride se heurtent le tempérament explosif du midi, la passion lente et forte du nord, la profonde sentimentalité de l'Ecosse et l'instinct aventurier du coureur des bois." (p.13) Later, he talks about the ancestors, the French Canadians that were left to themselves after the 1760 Conquest. Although he rejects vehemently the ethos they subsequently adopted, Harvey considers them sympathetically because they had not yet been regimented by the priests, and because, given the conditions they had to face alone, they endured:

> Toute la nation repose sur ces obscurs qui ont été presque les seuls à vraiment souffrir pour la sauver. Ce qu'ils ont fait, eux, ils ne l'ont pas crié sur les toits, ils ne l'ont pas publié, ni hurlé dans les parlements: ils l'ont fait par devoir, sans espoir de récompense humaine. Abandonnés à la conquête, ... ils ont fait ce qu'on leur disait de faire. Ils n'ont pas maugréé; ils ont tout accepté, les yeux fermés, tout subit, tout enduré. Ils sont pourtant restés fiers, intelligents .... Il me semble que notre paysannerie est la plus civilisée qui soit au monde. (p.144)

Hubert is even tempted to celebrate the land in the traditional manner, but it is clear that his impulse stems from nostalgia, the world of his grandfather that can no longer be his: "L'air des montagnes! Qu'il fait bon de le respirer! La voici, la petite maison de grand-père! ... Elle était faite pour être là, cette maison. ... Elle n'avait rien à cacher, car tout en elle était pur." (p.139)

The fact that we feel strong overtones of the urbanite's facile romanticizing of the country underlines Hubert's own realization that the world of the present is not that of the past. The myths and illusions, the prescriptions and proscriptions that were necessary for a time, and so amply cultivated, no longer apply. Harvey's viewpoint is that the world has changed, something which the traditional leaders seem not to be aware of, since they persist in "back to the soil" movements and exhortations to maintain a state of siege at all costs. Cultural defensiveness has begun to take its toll. Indigenous talents are stifled, individuals are thwarted in their ideals. Harvey goes on to imply that future generations will experience only living death if the insistence on homogeneousness and authoritarianism is not set aside. For better or for worse, life is now led in the cities; more often than not in the early migration it is for worse. Moving to the city, the Huberts, and the Lacasses in Roy's *Bonheur d'Occasion* and the Bouchers in Lemelin's *Au Pied de la Pente Douce*, represent the new urban proletariat: "Vers le milieu de mes études, ma mère émigrait à Québec, où la pauvreté la conduisait. J'avais dix-sept ans. Nous habitions un logis sordide, dans un quartier grouillant d'enfants et de vermine." (p.29)

But, like other sons in the urban novel, Hubert sees in the experience of poverty the striking symbol of what the Messianic ethos has brought upon his people. He rebels against his condition and attacks those, he feels, who are responsible for this state of affairs: the clergy and the clerically-educated élite (who certainly acknowledged the brunt of the attack considering what befell Harvey):

> Me voici parmi les descendants de ce peuple que je trouve terriblement domestiqué. Une fois la conquête faite par les Anglais et les sauvages exterminés par les vices de l'Europe, nos blancs, vaincus, ignorants et rudes, nullement préparés au repos et à la discipline, n'eurent rien à faire qu'à se grouper en petits clans bourgeois, cancaniers, pour organiser la vie commune. On eut dit des fauves domptés, parqués en des jardins zoologiques, bien logés, bien nourris, pour devenir l'objet de curiosité des autres nations. (p.31)

This domesticity referred to makes for an uncomfortable homogeneity of thoughts and actions. Harvey, of course, has in mind the absence of intellectual freedom and the sense of imprisonment this has led to in Quebec; witness the lecture Hubert is given upon applying for a position at the university (Laval): "Je veux bien vous appuyer, dit-il. Si jamais vous entrez là, ne soyez pas trop frondeur, pas trop indépendant. Tout ce qui peut ressembler à l'indépendance de caractère, à l'émancipation de certains principes, est banni de l'université, gardienne de la tradition ... et de la vérité." (p.44) This absence of freedom is, moreover, vividly dramatized in a dream sequence. In it, liberty is allegorically represented as a woman who is gagged, tied-up and hung from a post:

> Sur une arête de roc, je vis un gibet auquel pendait, attachée par les pieds, une femme divinement belle. Des forcenés lui criblaient la poitrine de coups de fouet, tandis que des gamins sordides se balançaient, comme en des escarpolettes, au bout de sa puissante chevelure, qui pendait jusqu'à terre et le long de laquelle coulaient des ruisseaux de sang.
> Je reconnus cette femme.
> C'était la Liberté qu'on avait pendue! (p.50)

Leaving aside the denunciation of the general ethos, Harvey attacks one by one the sacred cows of its infrastructure. The Church, the stereotype of woman, the traditional role of sex, the historical interpretation *à la* Groulx are all lambasted. The Church, for instance, is severely questioned when it allies itself with the affluent middle class, showing its time-honoured adaptability to change:

> Hermann se demandait quel serait le Christ du vingtième siècle avec des temples magnifiques bâtis par l'argent des gueux sous la peur de l'enfer; avec des biens immenses cotés par la haute finance et ne rendant pas tribut à César, le César honni, à qui le pauvre Jésus rendait son effigie et son denier; avec un monopole sur les connaissances, les écoles, les institutions; avec le confort, le luxe et l'opulence édifiés avec la dîme du paysan ou du pêcheur. (p.119)

The woman, in one of the first instances in the French-Canadian novel, is portrayed as a mistress instead of as a wife or mother. Hubert, unlike François Paradis or Euchariste Moisan, is drawn towards the woman on a purely sexual level: "Moi, qui n'avais jamais vu que des paysannes vêtues de lourdes étoffes, ce spectacle me fascinait, et j'en restais la bouche grande ouverte." (p.20) Lines such as the following may appear embarrassingly naive, not to say inoffensive, but this is the type of dialogue that brought upon Harvey the full wrath of the archbishop of Quebec City: "Penses-tu qu'il soit nécessaire de nous épouser pour nous aimer? — Evidemment non." (p.69) Finally, the blanket of history, traditionally used to cover the wounds of the Conquest, is lifted:

*from* Québec-Presse *Archives*

> Nous en parlons trop de notre histoire. Nous imitons les Hindous qui, arriérés, crasseux, miteux et ignorants, s'efforcent par la lecture de vieux textes, de se persuader qu'ils valent les Européens qui les dominent et les bottent au derrière. Devant les Anglais et les Américains, ... nous allons nous cacher sous notre histoire comme des marmots humiliés sous la jupe de leur mère. (p.127)

The derogatory reference to the Indians is, of course, typical of the kind of intolerance Harvey will go on to cultivate in his old age and as a journalist, until his death in 1967. Nonetheless, it is interesting to note how close his pronouncement is to the one earlier quoted by Chamberland (see p.106); and how, eleven years before Lemelin, Harvey levelled the first serious attack in the urban novel against the old order.

Roger Lemelin's *Au Pied de la Pente Douce* (1944), an autobiographical novel about teen-agers growing up amid the proletarian life of their newly-transplanted rural fathers in Saint-Sauveur, a parish in the poor, lower-town district of Quebec City, reflects the opposition between the generations, the tension between the old and the new order characteristic of the modern culture. These poor urban-dwellers are the Quebec counterparts to Gabrielle Roy's Saint-Henri people. But whereas the Saint-Henri people, living in the same wartime epoch in a Montreal ghetto, tragically endure, Lemelin's are part of an animated slice of life.

In the bristling little world of Saint-Sauveur, the attitude towards the past is ambivalent. While the parents, for the most part, cultivate a nostalgic feeling for rural tranquillity and stability (in proportion to the frustrations experienced in the city), the children, by contrast, revolt against it and embrace the new order. Denis Boucher, Lemelin's protagonist, reflects this outlook as he walks through the streets:

> C'était bon de respirer enfin les relents des cuisines! Il avait un coup d'oeil familier pour chaque porche, reconnaissait chaque perron. Le Cap, La Haute-Ville, faisaient horizon. Il l'aimait mieux ainsi, la Haute-Ville, comme horizon, car il était trop déçu quand il y était plongé, comme ce soir. Sa paroisse, il l'exécrait pourtant ce matin. Il y rentrait avec allégresse, serrait St-Joseph, toute la paroisse sur lui, comme une houppelande préférée. Ici, on pouvait vivre sans fard, sans chichi, sans plastron. (p.156)

In that passage there is an overt double ambivalence: Denis' fear of the Haute-Ville's sophisticated, affluent, life, which he nonetheless craves, and his contempt for the world of his parish, too conventional and humble, which he nonetheless loves. Denis triumphs over his mixed feelings later, as he leaves Saint-Sauveur to conquer the affluent world on top of the *Pente Douce*. The implication, of course, is that in growing-up he has come to realize that the world of the parish is too self-enclosed, too much the world of the older generation that clings to this milieu in a manner evoking their rural origins; around the district they have erected spiritual defenses to protect them from the world of the Haute-Ville:

> Denis se retourna et contempla le quartier. Les bicoques pointaient comme des pieux calcinés sur une terre qu'on désespère d'avance de labourer. Il se dégageait des habitations tassées une odeur de vie tenace, rétive au progrès; et tout cela, malgré sa honte, refusait avec obstination tout changement, parce que tout changement est opéré par les autres. (pp.331-332)

Denis' view of his mother also reveals divided feelings. In the tradition of Mme Chapdelaine, she would want to maintain her rural role: an "earth mother" encompassing the life of the family, the land and symbolic of survival. But Denis rebels: "Encore? J'en ai assez! Je n'en veux plus de ta protection. Occupe-toi des petits, un peu. Quand j'étais jeune, tu n'avais d'yeux que pour moi, tu me nourrissais de coups de bâtons. Aujourd'hui pour me barrer le chemin, tu délaisses les autres, ...." (p.189) In addition to being conceived as an obstacle on the hero's road to self-knowledge, the image of the mother has, moreover, become quite tarnished. Mme Boucher's impulses obey the traditional format, but otherwise her actual actions are the opposite. The mythicized, faithful, obedient figure, full of maternal love and care has, in the city, metamorphosed into a possibly unfaithful wife. Early in the novel, Denis, returning home, finds his mother in the company of another man:

> Soudain son rire s'arrêta net: sa mère était encore à jaser avec ce gros gendarme! Immobile, les yeux voilés, le jeune homme humectait ses lèvres. Il se rappela son désespoir quand on lui avait appris que ce gardien de rues désertes avait été pendant quatre ans le prétendant de sa mère. Où était la belle légende d'amour exclusif qu'il avait cru exister entre ses parents? (p.19)

Ambivalence is likewise experienced with regard to religion. The curate of Saint-Sauveur sees himself in the traditional role of secular and spiritual leader to his flock. He manipulates power autocratically, therefore, believing in his unquestioned, God-ordained, leadership even here in the non-spiritual urban reality ("Il dirigeait donc son petit troupeau à coup de dénonciations de lieux maudits et de moyens de rachat monnayés." p.93). Yet the curate Folbèche is a remnant of the past, like Denis' parents. The pastor of an urban parish, he is still obsessed by the idea that defenses must be built for protection against an hostile, outside world. The curate's attitude makes for irony Lemelin does not fail to emphasize:

112

C'était son obsession, à ce bon curé Folbèche. Il exploitait sa petite paroisse comme une mine à vocation religieuse. Il aurait voulu faire de la soutane, du rabat et de la robe de bure une palissade contre le péché, un rempart sacré, une sorte de "no man's land" autour de sa paroisse, où l'on aurait vu poindre tonsures et coiffes comme des croix dans un cimetière. (p.88)

The young generation increasingly construes such prescriptions as irrelevant and self-defeating. Secularly-minded, the young people are indifferent to such admonitions; if they still go to mass on Sundays, it is more because of routine than conviction ("Les Braves Mulots, ... en étaient venus à considérer l'église comme un immense tronc où il fallait lâcher ses cents." p.92).

However, it is in the attitude towards education Lemelin most effectively contrasts the generations, the world of the past and that of the present. The young people lament the level of education they are receiving which does not prepare them for a functional role in the city, an education still geared to an era when intellectual and practical values were frowned upon. (7) There is, consequently, a deep sense of frustration and resentment smoldering against that traditional outlook identified, by Harvey in the thirties, as one of the main causes for the French Canadian's backwardness in all fields. The adults respond by contemptuously dismissing the young people's desire for an education. Molded by their rural origins, they fail to see the value of intellectual pursuit and they perceive a threat, for, as the young interpret their state, adults must be held responsible for their failures.

Denis, for example, experiences frustration when, upon applying for several positions, he is turned down for lack of qualifications. He then indicts the school system and the generation which long maintained it to be "the best in the world" (8):

Sa détresse dégénéra en honte. Que savait-il de la chimie? A l'école, on ne faisait qu'étudier les biographies des grands hommes, entre les heures de récréation. Il y avait aussi le catéchisme, dont il ne se rappelait que les deux grandes lignes: le péché mortel, le péché véniel.... Ah! qu'elle était puérile, la belle sûreté des maîtres qui avaient bloqué son horizon de leur idéal sténographique! (p.301)

The negative view of education instilled in the young is further illustrated by the opposition between the Gonzagues and the Mulots, two of Saint-Sauveur's teen-age groups. The Gonzagues are the "brainy" and studious ones; but, since they are seminarians (students for the priesthood), their pursuits are seen as befitting emasculated individuals and not the rambunctious and the rowdy such as Denis' Mulots:

113

Chez nos amis, la débrouillardise était reine, tandis qu'on sentait chez les Gonzagues le stigmate de l'école, l'esprit de soumission évasé sur leurs faces comme un fruit gâté. ... Colin avait accepté l'ignorance, les Langevin établi leurs limites, et Boucher renié ce qu'il apprenait. Ils ne voulaient pas être des Gonzagues. Ils auraient toutefois bien aimé avoir leur baccalauréat, surtout Boucher, mais ils ne s'en doutaient pas, et leurs études se poursuivaient hors des balises de l'esclavage et loin des instruments de l'emasculation. (p.60)

These inhibiting attitudes are compounded, and not alleviated, by the parents' reactions. Denis' father, Tit-Blanc, symbolizes and crystallizes the stance of a whole culture as he threatens his son Jean for spending too much time with books: "Il souleva donc le banc de la victoria, en sortit la grammaire que Denis lui avait prêtée. Il fallait cacher tous les livres, car Tit-Blanc, quand il était ivre, les brûlait, en invoquant l'ignorance des grand-pères, qui avaient tout de même vécu." (p.184) Of course, the reason for Tit-Blanc's attitude is the indictment he feels levelled at himself, the nagging fear, long repressed in the Messianic ethos, that his generation and the previous ones must bear responsibility for their indifference toward material necessities. Only that explains Tit-Blanc's irrational rages at the mention of "education": ("T'es encore dans l'instruction, fainéant! Je t'ai vu avec la Lévesque. C'est elle qui te rend fier. T'as honte de nous autres, t'as honte des vers." p.184).

Gabrielle Roy's *Bonheur d'Occasion* (1945) continues Lemelin's realistic vein and, more painfully, documents the failure of a generation, a culture, through the eyes of urban-born children. Set in the slums of Saint-Henri, in Montreal, on the eve of and during World War II, this novel chronicles the cycle of poverty in Azarius and Rose-Anna Lacasse's family where since a baby is born every spring, new lodging quarters have to be found while the head of the family is chronically out of work. Witnessing their parents' defeat, the city-born children desperately try to escape a similar fate, with mixed success.

Azarius Lacasse is of Samuel Chapdelaine's and Euchariste Moisan's mold, but, like Menaud, he is a misfit in the industrial world of the present, a non-provider for the twelve children he sired. A failure, he is yet the perennial optimist (one of O'Neill's indefatigable "pipe dreamers" in *Iceman Cometh*: the introduction here of a naturalistic note fitted to the American Dream myth recurrent in American literature is not gratuitous, as shall be seen later). The man refuses to consciously apprehend his actual situation as he nurtures the ideal:

Et cependant Azarius n'avait point encore perdu confiance. Il refusait toujours les petits emplois que des amis, par l'entremise de

Rose-Anna, cherchaient à lui obtenir, déclarant qu'il n'était point né pour des besognes de gagne-petit. Sa réputation s'était faite dans le quartier: un sans-coeur qui laissait sa femme aller au ménage plutôt que d'accepter un honnête travail. (p.216)

Despite his twelve children, Azarius is a non-entity as a father, a weak and sterile figure in the home who compensates in long-winded discussions with neighbourhood ne'er-do-well:

Il était ainsi dans sa famille, sans ressort comme en un nid d'épines où il ne donnait rien de vouloir en arracher une, tant elles se multipliaient autour de lui. Sa voix même n'était plus celle qu'il employait au dehors pour donner son avis, exprimer ses audacieuses et généreuses vues. C'était un timbre conciliant, presque humble et où l'on aurait pu saisir parfois un accent de contrainte. (p.121)

In the face of the father's defeat, the mother, Rose-Anna, valiantly tries to sustain the family. She is the hard-working, energetic, obedient, archetypal French-Canadian mother who in the past, always kept her husband's pace, and took over his role in his absence. Still, Mme Lacasse's archetypal virtues, though a source of solace and inspiration, are not enough to provide material necessities for her family; they are not enough to keep her family together in the womb of her protection: "Cette impuissance à retenir sa famille cette pénible sensation de voir les frêles remparts de leur intimité céder, s'écrouler, et de se découvrir à la dérive parmi le flot turbulent et triste d'être pareils à eux ...mon Dieu, elle ne pouvait supporter cette épreuve." (p.374) Her world collapses. She fears for the future of her progeny when she observes that Azarius' emasculation, as husband and father, threatens to be passed on to her children: "Et voici que de plus elle remarquait chez ses enfants ce penchant de leur père à vivre dans le vague, en dehors de tout détail pratique." (p.223)

Rose-Anna finds momentary refuge in the remembrance of the world of the past; that of her childhood spent in the country. The dichotomy previously observed in *Menaud* is again presented: the misery of the present contrasted with the felicity of the past. Springtime, for instance, in the city means two things: the additional plight of moving to quarters as shallow and decomposed as before, if not worse; and the arrival of another child in an already large family that cannot be provided for: "Le printemps! Qu'est-ce qu'il avait signifié pour elle? Dans sa vie de mariage, deux évènements s'associaient au printemps: elle était enceinte et, dans cette condition, il lui fallait se mettre sur le chemin pour se trouver un logis. Tous les printemps, ils déménageaient." (p.125) Whereas springtime in the country meant something else. The world of childhood is briefly re-entered when, contemplating a visit to some country relatives, Mme Lacasse relives the spring of her youth: "Et pourtant, elle se voyait déjà là-bas, dans les lieux de son enfance; elle avançait à travers l'erablière, dans la neige molle, vers la cabane de sucre et, oh, miraculeusement! elle avançait à longues foulées, avec sa démarche de jeune fille svelte, allant, cassant des branches au passage...." (p.231) She becomes ecstatic as she approaches the haven of her childhood: "Elle ne cessait de voir surgir, se recomposer, s'animer, s'enchaîner les délices de son enfance. ... C'était gai, clair, joyeux, et son coeur battait d'aise. ... Rose-Anna percevait encore le pétillement du grand feu de la cabane; elle voyait la sève blonde dans les bassins, ...." (p.232)

Yet this return home turns out in reality to be a jolting meeting of Rose-Anna's two worlds, the rural and the urban, the past and the present, childhood and adulthood, the spiritual order and the material order. It occurs not just in the painful reminder of a fallacy nurtured by the country relatives ("Là-bas, on les croyait à l'aise" p.234) but in the evident contrast between her children and their cousins. As Rose-Anna rushes to rescue one of her brood being mishandled by a sturdy and well-nourished country cousin, she is forced to admit the evidence of her family's defeat: "Elle fit le tour de ses enfants, d'un regard craintif, effaré; et elle se demanda si elle les avait vraiment vus jusque là tels qu'ils étaient, avec leur petit visage et leurs membres fluets." (p.263)

Witnessing the defeat of their elders, the young reject their world and their values. This rejection is dramatized in the oldest Lacasse child, Florentine, and, more forcefully, in Jean Lévesque, the orphaned, ambitious, young engineer with whom Florentine falls vainly in love. The eldest of the Lacasses' twelve children, Florentine works as a waitress in a restaurant. She observes the kind of life her mother leads at home; like Maria Chapdelaine , she understands that it is expected of her to follow in her mother's footsteps. But, like Maria, she is also tempted by the values of the material world. Similarly, she identifies her mother's lot as hopeless and wants no part of it: "C'est qu'elle apercevait la vie de sa mère comme un long voyage gris, terne, que jamais, elle, Florentine n'accomplirait; et c'était comme si, aujourd'hui, elles eussent en quelque sorte à se faire des adieux. Leurs routes peut-être ici même se séparaient-elles" (p.158). She sees in Jean Lévesque (Maria's Lorenzo Surprenant) the symbol of the new way of life she desires to embrace, to the extent of sacrificing her virginity. But, whereas Maria had to renege on her intentions, Florentine steadfastly clings to hers; in the urban environment, the voices of etherealness cannot be heard over those of the cash-register: "Moi, je ferai comme je voudrai. Moi, j'aurai pas de misère comme sa mère" (p.117). Though she is eventually rejected by Lévesque, Florentine does not resort to an impossible return to an equally impossible ethos. She marries perhaps a less dashing and romantic figure, but her marriage to Emmanuel, who gives his name to the child fathered by Lévesque, is nonetheless an entry into the middle class. Florentine does escape the working-class ghetto symbol of her parents' defeat.

Jean Lévesque is the paramount symbol of the new order, both for the values he stands for and for his origins. His origins are not archetypal: he is not of a big family whose roots are in the rural framework; he does not partake of a paternal inspiration (or lack of) that prepares for a destined path in life. Indeed, Lévesque has no family, he is a man without roots. Raised in an orphanage, he never related to any traditional set-up, much less to the tenets of the faith. A man without past, Jean Lévesque exists in the present only, fully aware that only thus can the promises of the future be fulfilled. His lifestyle is based on that premise: in order to achieve anything he has to be pragmatic, to act according to the laws of the environment he inhabits. And since the laws of the industrial age are cold, factual, emotionless in the pursuit of efficiency and material success, Jean Lévesque responds accordingly. Prototypifying the replacement of the Messianic myth by the American Dream, and like many Horatio Algers and Sammy Glicks (by contrast, Azarius' emblem in defeat is Willy Loman), Lévesque is ruthless and single-minded in his desire to "get ahead". Benjamin Franklin (the aphorist of *Poor Richard's Almanach*) would have approved of his Spartan life, living in a small room, working in a factory during the day and going to night school:

> Car tout tendu vers le succès, tout dévoré d'ambition, une seule chose lui paraissait vraiment importante: l'emploi judicieux de son temps. Et jusqu'ici il l'avait consacré sans sacrifices pénibles, sans regret même, à l'étude, une étude opiniâtre et acharnée. (p.30) [The puritan work ethic has no doubt replaced Messianism when the description continues:] Cet être pragmatique qui aimait le travail, non pas pour lui-même, mais pour l'ambition qu'il décuple, pour les succès qu'il prépare, ce jeune homme sans rêve qui s'était donné au travail comme à une revanche. (p.31)

Jean instinctively recognizes Florentine as representing that which he is working hard to leave behind: the tradition, closeness, warmth and security of organic culture which has molded Florentine through her extended family. Should Lévesque relate to Florentine deeply, he knows he would have to espouse the values he feels are embodied in the girl; it matters little to Lévesque that she, like him, loathes these values. He suspects her hate is tainted by her parents' poverty; not, according to Lévesque, a pure rejection of the fundamental insignificance of such values in the industrial age; and *that* may thwart his ambitions. Thus, after coolly weighing what Florentine has to offer him (nothing) and what his endeavours will get him (everything "upwardly mobile"), Lévesque forsakes her.

Lastly, one may contrast the guiltless a-religiosity of Lévesque, Florentine and the other young people with the religiosity of the elders. Again, the

117

antithesis is stark. In the urban environment, Mme Lacasse has followed the prescribed rural pattern: she has obeyed God's design by having a good number of children: "J'ai fait mon devoir, Notre-Seigneur, j'ai eu onze enfants." (p.134) But God has not rewarded her travails to the proportionate level of material abundance expected. Mme Lacasse, attending Church to express her disappointment and to still pray for better days, gathers only the impression that the presumed old rapport has disappeared, God is not listening: "Notre-Seigneur, écoutez moi!" (p.133) What is implied in that 'impression'is illustrative of the overall scission that occurs in migrating to the city: although Mme Lacasse's spirituality is the same as in the old order, existentially, in the city pregnant with material contingencies, God seems to be dead. At any rate, he is absent for Rose-Anna, who cannot conceptualize him in her prayers; indeed, she is not far from grasping the primary consciousness of existential despair:

> Mais, Dieu, Dieu lui-même, elle ne se le représentait pas, elle ne se l'était pas représenté depuis des années à cause de l'effort que cela demandait et, surtout, parce qu'au delà de tous ses efforts, elle n'apercevait rien, rien que des nuages blancs comme des tas d'ouate où survolait une colombe. (pp.133-134)

This notion of 'existential despair' brings us to three novels of the sixties owing much to such a consciousness: Bessette's *Le Libraire* (1960); Renaud's *Le Cassé* (1964); Aquin's *Prochain Episode* (1965).

Gérard Bessette's *Le Libraire* is a powerful indictment of the old order as it exists in modern rural Quebec, or, at least, as it existed in the fifties under Duplessis. The story is set in a small town and focuses on the dilemmas besetting a free thinker whose liberalism brings upon him the opprobrium of the local establishment. Thematically, Bessette resumes Jean-Charles Harvey's protest against the absence of intellectual and moral liberties in a province that stifles freedom when it strives to maintain an homogeneity of thought and action which, instead of protecting the people from a presumed outside threat, kills them from within. To dramatize his point, Bessette utilizes the paradigm of Socrates' fate when the townspeople, led by the curate, accuse Jodoin, the bookstore clerk, of corrupting youth, (he sold a book on the Church's Index to a student) when they expel him from town.

The novel opens with the description of a milieu contaminated by what the "collective shell" has bred through the years: fear, sheepishness, a sense of paralysis, that have consecrated mediocrity and ignorance. This atmosphere is readily evidenced when M. Chicoine, the bookstore owner, shows Jodoin, a blasé former schoolteacher, his bookshelves. As he reveals his 'forbidden' books (those on the Church's Index), Chicoine displays the suspiciousness and fear sown by years of living in the shadow of the Church:

118

"Ses yeux perçants, un peu hagards, me fixaient un instant pour glisser sur les rayons de livres et revenir à moi. Je compris soudain qu'il avait peur." (pp.51-52) Other townspeople are likewise dominated by fear; such as the clients who want to buy books other than the approved ones: "Je n'ai pas eu de difficulté à les reconnaître. Ils s'approchent de moi avec des airs de conspirateurs et me glissent à l'oreille quelque titre ou nom d'auteurs du ton dont on demande un condom ou un suppositoire chez le pharmacien." (p.71) Jodoin quickly perceives that these individual attitudes are the reflection of a collective conditioning. Chicoine tries to explain that though freedom of thought may be stifled in some cases, this is only a negative side-effect of an overall positive molding that preserved the freedom of the people as it protected them. Jodoin does not see the problem that way. His attitude is that this ethos is based on a fundamental negation of individual freedom that he, as an intellectual, cannot accept:

> Je le rassurai sur ce point en lui faisant toutefois observer que ces deux sortes de liberté s'opposaient souvent; que, dans bien des cas, les individus dont la majorité, fatalement, exprimait l'opinion générale "officielle" étaient tellement tiraillés, ballottés par des craintes, par "certaines pressions" selon son expression, que leur prétendue liberté collective était le résultat de leurs servitudes individuelles. (p.87)

That Jodoin's reading of the town's notion of conformity is accurate is demonstrated in his comeuppance, when he sells an 'indexed' book to a student. The student, who is attending a nearby college, is caught reading the book by a priest. An Inquisition-like investigation is launched, during which the town's gossip mills run riot and point inevitably to the store clerk. Amazed that a little book can cause such havoc, Jodoin makes a highly symbolic utterance, virtually using the same words articulated in the accusation against Socrates: "Est-ce que je voulais passer pour un débaucheur de collégiens?" (p.134) Matter-of-factly, in these Duplessis days in a rural town of Quebec, Jodoin suffers, albeit symbolically, Socrates' fate; like the Greek philosopher, he ends up the victim of the forces of obscurantism and superstition against which he tried, meagre clerk that he was, to shed some light:

> M. Chicoine me réitéra son "absolue confiance dans mon avenir", mais crut opportun de souligner que Saint-Joachim ne constituait peut-être pas le champ d'action idéal pour un homme tel que moi: éclairé, brillant, d'une vaste culture humanitaire, champion de la liberté individuelle, etc., etc. (p.155)

Jodoin, like Harvey's Hubert (and Bessette in real life is a university profes-

119

sor who since the fifties has taught outside of Quebec), is forced to leave a self-enclosed order that is not yet ready to open its doors to the outside world. Facing the Inquisition tactics of the priest who questions him about keeping 'forbidden' books in stock ("—Vous savez bien ce que je veux dire, voyons! Des livres qu'il ne faut pas mettre entre toutes les mains" p.79), or ominously warned by an old townsman: "moué, ça fait soixante-deux ans que je promène ma carcasse. Eh bien, c'est pas bon pour la santé icitte de contrer les curés. Les ficelles, c'est eux autres qui les ont, vous comprenez..." (p.126), Jodoin, like Max Hubert, feels intellectually bound to rebel.

Ti-Jean, the protagonist in Jacques Renaud's proletarian novella, *Le Cassé* (1964), is compelled to rebel also. But Ti-Jean's revolt is visceral, crude and forceful in its ugliness. This reflects the difference between Bessette's generation (which is Pierre Elliott Trudeau's and that of all those intellectuals who opposed Duplessis and came to be called "architects" of Quebec's "quiet revolution" in the immediate post-Dupplessis years) and Renaud's; the former relying on a liberal humanist tradition of freedom of thought and action, the latter on a radical Third World assertion in the name of 'the wretched of the earth'.

Jacques Renaud's world in *Le Cassé* (French-Canadian slang meaning "the man who is flat-broke") is that of the pavements and slums of the city, Montreal. It is rooted in the secular new order in which Ti-Jean, like other *déclassés* is not equipped to compete. Contrary to Lacasse, but like Denis Boucher, Ti-Jean is a product of the city. He suffers from a legacy of disqualification. Devoid of the ambitions of Lévesque, but, like him, a rootless man, unattached to any family, Ti-Jean does not know whom to blame, or what to hold responsible for his lot. Unemployed, he lives from one expediency to the next in the slums of the East End of Montreal, unable to see any future to speak of and becoming increasingly enmeshed in his frustrations. Embodied in this *déclassé*, (the alter ego of Pitou and Alphonse in *Bonheur d'Occasion*, who at least could name the war as responsible for their situation), there is a vehement revolt against all that the old order stood for.

The first value thoroughly dismissed is that of the family. Whereas sex was traditionally kept within the framework of reproduction, emblematic of God's design, here the instinctive imperative of the flesh is, in its most brutal form, affirmed. The passage describing the meeting of Ti-Jean and Philomène, his mistress, needs to be cited:

> Ça date du temps de leur première rencontre. Il avait pris sa petite main dans sa grosse patte. Tu viens avec moé Mémène? On va s'en passer une? hum? Viens, viens-t'en! Ti-Jean avait insisté. Philomène avait suivi. Quand y veut, Ti-Jean y a pas moyen de l'faire démordre. C'te nuit là, Ti-Jean était venu trois fois. (p.24)

The second value negated is religion. To say so is really to understate the case. For the world of Ti-Jean, oozing with fetidness, has escaped divine benevolence; it either has no place for God, or God has no use for it. If God is mentioned at one point, as Ti-Jean remembers his youth, it is better to spew blasphemy on him: "J'ai dit à Jésus-Christ d'manger d'la marde longue de même pis j'ai commencé à m'crosser en pensant à Marie Madeleine." (pp.83-84)

If something is jarring in the grammar, notwithstanding the diction, of the above quotation, it is because the French language, conceived as one of the essential values protecting the identity of the Québécois, is used in this novella, by negation, as a means of protest. Many of the mid-sixties novelists and poets (specifically the *Parti Pris* group) believe that 'good' French does not reflect the real condition of the people of Quebec who, in their daily activities, speak a fractured French called *joual*. (9) They agree with Gerald Godin on "speaking horse" when he says: "Le bon français c'est l'avenir souhaité du Québec, mais le joual c'est son présent. J'aime mieux, pour moi, qu'on soit fier d'une erreur qu'humilié d'une vérité." (10) These writers feel that the use of *joual* is best for the depiction of contemporary Quebec reality, which they want, foremost, to denounce: hence abomination in syntax, diction, taste, nay, *form*, is perfect for the reflection of a reality deemed abominable. To quote Godin again, such is "la véritable situation coloniale des québécois." (11)

*Le Cassé*, from beginning to end, aims at fulfilling this new aesthetics. Any passage can be taken at random to illustrate. Ti-Jean, for instance, is talking about the government and says:

> Ch' peux pas crouère qui sont assez caves pour pas savouér que l'quatre piasses m'as l'garder pour moé. Ou ben donc y s'en sacrent... Pour moé c'est ça. (p.37) (Translation: I can't believe they're that dumb that they don't know that I am going to keep the four bucks for myself. Or else they don't give a damn... I think that's it.)

Later, after having a fight with Philomène, he says:

> Je l'ai pitchée dehors... la chienne! J'voudrais qu'a soye pus r'gardable... Que pas personne mette la patte dessus... Excepté moé... Moé! Rien qu'moé! crisse! (p.47) (Translation: I threw her out... the bitch! I'd want her to be a pain to look at... So no one would lay hands on her... Except me... Me! Only me! Christ!)

As the modern novelists of revolt negate their traditional culture, as they reject the very core of what once was French Canada, there is often-times a concomitant "wish to escape". A number of protagonists are obsessed with that wish: this is the case for Denis Boucher, Jean Levesque, Florentine, Aquin's nameless hero (the same is true for Maria Chapdelaine, Ephrem Moisan, and even one suspects, Menaud's daughter, Maria — the first signs of dissatisfaction with the old ethos). Ti-Jean, "down and out" as he is, is also obsessed with that wish. Tied to the harsh realities of ghetto-life, this wish becomes most exacerbated, as its fulfillment cannot be envisioned. The slum-dwellers in *Bonheur d'Occasion* and *Au Pied de la Pente Douce*, like Ti-Jean, see that escape from the point of view of socio-economics, and Florentine's final entry into the middle-class typifies their aspirations. But escape often means a spiritual longing for an *ailleurs*, anything really, away from Quebec, but, ambiguously, something which contains Quebec as well. Ti-Jean indicates this by referring to a voyage of discovery of *le pays*: "..., la partance, le goût parfois obsédant de tout crisser ça là pis d'partir. Disparaître. Le pont Jacques-Cartier. La campagne. Québec. Les filles. Et plus loin encore, plus loin, jusqu'à Percé." (p.18) This need for escape is undeniably tied, one suspects, to the pervasive consciousness of exile earlier discussed. Which brings us to Hubert Aquin.

Escape (not escapism) is not only indulged but apotheosized in a constant state of pursuit in Hubert Aquin's *Prochain Episode* (1965), a bewitching mixture of fact and fiction, that portrays a French-Canadian revolutionary carrying from Bagotville, Quebec, to Berne, Switzerland, the flame of a coming revolution in Quebec. Pursued by "enemies" from without (the Corporate Establishment, represented by H. de Heutz) as well as from within (the unconscious resignation and defeatism), the nameless revolutionary tries to elude and defeat them. The eradication of an historical state of defeat in Quebec is envisioned through a novel consciousness of past traumas, which are to be overcome mainly in a rediscovery and celebration of the land, and through the woman whose possession by the revolutionary signals the birth of a new Quebec.

*Prochain Episode* presents a radical solution; just as the hero comes to grips with the opposing forces of his battling self, Quebec must undergo a parallel confrontation, the outcome of which is to bring about a new awareness, a reconciliation of divisions present since 1760. Aquin's novel is therefore a quest for liberation, both personal and collective, the two being indivisible on the psychological as well as political levels.

The traditional value of the preservation of the family is, of course, negated. The mother is nowhere to be seen, but the narrator's mistress, K, is celebrated throughout. Curiously, the traditional alliance of the land and of woman (cf. *Maria Chapdelaine, Trente Arpents*) is here maintained, albeit for a completely different purpose. While in the rural tradition it was symbolic of divine purpose, allied to divine prescription, in *Prochain Episode* K's alliance with Quebec constitutes the lyrical flame of the coming revolution. Conversely, the narrator's ultimate defeat is explained by the beguiling discovery, when in the pursuit of his nemesis, H. de Heutz, that K.

is also the latter's companion. The painful irony of the end defeat is best explained when the narrator's love for K (diminutive for the old appellation "Kébec") has been measured. Early in the long flashback that constitutes the core of the novel, the narrator, from his prison cell, writes (obviously still believing in K's sincerity, when in fact it is *her* betrayal that has brought him there): "Je t'écris infiniment et j'invente sans cesse le cantique que j'ai lu dans tes yeux; par mes mots, je pose mes lèvres sur la chair brûlante de mon pays." (p.70) He elaborates on the land symbolism when he later reminds her of the night of the 24th of June (St. John the Baptist Day, named after the patron saint of the French Canadians), when, as the two were making love, the spark of revolution was ignited:

> J'ai beau tracer sur ce papier le fil enchevêtré de ma ligne de vie, cela ne me redonne pas le lit encombré de coussins colorés où nous nous sommes aimés un certain 24 juin, tandis que, quelque part sous notre tumulte, tout un peuple réuni semblait fêter la descente irrésistible du sang dans nos veines. ...Quelle violente et douce prémonition de la révolution nationale s'opérait sur cette étroite couche recouverte de couleurs et de nos deux corps nus, flambants, unis dans leurs démence rythmée. (p.72)

Slightly paraphrasing Baudelaire in the final two verbs ("t'aimer et mourir," cf "L'Invitation au Voyage"). the narrator accentuates the symbolic sameness of the land and of woman when he laments his separation from them: "Où est-il le pays qui te ressemble, mon pays natal et secret, celui où je veux t'aimer et mourir." (p.78) Again and again the narrator ambiguously reasserts his attachment ("Laissez-moi me coucher encore une fois sur le sol chaud du pays mon amour et dans le lit vulnérable qui nous attend" p.79), although the fact of his writing from jail — because he is put there by K — should preclude this.

While, upon first impression, *Prochain Episode* seems to be a very passionate call for violent revolution, it really is an aesthetic statement on the need for self-liberation. Admittedly, we have throughout the novel a dual progressive quest for liberation: the narrator vis-à-vis his self, and the collective self vis-à-vis its internal and external menaces. We have dealt up to now, through the K symbolism, mainly with the latter quest; but the former is the more profound. The opening lines indicate this journey into the self — reminiscent of Cesaire's in *Cahier d'un Retour au Pays Natal* — as the narrator says: "Cuba coule en flammes au milieu du Lac Léman pendant que je descends au fond des choses. Encaissé dans mes phrases, je glisse, fantôme dans les eaux névrosées du fleuve et je découvre dans ma dérive, le dessous des surfaces et l'image renversée des Alpes."(p.7) Indeed the recreation of the narrator's revolutionary commitment (the long flashback which is the plot of the novel) serves as therapy for the narrator's present illness, as he indicates that his schizophrenia is also his people's. Repeatedly, the narrator reminds us to interpret his personal history with that of his people. But then the author, Aquin, intervenes and says that the story told by the narrator is indissociable from what happened to him (Aquin was arrested in the summer of 1964 for subversive activities, put under mental observation, and like the narrator, wrote a book, *Prochain Episode*, during his imprisonment) (12):

> Je suis ce livre d'heure en heure au jour le jour; et pas plus que je ne me suicide, je n'ai tendance à y renoncer. Ce livre défait me ressemble. Cet amas de feuilles est un produit de l'histoire, fragment inachevé de ce que je suis moi-même et témoignage impur, par conséquent, de la révolution chancelante que je continue d'exprimer, à ma façon, par mon délire institutionnel. Ce livre est cursif et incertain comme je le suis; et sa signification véritable ne peut être dissociée de la date de sa composition, ni des évènements qui se sont déroulés dans un laps de temps donné entre mon pays natal et mon exil, entre un 26 juillet et un 24 juin. (pp.92-93)

Considering, therefore, this book as the product of a real imprisonment, as the therapy Aquin needed to keep his sanity (he said so in so many words in a volume of essays, *Point de Fuite*, (13) we may understand this novel-within-a-novel, complicating and infuriating as it is, to be primarily an aesthetic metaphor for one man's self-liberation. The spy story with H. de Heutz and assorted characters, the mystifying use of identities, serve as surrogates. And if the process of creation itself is Aquin's lasting statement, we can understand the value placed on the medium of language. In striking contrast to *Le Cassé*'s, the language here is highly polished, in the finest French literary tradition. Language is deliberately not conceived of as the sort that is ordinarily spoken, or that which would relate to any existential context; rather, in its highly poetical articulation, it cannot but be correlated with the aesthetic design. Creative language for the imprisoned narrator is one of the essential means to preserve his freedom. Language, in fact, is liberation. It is as if the more polished and poetic (and interpretative of the narrator's intimate feelings), the closer the narrator is to freedom.

We have come a long way from the first trials and defeats in the urban environment of the forties. But, in order to understand correctly the composite of "revolt", we cannot consider only the decadence of the Messianic myth; we must consider the actual conditions experienced in city life which more than anything else brought about its demise: the sordidness that breeds violence.

As said earlier, the world of the fathers is a reflection of the spiritual and vital inadequacy they confront as they migrate from the country to the

124

city. Whether it is Saint-Sauveur, Saint-Henri, or Montreal's East End, the ghetto is a physical environment illustrative of this inadequacy. The ghetto is envisaged by the city-born children as a world that reeks of conservatism and defeat. Fearful that they may get caught up and follow the pattern traced by their elders, while in opposite fashion, attracted and stimulated by the general overall secular environment they want to dominate, the new generation rebels against the ghetto.

Denis Boucher, for instance, though he gaily moves about the streets of Saint-Sauveur, in Lemelin's novel, as an acknowledged "gang leader", nonetheless considers this environment as humiliating. The more so when he dreams about his future as a successful man and , particularly, when, during the summer season tourists come to ogle and be pursued by children begging for money. Denis angrily berates the tourists, but his anger is really directed against an environment that breeds such humiliations:

> On ne vous les a jamais demandés, vos cents. Filez puants! Il saisit une pierre et la lança sur le tramway. Les mamans, dans les portes, le huèrent. Les étrangers viendraient plus jeter des cents. Elles faisaient apprendre aux petits, en même temps que: "Je vous aime mon Jésus," "Give me five cents, please." (p.176)

Denis becomes increasingly critical and he identifies this world as a consequence of his elders' defeat, the product of those who never dreamt of trying to move up to the upper part of town Denis vows to dominate. (14) He understands, then, that if he does not leave the ghetto his ambitions will be stifled:

> Boucher se débattait en vain contre ce "quelque chose" qui le dénonçait au néant, d'en haut. Le passé se pressa devant ses yeux, significatif. La paroisse le trahissait d'une façon autre qu'il n'avait cru.... Boucher était la victime de la somnolence malheureuse d'une classe de gens pour qui l'éducation est un soulier, ou un chapeau. (p.301)

An educated man compared to the rest of the people in the district, Denis grows in the awareness that he is too talented and ambitious to limit his horizons to Saint-Sauveur. He will be true to the vow he made to his girlfriend early in the novel: "Elle et lui fuiraient ce sale faubourg, s'éleveraient jusqu'à des nues superbes où il ne serait plus question de s'élever." (p.71) Though he suffers various setbacks (with fortitude and perseverance, if stimulated by the dreaded prospect of having to settle for his elders' defeat), Denis at the end of the book has published his first novel. He is starting to make money and to be known in the Haute-Ville; and since his story is in fact Roger Lemelin's who, after being for over a decade

125

Quebec's best known T.V. serials writer, became the prosperous businessman he is now — its successful ending could not be more in the Horatio Alger grain.

This is not really so for the Lacasses in *Bonheur d'Occasion*. Rose-Anna is walking the streets, in her yearly search for a flat; the author provides a powerful picture that speaks for itself:

> Une nuée d'enfants dépenaillés jouaient sur les trottoirs au milieu de paquets de débris. Des femmes maigres et tristes apparaissaient sur les seuils malodorants, étonnées de ce soleil qui faisait des carrés de lumière devant chaque tonneau de déchets. ...Partout des voix aigres, des pleurs d'enfants, des cris qui jaillissaient, douloureux, des profondeurs de quelque maison, portes et volets délabrés, rabattus, morte, murée sous la lumière comme une tombe. (p.132)

The last image is meaningful: the ghetto is a grave in which the elders rot and the children are in the process of dying. Although there seems to be life, in the restaurants, in the streets, judging from the rantings going on (at which Azarius excels), the impression remains that this is the visceral world of the dead cerebrally investigated by the poetess Anne Hébert in "Le Tombeau des Rois", a world of mute oppressed vitality. The conversations reflect this:

> Barquiens! reprit l'homme à tête chafouine, c'est la soupe pour les vieillards, la Saint-Vincent-de-Paul et pis le chômage; un tiers de la population sur le secours direct et des pauvres diables qui travaillent dans les rues à treize cennes de l'heure pendant quatre, cinq jours au printemps. La v'là la démocratie! (p.56)

Azarius Lacasse's incapacity symbolizes this:

> Le chauffeur, comme sa fille, se sentait peu fait pour sa besogne et mal ajusté à la vie quotidienne. Tant qu'il jonglait avec les mots, se retenait à de grandes causes qu'il estimait nobles, tout allait bien, mais dès qu'il s'agissait de reprendre contact avec la réalité de tous les jours, il perdait pied. (p.61)

Florentine looks at the diners in her restaurant and knows: "Ainsi, jamais elle n'avait remarqué comme aujourd'hui la dolente résignation écrite sur les visages des pauvres attablés. Jamais d'ailleurs elle ne s'était sentie si près d'eux et si haineuse de cette ressemblance! Jamais toutes ces odeurs...." (p.153) Jean Lévesque is similarly conscious when in Florentine's home he muses:

126

Il savait maintenant que la maison de Florentine lui rappelait
ce qu'il avait par-dessus tout redouté; l'odeur de la pauvreté, cette
odeur implacable des vêtements pauvres, cette pauvreté qu'on
reconnaîtrait les yeux clos. Il comprenait que Florentine elle-
même personnifait ce genre de vie misérable contre laquelle tout
son être se soulevait. (p.280)

Rebelling against the ghetto, Lévesque has to forsake Florentine since
her image would always remind him of that which he wants to leave behind
in his drive for success. Like Denis Boucher, his energies are harnessed for
the conquest of the 'upper' part of town (here Westmount, a posh
traditionally Anglo-Saxon residential area on the western slope of the
Mount Royal in the centre of Montreal); his ambitions are galvanized by
contemplating Westmount from Saint-Henri, in the lower part of town: "Ici
le luxe et la pauvreté se regardent inlassablement, depuis qu'il y a
Westmount, depuis qu'en bas, à ses pieds, il y a Saint-Henri. ... Il était à la
fois haineux et puissant devant cette montagne qui le dominait." (p.45)
   Florentine similarly fixes her eyes on a world different from her family
origins: one of affluence and determination, which she identifies with Jean
Lévesque, and to which she finally gains access through her marriage to Emmanuel: "A travers cet inconnu [Jean Lévesque] que les lumières lui parais-
saient brillantes, la foule gaie, et le printemps même, plus très loin, à la veille
de faire reverdir les pauvres arbres de Saint-Henri." (p.23) But not all the
children succeed in their revolt. The trio of Alphonse, Pitou and Boisvert is
not aware of the stamina and ruthlessness required to make a decent living.
In contrast to Jean Lévesque, these young men naturally expect to obtain
from society the positions and rewards guaranteed by their albeit minimal
education and the advertisements and the lavishly decorated store windows
they see around them. When they discover the truth — that a mass society's
promises are out of proportion with its actual rewards; that its 'rewards' are
never given but ruthlessly competed for by 'achievers' in the mold of Lévesque — they are bitterly disappointed. They become their father's alter egos;
numbed victims of a reality whose laws they have not understood:

Qu'est-ce qu'a nous a donné à nous autres, la société? Rien.
Pis, si t'es pas encore content, regarde Pitou. Quel âge qu'il a
Pitou? Dix-huit ans... eh! ben, il a pas encore fait une journée
d'ouvrage payé dans sa vie. Et v'là betôt cinq ans qu'il est sorti de
l'école à coups de pied dans la bonne place, et pis qu'y cherche.
C'est-y pas de la justice, ça? ...Et v'là not' Pitou qui fume comme
un homme, mâche comme un homme, crache comme un homme,
mais y a pas gagné une tannante de cenne toute sa saprée vie.
Trouves-tu ça beau, toi? Moi, je trouve ça laite, ben laite. (p.72)

The prospect is grim. The Pitous and Ti-Phonses seem condemned to live in a world of verbose discontent, hopeless idealization, wishful thinking. The post-Depression context (whose economic plight is lifted by the advent of World War II; a fact whose bitter irony Mme Roy deftly uses in the conclusion of the novel) is essential, of course, for the interpretation of these young men's defeat. But, just as they recall earlier figures of defeat, they seem to be forerunners of the malcontents of the sixties who, far from humbly resorting to a spirit of resignation, rage against their underprivileged condition.

Let us take *Le Cassé*'s Ti-Jean, for example. Penniless, unemployed, uneducated, Ti-Jean lives under the constant threat of hunger and thirst. Dispossessed of moral, intellectual and material values, Ti-Jean, in his despair, is driven to revolt in the most violent manner. For Ti-Jean, with no family and roots, the ghetto is not the world of the fathers. He cannot blame his condition on them, or use them as motivation for escape, in the manner of Boucher, Lévesque and Florentine. His revolt, hence, is directed at everything and at nothing in its nihilism. His despair is so all-encompassing that he rebels against the world as it appears to him from his dilapidated quarters, in the personage of his mistress, in that of Bouboule, and in the image of himself he would like to destroy.

The ghetto, as in *Bonheur d'Occasion*, is presented in photographic fashion: the picture of a totally dismal way of life. Ti-Jean's room seems to be, in fact, the microcosm of Montreal's East End:

> Aucun drap sur le lit. Aucune couverture non plus. La literie n'est pas fournie. Le matelas taché de grandes flaques brunes et jaunâtres. Des trous de cigarettes dans dette chaise bleu-déteint. Une coquerelle sort de l'un des trous comme une grosse bébite d'un trou de balle dans le ventre luisant d'un chien abattu. Lourde et saoule coquerelle. (p.17)

But the definitive jolting symbol of the ghetto is introduced in the image of Bouboule, the dope pusher of the district, whose characterization as evil incarnate is a throwback to the Mestizo in Graham Greene's *The Power and the Glory*:

> Bouboule rit, râle, se lèche les babines, cale son quatrième [he is drinking beer]. Quand il rit, on aperçoit ses deux incisives à la mâchoire supérieure, petites, fragiles, collées l'une contre l'autre, isolées, toutes les autres dents de la mâchoire supérieur manquent. Ça lui fait une bouche de lapin. Ses cheveux sont noirs sales, grisâtres, des poils follets au menton, sur les joues, une tête à mourir bientôt, une face à fesser d'dans. (p.55)

The words "une tête à mourir bientôt" are ominous. In Bouboule, Ti-Jean sees the image of degradation he would like, but is unable, to escape; therefore he tries to wreak revenge on society by destroying the dope pusher, the arch symbol of its rottenness. Everything Ti-Jean has been rebelling against in vain (hunger, unemployment) is projected onto Bouboule.

It is interesting to observe the pattern leading to, and going beyond the need for, an object to destroy. Philomène (Ti-Jean's mistress) at first appears to be an obvious target, but she is spared and allowed to live, estranged from Ti-Jean. Next, as Ti-Jean's resentments grow upon his discovery that Philomène is having a lesbian affair with a "bourgeoise" from Outremont (the French Canadian counterpart to Westmount), he turns his potential for violence onto himself: "Il a frappé à coups de pieds dans la portière du frigidaire. Une bosse, puis à coups de poings. Ses jointures sont tuméfiées. Son poignet droit lui fait mal. Il se jette la rage au coeur sur le lit. Il se tire les cheveux à pleines mains." (p.60) Finally, Ti-Jean finds the right channel for his all-destroying rage: Bouboule. He decides to kill him, ostensibly because Bouboule also is having an affair with Philomène, but, more likely, in order to find release from despair, in a manner not altogether different from Bigger Thomas' in *Native Son*. The climactic raw violence, enhanced by the clinical description of the killing, attains an almost epic proportion. It serves, it would seem, as a kind of ritual through which Ti-Jean is to achieve purification of a sort (15):

> Bouboule est étendu sur le dos. Il geint. Il commence à chialer un peu plus fort que tout à l'heure. Les deux incisives: Ti-Jean lui bouche la gueule d'un coup de talon. Les deux lèvres ont fendu. Ça saigne. Bouboule saigne trop fort. Ti-Jean s'agenouille sur ses épaules, il lui plante la tige du tournevis dans le palais. Envoyéye! Dans la gorge via la bouche gluante. Ti-Jean jouit à imprimer au tournevis un mouvement saccadé de va-et-vient. Le sang gicle par le nez. Un coq saigné. (p.69)

Soon enough, the revolution called for, in *Prochain Épisode*, is identified as the recourse to violence. While in *Le Cassé*, it operates as one man's outlet for frustration, here violence is celebrated as the necessary catharsis for a collective *and* individual state of discontent. We are presented with a lyrical view of violence whereby the narrator succinctly states: "Tuer confère un style à l'existence." (p.23) Violent revolution is seen as a creative act for the people and for the writer, since an historical gap between the élite and the masses is thus bridged. The writer, particularly, finds in it an outlet from the gnawing sense of exile: "Notre histoire s'inaugurera dans le sang d'une révolution qui me brise et que j'ai mal servie: ce jour-là, veines ouvertes, nous ferons nos débuts dans le monde." (p.94) But it is this call for violence, which in its stridency associates itself with a process of purification

129

that retains our attention. Aquin asserts that, in its absolute, violence is a philosophy, an aesthetic programme, a love project, as he says:

> Le temps sera venu de tuer et celui, délai plus impérieux encore, d'organiser la destruction selon les doctrines antiques de la discorde et les canons de la guerilla sans nom! Après deux siècles d'agonie, nous ferons éclater la violence déréglée, série ininterrompue d'attentats et d'ondes de choc, noire épellation d'un projet d'amour total. (p.172)

One can argue that such words should not be taken literally; that they are modulated by a time honoured rhetorical tradition, particularly in the French language. Yet five years after their publication, the Quebec Minister of Labour was murdered. (16)

The celebration of violence as the expression of a collective wish for political independence culminates within an aesthetic frame, in *Prochain Episode*; revolt therein attains its most extreme form in the French-Canadian novel. This, however, does not imply that would-be revolutionary commitment is a phenomenon chiefly of the sixties in Quebec. That there always were underlying sentiments and attitudes claiming sovereignty as a solution to the French-Canadian historical sense of defeat can be seen, in a range of works, from the nineteenth century historical novels, which re-arrange the war of Conquest to suit nationalist sentiments, to those of the Messianic mold. Groulx's *L'Appel de la Race*, for instance, in portraying the trials of French Canadians have to undergo in Ontario, and the impossibility of a mixed marriage, certainly leads to such a conclusion. Savard's *Menaud* ominously ascribes Menaud's tragedy to the increasing dispossession of his woods by foreign entrepreneurship. His hate for his daughter's suitor, Délié, his severe reprimanding of his daughter, Maria, and his eventual insanity stem from the clash between his traditional heritage and the threat of the outside world. His resentments grow to the extent of contemplating violence to seek redress from real or imagined wrongs. Lighting a camp fire at one point in the book, Menaud sees in the flames an omen of deliverance through the ritual of fire:

> Cela se ferait un jour, partout! On verrait ce signe s'allumer sur toutes les buttes de l'immense pays! Ce drapeau vivant et clair jaillirait du sol pour le ralliement de la race! Il serait le signal de la délivrance; le peuple briserait les liens dont la trahison, la veulerie l'avaient chargé. (pp.112-113)

And the novel ends with the threatening note sounded by the villagers' chorus-like commentary in the face of the protagonist's final insanity: "C'est pas une folie comme une autre! Ça me dit, à moi, que c'est un avertissement." (p.265)

But the ultimate pre-1960 call for independence is contained in an unabashedly fascist novel published in 1942, Rex Desmarchais' *La Chesnaie*. It is the story of the creation of a revolutionary movement in Quebec whose leader, Hugues Larocque, is grandiloquently presented as the would-be dictator of a free and autonomous Quebec. The organization is located in the suburbs of Montreal and vows to resume the aims of the 1837 rebellion. However, due to internecine quarrels, the movement disintegrates before achieving its goal.

A look at the revolutionaries' programme reveals some disturbing similarities. As in *Prochain Episode*, the road towards sovereignty lies through violent revolution: "On se battrait de nouveau ici. 1837 n'était qu'un prologue. Tout était suspendu; rien n'était fini. L'affranchissement de la nation canadienne-française et la confirmation de son indépendance parachèveraient le sacrifice des patriotes de 1837." (p.62) Revolution is said to be necessary for catharsis, like in Aquin's novel, for the people are in a state of apathy and defeat which can only be shaken by violence: "Le plus affreux, poursuivit Larocque, c'est l'avachissement inénarrable des descendants des victimes de 1837. Ils ont perdu la mémoire de ces heures tragiques. Ils ne savent plus, aujourd'hui qui avait raison des bourreaux ou des victimes." (p.145) Finally, revolution is to liberate the writer from his situation of exile. Interestingly, Hughes Larocque is a frustrated writer whose lack of creativity, he tells us, is to be blamed on the presumed absence of political freedom in Quebec. (17) Conversely, thus, a free Quebec will liberate the artist's Muse:

> Mais sa persuasion raisonnée, c'est que le Canadien Français ne produira des chefs d'oeuvre que le jour où il sera le fils d'une nation libre et fière, riche et assurée sur le sol de la patrie. Il n'y a qu'une tâche urgente: affranchir la nation, établir, confirmer sa force et sa prospérité. (p.45)

But there is an added justification for independence, the dominant one in fact in Desmarchais's book. Writing at a time when totalitarianism was on the rise, Desmarchais does not shy from symbolizing the quest for political power in the "superman" figure of a dictator whom he sees as the ideal ruler of a free Québec: "Le Chef, capable, lorsqu'il fallait de toutes les subtilités de la diplomatie, marchait droit vers son but. Il trainait la nation à sa suite. La nation: ce misérable troupeau de mous, de faibles, d'indécis, de lâches,...." (p.260) For this ideal "Chef" Desmarchais sees a model in the late Portuguese dictator, Salazar ("A quarante, à quarante-cinq ans, je le vois comme le Salazar des Canadiens Français. Il organise la nation, il restaure son caractère catholique et français" p.33).

The lunacy of Desmarchais is quite evident. The fascist and antisemetic references that pollute his novel are reflections, probably, of an era in

Quebec's history when such attitudes prevailed and were condoned by the clergy. (18) What is less evident, and appears now in retrospect of particular importance for Quebec's cultural evolution, is that dictatorship, the "Chef" syndrome, came about two years after the publication of this novel, without the need for revolution and the resumption of the 1837 rebellion. Maurice LeNoblet Duplessis saw to that from 1944 to 1959. (19)

1 Paul Chamberland, "de la Damnation à la Liberté", *Parti Pris*, p.70.

2 Pierre Elliott Trudeau, *La Grève de l'Amiante*, p.11.

3 Mason Wade, *The French Canadians 1760-1945*, p.47.

4 This is the central argument in P.E. Trudeau's essay, "Les Séparatistes: des Contre-Révolutionnaires".

5 See Samuel Baillargeon's *Littérature Canadienne-Française*, p.280. Also Guildo Rousseau's *Jean-Charles Harvey et son Oeuvre Romanesque*.

6 See Robert Vigneault's devastating review of Rousseau's book in *Livres et Auteurs Québecois 1969*, pp.132-134.

7 See Jean-Paul Desbiens' *Les Insolences du Frère Untel*, pp.37-54.

8 *Ibid.*, pp.35-36.

9 Jean-Paul Desbiens gives a full account of the origins of the term and the structure as well of this vernacular speech, see *Les Insolences*, pp.23-36.

10 Gérald Godin, "Le Joual et Nous", *Parti Pris*, p.19.

11 *Ibid.*

12 Hubert Aquin, *Point de Fuite*, p.15.

13 *Ibid.*, p.16.

14 Cf. Vallières' account of his own childhood, particularly his mother's leitmotiv, "Quant on est né... pour un petit pain... il faut savoir s'en contenter". *Nègres Blancs d'Amérique*, p.187.

15 The source for the celebration of violence as a "purifying ritual" in the literature of the sixties, as it appears here in Renaud's novel, and, more evidently, in Aquin's seems to be the opening chapter of Frantz Fanon's *Les Damnés de la Terre*, "De la Violence", where cathartic significance for the colonized group and individual in Third World countries is said to lie in finding release for frustrations and oppression in revolutionary upheaval. See Fanon, pp.5-62. Discussing the would-be revolutionary stance of the separatists, Trudeau finds also that the most violent among them seem to have stopped their reading of Fanon with this first chapter, see "Les Séparatistes: des Contre-Révolutionnaires", *Le Fédéralisme et la Société Canadienne-Française*, pp.226-227.

16 I am not suggesting, of course, a cause-and-effect relationship between Aquin's novel and Laporte's death. Rather, I wish to

point out that when a certain "Zeitgeist", that of the sixties, is nurtured by violence — be it the rhetoric of writers — there appears to be a connection between the artifact of language and violent deeds.

17  This same idea is repeated throughout the sixties by writers of the "pays" group. Jean-Guy Pilon, for instance, writes: "Le jour où cette minorité culturelle qui a été tolerée en ce pays deviendra une nation à l'intérieur de ses frontières, quand cette minorité sera indépendante, notre littérature connaîtra un formidable bond en avant. Car l'écrivain, comme tout homme de cette société, se sentira libre". Cited in Trudeau's "La Nouvelle Trahison des Clercs", *Le Fédéralisme et la Société Canadienne-Française*, p.183. Ironically, the "great leap forward", in French-Canadian literature, to use Pilon's words, was taking place in the very decade, if not at the very moment, during which he was speaking; that is to say the *anticipation* rather than the *realization* of the "pays" in political terms gave a much needed boost to writing in Quebec. That this spirit of revolt is more complex than Pilon *et al.* would lead us to believe, I think, can be seen in the novels under discussion. And that this revolt culminates, as it should, in one of the imagination, I hope to show in the chapter on "self-articulation".

18  See André Laurendeau's *La Crise de la Conscription, 1942*, pp.92-95.

19  Duplessis was first elected in 1936, and voted out of office in 1940 over the Conscription issue. When the Duplessis era is referred to in Quebec the period in question is likely to be the latter and more important stage, from 1944 to 1959.

# RELIGION

# AND THE BLACK

As early as Brown's *Clotel*, a concern with religious beliefs and rituals is introduced in the Black novel. Since the Abolitionist movement steeps itself in Christian ethics to inveigh against the inhumanity of slavery, Brown highlights this attitude to reinforce the pathos of the mixed-blood's predicaments:

> This was a Southern auction, at which the bones, muscles, sinews, blood, and nerves of a young lady of sixteen were sold for five hundred dollars; her moral character for two hundred; her improved intellect for one hundred; her Christianity for three hundred; and her chastity and virtue for four hundred dollars more. And this too, in a city thronged with churches, whose tall spires look like so many signals pointing to heaven, and whose ministers preach that slavery is a God-ordained institution! (p.48)

To buttress his didactic aim, Brown relentlessly attacks the white preachers who have distorted the Bible and their offices to sanction the institution of slavery. The following scene typifies the smugness and condescension the plantation writers will use as a credo in their defense of the "southern way of life":

> Lastly, you should serve your masters faithfully because of their goodness to you. See to what trouble they have been on your account. Your fathers were poor ignorant and barbarous creatures in Africa, and the whites fitted out ships at great trouble and expense and brought you from that benighted land to Christian America, where you can sit under your own vine and fig tree

and no one molest or make you afraid. Oh, my dear black brothers
and sisters, you are indeed a fortunate and a blessed people. (p.72)

Generally, though, moral indignation in the post-Abolitionist Black novel is
directed against Black ministers who wittingly or unwittingly seem to follow
in the footsteps of their White counterparts. From Jean Toomer to Ralph
Ellison, the Black preacher, like the French-Canadian curate, is indicted for
keeping the eyes, hopes, miseries of his flock turned toward heaven, while
their alienation and dispossession, however sublimated thus, were left
unattended in the material order. But the very terms of the indictment
reflect ambivalence. The stance which kept the Negroes impervious to their
social malaise served also as a primordial mode of survival.

One cannot forget that Caliban, more than being a foul-mouthed rebel,
is also, and principally, a dreamer who hears voices unheard by Prospero.
On the one hand, he reveals the extent of his quarrel with Prospero, now
carried over in the latter's power of conditioning his spiritual beliefs; on the
other hand, the 'voices' that are his own manifest themselves. But let us first
analyze the religious extension of Caliban's quarrel with Prospero, the
consciousness by Black authors of a systematic debasement carried both in
the secular and the religious fields. The consequent attitude is succinctly
expressed by James Baldwin in *The Fire Next Time*:

> It is not too much to say that whoever wishes to become a
> truly moral human being (and let us not ask whether or not this is
> possible; I think we must believe that it is possible) must first
> divorce himself from all the prohibitions, crimes and hypocrisies
> of the Christian church. (1)

*Cane*'s "Kabnis" introduces, in fact, the factors that culminate in
Baldwin's rejection. After hearing of a lynching which Blacks helplessly
witnessed, a character expresses one of these seminal factors: the emasculation religion has reduced the Negro to: "Can't something be done? But
of course not. This preacher-ridden race. Pray and shout. They're in the
preacher's hands. That's what it is. And the preacher's hands are in the white
man's pockets." (pp.173-174) But the indictment of Christianity is mainly
conveyed in Toomer's characterization of Halsey's blind grandfather who
resides in a "hole", symbolic of hell, into which Kabnis, Orpheus-like,
descends to confront his demons. The confrontation is dramatic both for
the mixed-blood, who regains his identity, and Father John (the
grandfather), who is subsequently able to name the "horror" he has seen.
The two are shown to have been twin-like figures in their delusions. Father
John's Christian beliefs and Kabnis' neuroses, derived from the social impact of his hybridity, are elements of the same problem. Kabnis' violent
abuse of the grandfather emphasizes the fact that the traditional religion
136

steeped in the Negro's soul is coupled with some dark, unknown, forces that may very well destroy the Negro who embraces it as innocently and as ardently as the grandfather did:

> Slave boy whom some Christian mistress taught to read the Bible. Black man who saw Jesus in the rice fields, and began preaching to his people. Moses — and Christ — words used for songs. Dead blind father of a muted folk who feel their way upward to a life that crushes or absorbs them. (p.212)

Kabnis' gratuitous abuses are explained shortly by the fact that he senses in the old man's dark forces a correspondence with his own, that he has yet to confront consciously. Lewis understands Kabnis' predicament and says: "The old man as symbol, flesh, and spirit of the past, what do you think he would say if he could see you? You look at him, Kabnis." (p.217) As Kabnis is in the process of releasing his demons by verbally assaulting the old man, the latter remains a fixed, rigid, death-like figure. Suddenly he starts breaking his long-held silence (the old man has not spoken in years), and he is led to express himself in language similar to Kurtz's in *Heart of Darkness*, when the dejected European finally assessed his journey in the darkness of his self as "the horror...." (2) Here the "horror" is the traumatic disillusionment that deprived Father John of sight and speech, when he realized the destructive process he was engaged in as a preacher for an institution that condoned the oppression of his people: "Th sin whats fixed... ...upon th white folks — ... — g tellin Jesus — lies. O th sin th white folks 'mitted when they made th Bible lie." (p.237) Spluttering and almost incoherent, Father John nonetheless, finally grasping the meaning of his fate, stands in Toomer's design as symbolic of the Negro's spiritual destruction. Father John's sin is his participation in a process of deception. Kabnis likewise recognizes his sin, the destruction of his soul, through the deceptive lure of "passing" in the North. As Father John exorcizes himself, Kabnis too is liberated; Father John is, in fact, a symbolic *alter ego*: Kabnis' repressed and denied dark self.

Nowhere does McKay deal explicitly with Christianity. This is not surprising since he is concerned to celebrate the exact opposites of what it stands for. Nevertheless one cannot fail to see the rejection that is implied in the depiction of the Negro's primitivism or Africanness. Just like other (presumed) white products of civilization, — intellectualism and abstractions — Christianity, apparently, stands alien to the Black experience. (That this point of view is historically and culturally false, we shall see shortly.)

Conversely, in *Native Son*, Christianity is referred to, in no uncertain terms, as one of the main causes of the Negro's dispossessed state; it is responsible for the plight of Bigger to a great extent, says Wright. As Bigger is in jail, reflecting upon his life, resignation and defeatism are associated with the maternal symbolism of his mother and the Church. And both are assessed as negative factors, for they belong to the world of the Southern past which accepted, without contesting, the Black man's assigned role in the order of things. Since Bigger is precisely fated to question this tradition, in the most direct manner, it is a natural consequence that his mother's world is judged to be irrelevant in his urban secular experience:

> Would it not have been better for him had he lived in that world the music sang of? It would have been easy to have lived in it, for it was his mother's world, humble, contrite, believing. It had a center, a core, an axis, a heart which he needed but could never have unless he laid his head upon a pillow of humility and gave up his hope of living in the world. And he would never do that. (p.238)

The association of the Negro's Christianity with the White power structure, the consequent betrayal by Black religious leaders (or the potential danger of such an occurrence due to the Black preacher's very ambivalent role, as Gunnar Myrdal noted in his classic study of the White-Black conundrum, *An American Dilemma*), (3) is carried in the scenes near the end of the novel, as a preacher tries to talk to Bigger:

> Bigger stared unblinkingly at the white wall before him as the preacher's words registered themselves in his consciousness. He knew without listening what they meant; it was the old voice of his mother telling of suffering, of hope, of love beyond this world. And he loathed it because it made him feel as condemned and guilty as the voice of those who hated him. (p.263)

Later, the preacher tries to intervene between Bigger and Jan, his communist friend. The contrast that emerges between the worlds represented by the Reverend and the revolutionary is extended to the level of caricature, which comes about in the very language used by the preacher, pregnant with time-honoured submissiveness:

> "Ah don't wanna break in 'n meddle where Ah ain' got no bisness, suh," the preacher said in a tone that was militant, but deferring. "But there ain' no usa draggin' no communism in this thing, Mistah. Ah respecks yo' feelin's powerfully, suh; but whut yuh's astin' jus' stirs up mo' hate. Whut this po' boy needs is understandin'.... (p.269)

In the face of such emasculation, Bigger again resorts to revolt. He throws away a cross left by the preacher. And to the latter's "Son, don't spit i.1

138

Gawd's face!" — he threateningly replies: "I'll spit in your face if you don't leave me alone!" (p.314)

The correlation between the indictment of religion and the recourse to violence is indeed an intimate one. It recurs in Attaway's, Demby's, and Ellison's novels; and it is implied in Himes', Gardner Smith's, and Petry's in the vehemence of the violence depicted. Attaway's Big Mat is a religious person used to reading his Bible every day. One day, as Melody observes, Big Mat stops that practice: "In all the time that Melody had known him there had never a day passed that Mat hadn't studied the word." (p.145) Thereupon a noticeable change, which his brothers do not fail to perceive, ensues in Big Mat's behaviour. This change appears immediately in his relations with his Mexican mistress. But the new surrogate of violence equally extends to his fellow workers, as we saw earlier. The equation is clear: so long as religion was resorted to, Big Mat could sublimate the awareness of his dispossessed condition, but the moment the deputy's badge has been substituted for the power of the 'word' Big Mat becomes Bigger's *alter ego*. Similarly, Demby has David, in *Beetlecreek*, identify the rituals of the Church with the cycles of alienation. The Church is another place where the feeling of "asphyxiation" engulfs David. Because of this, and the Church's "death" symbolism, the association is made with the existential conditions that cause what Ellison and Demby call the "death" of the Negro: "— the suffocation he had felt in church, the undercurrent of secret excitement he knew they felt partaking of the death ritual, the secret envy for the escape death offered, the jealousy of the escaped one; the hunger to be joined together in something, anything, even the celebration of death." (p.78)

Ellison carries the correlation to its ultimate point. The world of the South is dominated by Church rituals, that of the North by riots. As in *Native Son*, the South is the maternal world of the family and of the Church, while the North is the paternal one of material dispossession. Early in *Invisible Man* there is a scene where the hero is in the Negro college's chapel, and the choir is about to sing for the white trustees led by Norton. The expected Negro spirituals are representative of the overall submissiveness the Negro must profess: "Loved? Demanded. Sung? An ultimatum accepted and ritualized, an allegiance recited for the peace it imparted, and for that perhaps loved. Loved as the defeated come to love the symbols of their conquerors. A gesture of acceptance, of terms laid down and reluctantly approved." (p.100) The first mass secular experience the hero undergoes in the North is a riot in Harlem. The riot comes as a consequence of an eviction. Interestingly, the evicted ones are two old Negroes, originally from the South, who cling to a Bible as they beg the white marshals to allow them a few minutes' delay so that they can pray. The hero, moved by the sight of the couple, takes up their defense. He makes a speech, referring to the Church, to the meaning of religion for these old people — all of this for the purpose

139

Gospel Singers                                    *(lee Friedlander)*

of convincing the marshals of their inoffensiveness: "They don't want the world, but only Jesus. They only want Jesus, just fifteen minutes of Jesus on the rug-bare floor. How about it, Mr Law? Do we get our fifteen minutes worth of Jesus? You got the world, can we have our Jesus?" (p.242) The marshals, of course, refuse, wherefore violence erupts.

But we did mention, at the beginning of this chapter, that there is more than discontent in the Black American's involvement with Christianity. This appears in terms of the cathartic Church meetings (revival meetings), and the lore of the Gospel (in singing, testifying and preaching), through which the meaning of religion is made present for the Negro. Because of the historical, psychological and cultural reaches of this meaning, the Negro's experience of Christianity, in truth, is one whereof he has taken a body of alien rituals and beliefs and made them into *his own*, the profound expression of *his* vision, outlook, and experience of life in America. (4) Far from being a negative frame of reference (as the authors previously quoted would have us believe), the Church, in all that it represents, is perhaps the most positive institutional and cultural frame of reference that he has; since every secular art form that is distinctively originated in Black American culture (the Blues, Jazz, "soul" music, the Charleston and its derivatives, the rhetoric of Black leaders, etc.) stems in no uncertain manner from its grounds. (5) It is significant that it is no other than James Baldwin who, while rejecting the Church in one context, exaltingly celebrates it in another — in such rarely matched flow of lyricism as:

> The church was very exciting. It took a long time for me to disengage myself from this excitement, and on the blindest, most visceral level, I never really have, and never will. There is no music like that music, no drama like the drama of the saints rejoicing, the sinners moaning, the tambourines racing, and all those voices coming together and crying holy unto the Lord. There is still, for me, no pathos quite like the pathos of those multicolored, worn, somehow triumphant and transfigured faces, speaking from the depths of a visible, tangible, continuing despair of the goodness of the Lord. I have never seen anything to equal the fire and excitement that sometimes, without warning, fill a church, causing the church, as Leadbelly and so many others have testified, to "rock". Nothing that has happened to me since equals the power and the glory that I sometimes felt when in the middle of a sermon, I knew that I was somehow, by some miracle, really carrying, as they said, "the Word" — when the church and I were one. Their pain and their joy were mine, and mine was theirs — they surrendered their pain and joy to me, I surrendered mine to them — and their cries of "Amen!" and "Hallelujah!" and "Yes, Lord!" and "Praise His name!" and "Preach it, brother!" sustained and

whipped on my solos until we all became equal, wringing wet, singing and dancing, in anguish and rejoicing, at the foot of the altar. It was, for a long time, in spite of — or, not inconceivably because of — the shabbiness of my motives, my only sustenance, my meat and drink. I rushed home from school, to the church, to the altar, to be alone there, to commune with Jesus, my dearest Friend, who would never fail me, who knew all the secrets of my heart. (6)

Is it surprising, after hearing this searing confession, to find out that Baldwin's two most-acclaimed works of fiction, the play *The Amen Corner*, and the novel *Go Tell It On The Mountain*, are works which are very much autobiographical and steeped in the world of the Church? Or that Baldwin, as a writer, is celebrated for the quality of his prose, one that owes, in its power and breath, a great deal to the oracular tradition of the Negro church? Or, that Baldwin's fame rests firmly on collections of essays such as *The Fire Next Time, Nobody Knows My Name*, and, *Notes of a Native Son*, where the conscience and the voice that are brought to bear on the dilemmas of the American scene — are those of a fire-breathing preacher in disguise? It should not be. And as a matter of fact, given the profound and far-reaching truth of Baldwin's confession, all the Black authors seen so far, and especially the most revolted ones, would recognize that behind their vision — helping to shape it — lies the religious meaning Baldwin speaks of.

It is obvious that the feelings revealed in the above excerpt are not those of a parishioner paying lip-service to an institution existing *outside* of himself. On the contrary, the exaltation is expressive of a central core of experience which is Baldwin's, and not an institution's; which is archetypal, by this I mean a core of experience that is the Black American's, and not any Christian's — because, ultimately, such a transcendent symbiosis of the *I* and the *Other*, of the *here* and the *hereafter*, is rooted in the Black American's African ancestry. There lies, in a culture primordially spiritual where all of the living and the dead, the familial as well as the societal institutions, are linked in a spiritual continuum with all of creation, there lies the unmistakable *quality* of the spirit that has struck and puzzled more than one observer of peoples of African descent, be they Black American, Afro-Cuban or Afro-Brazilian, Haitian or Trinidadian.

Long before Baldwin, James Weldon Johnson showed in his *Autobiography of an Ex-Coloured Man* that it is such a "core of experience" that reconciles, for a while, his narrator's divided self (upon his return from Europe, as he goes to the South to do research in Black culture):

The sentiments are easily accounted for; they are mostly taken from the Bible; but the melodies, where did they come from? ... And so many of these songs contain more than mere melody;

there is sounded in them that elusive undertone, the note in music which is not heard with the ears. ... Any musical person who has never heard a Negro congregation under the spell of religious fervour sing these old songs has missed one of the most thrilling emotions which the human heart may experience. (p.181)

Johnson, like Baldwin, is content to dwell in the rapture of mysterious melodies or in the "spell" of a revival meeting. Interestingly enough, such African observers as Leopold Senghor and Ezekiel Mphahlele have not hesitated to recognize an African echo in this "quality of the spirit" referred to in some quarters as "soul". Senghor, in an essay on Black American poets of the Negro Renaissance (including James W. Johnson), asserts:

L'esclave noir avait, certes, oublié toute langue africaine, et aussi, à un moindre degré, le folklore africain. Il avait conservé l'essentiel: une extraordinaire perméabilité aux courants du monde extérieur, un sens aigu des forces cosmiques. Cette sensibilité, cet *animisme* a fécondé le folklore en même temps qu'il le ratt chait, par des liens profonds, à la tradition ancestrale.

Les plus anciennes manifestations du folklore négro-américain sont les *Spirituals*, chants religieux qui tiennent du cantique protestant et de la mélopée africaine. (8)

But, because it is difficult to marshal a systematic factual set of evidence to back up such assertions, a number of Black authors (Baldwin, Wright, Ellison, to name just a few), have remained unconvinced in the past, at least, before the contemporary glorification of the Black American's African roots. One suspects that such scepticism has to be taken into the context of the pre-1960 period, when, after much ostracization, integration, or rather assimilation, into the mainstream of American culture was the goal pursued. (10) However, one need not refer to the pioneering work of a Herskovits to agree with the conclusions of Ezekiel Mphahlele, after his first trip to Harlem:

The fact is that there *are* African survivals in American Negro life. You see them in the Negro's gait; in his bodily rhythm in a dance; in his "separatist" religious worship where he is not ashamed to surrender himself to the emotional intensity of the devotional moment; in the abundance of his laughter when he is really tickled. For the Negro writer to admit this is not necessarily to deny that he is the synthesis of historical processes and present-day experience. (11)

Thus a book such as Baldwin's *Go Tell It On The Mountain* uses a revival meeting in a Harlem storefront church as the dramatic locus for the coming-to-grips of four sinners with their past life. Their yearning for grace conveys the deep psychic meaning religion fulfills for ghetto Blacks (who are, of course, uprooted Southerners, as in most of the novels examined so far). A striking feature of the novel is the ambiguities carried throughout in the characters of Roy and John, who rebel against the authoritarian figure of their Deacon father, Gabriel. They remind one of a number of "sons" in the African novel. (12) And the dilemma is the same: how to reconcile the fundamental spiritual, or religious, roots of one's culture with the temptations, or necessities, of the material order; to reconcile a world identified as that of the fathers, the past, and one identified as progress in a materially-acquisitive society? The protagonist in Sheikh Hamidou Kane's novel, *L'Aventure Ambiguë*, never successfully resolves the ambiguity of his condition, and his death in fact comes as a consequence. Yet, in a scene with a French girl full of Marxist belief in the subjugation of everything to the dialectical process of matter, Samba Diallo expresses his opposition to materialism as a philosophy and stresses what his African culture stands for:

> Tu ne t'es pas seulement exhausée de la nature, voici même que tu as tourné contre elle le glaive de ta pensée, ton combat est pour l'assujettir n'est-ce-pas? Moi je n'ai pas encore tranché le cordon ombilical qui me fait un avec elle, la suprême dignité à laquelle j'aspire aujourd'hui encore c'est d'être sa partie la plus sensible, la plus filiale. Je n'ose pas la combattre étant elle-même, jamais je n'ouvre le sein de la terre cherchant ma nourriture que préalablement je ne lui en demande pardon en tremblant. Je n'abats point d'arbre combattant son corps que je ne le supplie fraternellement. Je ne suis que le bout de l'être où bourgeonne la pensée. (13)

Even at the cost of never escaping a condition of being torn apart by two cultural poles, Samba refuses to deny his roots. One wonders whether Baldwin's characters are not only conscious of living an ambiguous condition also but willing to pay for it if they must, for the book ends with grace having come to the sinners. Two "Sisters" (female members of the congregation) sum up the cathartic ceremony they have all been through:

> "Well, amen," said Sister Price. "Look like the Lord just wanted this church to *rock*. You remember how He spoke through Sister McCandless Friday night, and told us to pray, and He'd work a mighty wonder in our midst? And He done *moved* — Hallelujah — He done troubled *everybody*'s mind."
>
> "I just tell you," said Sister McCandless, "all you got to do is *listen* to the Lord; He'll lead you every *time*; He'll move every *time*.

Can't nobody tell me *my* God ain't real." (p.180)

Indeed not, one is tempted to add. Considering the reaches of the religious in his cultural make-up, the Black American, like the African, is not about to cast away that without which he can only be an Ellisonian "invisible man", or a psychotic Bigger Thomas.

But if he is seriously bent, Baldwin *et al.* seem to say, upon exploring the positive and far more rewarding side of his Calibanness, the Black American cannot negate the 'voices' that have sustained him in his exile and dispossession. These 'voices', much more than his revolt against Prospero, it would appear, will free him of the metropolitan man's subjugation. We seem to be a far cry from Bigger's alienation, but that and Gabriel's yearning for grace are in reality the "rind" and the "heart" of Caliban, as Ellison might say. When Caliban acknowledges the two and asserts himself accordingly then he will have emancipated himself from Prospero's hold.

1  James Baldwin, *The Fire Next Time*, p.67.
2  Joseph Conrad, *Heart of Darkness and the Secret Sharer*, p. 147.
3  Myrdal says: "The Negro preacher's stand on problems of caste and on all 'political' problems is equivocal. On the one hand, he must preach 'race solidarity' .... On the other hand, he is not only a focus of caste pressure, but his position of leadership depends upon the monopoly given him by segregation". See Gunnar Myrdal, *An American Dilemma*, p.940.
4  E. Franklin Frazier, *The Negro Church in America*, pp.72-75.
5  *Ibid.*
6  Baldwin, *The Fire Next Time*, pp.49-51.
7  For the pervasive spiritualism of African culture, see John S. Mbiti's *African Religions and Philosophy*; Basil Davidson's *The African Genius*. For a study that uses the Bantu concept of "Ntu" (universal force) as the connecting link between peoples of African descent, see Janheinz Jahn's *Muntu An Outline of the New African Culture*; see also Jahn's *Neo-African Literature* that traces that same "force" in verbal structures of rhythm and repetition in the literature of these same peoples (American, West Indian of French, English and Spanish expression).
8  Léopold Sédar Senghor, *Négritude et Humanisme*, p.105.
9  See Richard Wright's account of his journey to pre-independence Ghana, *Black Power*, a book replete with condescending generalizations. See James Baldwin's essay on the first "Congrès des Ecrivains et Artistes Noirs" convened by the *Présence Africaine* group in 1956 at La Sorbonne, "Princes and Powers", *Nobody Knows My Name*. Like Wright, in the presence of Africans and West Indians, Baldwin cannot help resorting to an

"Americanness" of spirit that differentiates him from the surrounding Blacks. Baldwin goes on to make the unbelievable statement that the reaction he had listening to the great Martinican poet, Aimé Césaire, was, "I myself felt stirred in a very strange and disagreeable way." (p.40) — to a speech that indicted the colonial policies of Europe. It is interesting to note also what according to Baldwin, Wright had to say to the Africans (that *they* were not "free from their 'irrational' past"). Lastly, see Ellison's insistence on the Black American's "Americanness" that dwarfs his (if such a thing there is, Ellison *dixit*) "Africanness", "Indivisible Man", *The Atlantic,* pp.50-51.

10 See, for instance, the conclusion to Margaret Just Butcher's *The Negro in American Culture.*

11 Melville Herskovits is, of course, the author of the pioneering *The Myth of the Negro Past* which successfully established that in some regions in the South with a historically-stable Black population there were indeed African-inherited practices and beliefs. Ezekiel Mphahlele, *The African Image*, pp.47-48.

12 See Margaret Laurence's study of the Nigerian novel, particularly Chinua Achebe's, in *Long Drums and Cannons*, pp.97-125.

13 Sheikh Hamidou Kane, *L'Aventure Ambiguë*, p.167.

# BLACK SELF

# ARTICULATION

From the Black novel's inception with William Wells Brown's *Clotel* (1853), to its flowering with Ralph Ellison's *Invisible Man* (1952), two broad interrelated spheres might resume the dramatized experience of Black life in America: the psychological and the social. First, problems of identity are obsessively dealt with in the "tragic mulatto" novels. In Charles Waddell Chesnutt's *The House Behind the Cedars* (1900), and Jean Toomer's *Cane* (1923), the Renas and the Kabnises are misfits, psychologically crippled in that they are seen (until they *see* themselves which, except for Kabnis, is never the case) as deprived of identity. Hence their attempt at gaining an individual identity, at the expense of negating the other element of their biological duality, results in failure. Not until the Depression years does concrete reality impose the evidence that individual psychology is molded by environment. And when it is considered that the same factor (race) explains the tragedy of the mixed-blood and that of the economically underprivileged, it follows that the attack, for the novelist's part, must be directed against the environment. But by the time we get to Ellison, the Negro reaches the awareness that neither appeals to pathos nor calls for upheaval change a root situation. If in Bigger's revolt there is the expression of a Promethean quest, in the "invisible man's" sardonic view of humanity we come close to Sisyphus, as understood by Sartre, Beckett and Camus.

Man lives in an environment that labels him, defines him, oblivious to *his* view of self. The individual turns a deaf ear to the claims of race, nation, religion, because he is conscious of his primordial solitude. As a matter of fact the group is more the locus of evil than the presumed threat that calls for group cohesion. Hell is indeed others. (1) And for the "invisible man" "others" are Black Nationalists in the mold of Ras the Exhorter, as well as the well-meaning Marxists in the "Brotherhood". The only way out of the

149

existential conundrum, according to Ellison, is to escape from it all ("to live out one's own absurdity rather than to die for that of others" p.484), albeit after confronting the evil one wants to run away from. Thus the resolution in the hero's refuge in a coal-cellar where he will, presumably, spend the rest of his life.

But someone has been misreading either Sartre and Camus or the history of his own people in America. Sartre says "Existence comes before Essence." (2) That is, since man exists in the inevitable environment of other people, institutions, and laws, it is in such public arena that he must try to define himself, or see himself. Since, moreover, it is not what one thinks of oneself that matters when the Joseph Ks, Roquentins, Meursaults are *en situation* in regard to other people and institutions, but how others see them and so judge them — there is no escaping the premise that the eyes of others must first be taken into account in any self-evaluation. All this is hardly news to Black people. From their violent past they know a thing or two about being defined by others; from the feeling of alienation that runs from Rena Warwick to the "invisible man" they have the consciousness of the fundamental dichotomy between the "regardant" and the "étant regardé," or the "être-étant-pour-soi" and the "être-étant-pour-autre." (3) But, more profoundly, their very survival indicates that long before Camus they answered the only serious philosophical question in the face of absurdity: "la vie vaut-elle la peine d'être vécue?" (4) In answering yes, in their ignorance of learned intellectual exercise over a condition of life borne in their very bones, the American Blacks have never seriously contemplated escaping their condition, either historically, in any Garveyist back-to-Africa movement, or, in dilettantist luxury, by hiding in some coal-cellar. Thus, in the end, one is tempted to fault Ellison's resolution on the two essential grounds that otherwise give his novel its importance: the Black historical consciousness, and the existential attitude. Alienation has simply been too deeply traumatic and concrete an experience for the American Negro to end up in an ambiguous form of evasion. One which would appear to Ellison's most ardent European admirers as, to use Camus' phrase, "un saut dans l'absurde." (5)

If Ellison's existentialism, as a culmination of the psychological malaise that reigns in the Black novel, does not offer a viable alternative, what does? Marxism perhaps? As Daniel Aaron and others have pointed out, this social doctrine did appeal to Black intellectuals during the Depression years. (6) This explains Richard Wright's and Ralph Ellison's portrayal of the temptations offered by Marxism, as a comprehensive philosophy purporting to solve the racial problem. Marxism posits the premise that the capitalist structure of society, by hierarchizing classes and concentrating the rewards and the ownership of production into the hands of a few (who then enjoy the fruit of the masses' labour), gives birth to the subjugation of one race by another. Racial injustices being, then, offshoots of the larger injustice of society's structure, Marxism concludes that once capitalism is removed the racial problem will disappear. However simplistic such reasoning may seem in retrospect, one can see how this "two-birds-with-one-stone" strategy appealed to Blacks at the time.

Wright thus creates a character, Bigger, who suffers from economic and racial alienation which consequently lead him to commit murder. This justification is repeatedly, if not artlessly, brought home in the concluding trial scenes, when the Marxist in Wright gets the better of the artist. Bigger's lawyers sum up in neat Marxist dialectics the meaning of his condition, but in rhetorical excess that gives the distinct impression of having more to do with theoretical niceties than with the Black man under trial. Thus, Wright's social views boomerang in the cruel crowning irony of his protagonist's humanity being exploited and denied once more. Involuntarily, Wright indicates that Bigger's situation has not changed, even after two avowed cathartic murders.

Similarly Ellison's "invisible man" adheres to the Brotherhood because of the *nirvana* promised. Once the rhetoric is dispelled, however, the protagonist grows aware of what Bigger missed: his humanity is being denied by the "brothers". He discovers he is but a cog in the destructive technology of capitalism, as well as in the cold chess game of Marxist opportunism ("don't you think he should be a little blacker?" p.263). He flees consequently, to preserve his "sense of reality", as Ellison would put it.

Principally, the reason why Marxism fails is the same as outlined above for Existentalism. The failure lies in the concepts that subordinate race to class, racial alienation to economic exploitation. The question, to be sure, is a moot one. Even today it has not been satisfactorily answered (witness the Black Panthers programme): Is the Negro victimized because of his race, or because of his inferior economic position? Is money, as oddly enough both Marxists and Captialists would agree, the great equalizer? Or is there not something deeper, more in line with reality: that which tells of affluent Negroes being discriminated against, of poor Whites and poor Negroes at each other's throat? Simply, if we are to lend an ear to Konrad Lorenz's statements on innate human need for aggression, where are we to find the human society that has not one race, or one social or ethnic group, trying to dominate the other? (7) All these are ultimately academic questions. The historical fact reflected in the Black American novel up to Ellison concerns individuals who are brutally treated, or are psychologically incapable of coping with themselves, for no other reason than that they do not feel, as one of them says, any sense of control over their life. (8) Were we to leave it at that, modern anti-heroes such as Camus' Meursault and Beckett's Malone would be justified in claiming their share of human absurdity. The inescapable difference, though, is that the lack of control over their life bemoaned by the Negro character, is, first, not life with a capital "L", but *theirs*, meaning a relevant sense of identity at a particular basic level of being able to say "I". And this is so, second, because the Negro's invisibility, or

Harlem Storefront ca. 1964

visibility (it is the same really), has been defined in a consistent pattern of negation by a person, a group, a culture in a position of power (or control) over the Negro's life. So that the Negro cannot escape identifying his sense of oppression with his racial character.

Since Existentialism and Marxism ignore or dismiss this *sine qua non* of the Black experience, perhaps religion, being closer to the Negro's historical consciousness, offers a more viable point of departure for a philosophy relevant to this experience. Yet, as can be seen in a number of-Black novels, the Church, as an institution, has been severely taken to task, inasmuch as it is not the center of social relevance the Blacks feel they can turn to. On the other hand, religion, as a psychic reservoir perhaps archetypally related to the Negro's African past, lies at the root of his character. This being so, this latter phenomenon should be definable in terms larger than the Black American experience. But there are drawbacks. The dearth of solid evidence regarding authentic African traits, beliefs, rituals and modes of behaviour in America suggests that the reference to Africa may only be a subliminal one,

The present-day reality of Africa is one of largely independent nations emerging from their colonial past to confront alien spheres of experience which the Black American has historically had to live with. The contrast between traditional African culture and the modern Western polity makes for what I have referred to elsewhere as the "ambiguity" of the African novel. (9) Race, alienation derived from racial prejudice, revolt, are very limited features of the African novel. The African writer, instead of being concerned with what "others" have done to him and his people, is more preoccupied with articulating the new culture, what Jahn calls "neo-Africanism", the meeting of the oral tradition of Africa with the written one of the West. (10) It is hard to find in his work the insecurity that pervades the atmosphere of the Black American novel. The reason for this is obvious: in spite of some of the extreme forms of colonialism, of all the trials and troubles undergone, the African always had a "home" he could call his, an environment that historically, and in every other way, bore his stamp. So that in *reality* there seems to be little in common between Blacks in America and in Africa.

Where then is the missing link? Because of the common history of uprootment from the native continent, the "Middle passage," the experience of slavery and its legacy of racism, the Black American shares with all Blacks out of Africa the central consciousness of exile. (11) Within this state of exile, Black Americans and Haitians have been the first peoples of African descent to create and articulate a new culture. Consequently, it is towards them a number of West Indian and momentarily exiled African students looked when, hard put to resist the contempt meted out to them in Paris in the thirties, they urgently plunged themselves into the writings of the Negro Renaissance and claimed the heroes of the first successful revolution made for and by Blacks (Haiti's). Thus Négritude was born.

In this context *how* Négritude was born is less interesting than *why*. In what follows, I am less interested in the literary movement that more or less consciously followed in the wake of Aimé Césaire's 1934 coining of the term. (12) It is as a philosophy *for* and *of* the Black man in exile that I shall be discussing the term. Here I find an appropriate centrifocal point for the summation of the three strains under discussion so far: the psychological, the social and the religious. Let us posit that the relevance of Négritude to Black American culture is contained in its synthesis of these strains. Négritude is the child of Existentialism in its use of the dialectical movement of negation and affirmation, in its concern with "engagement", and in the light of its 1948 baptism, with Jean-Paul Sartre as godfather. (13) It is the child of Marxism inasmuch as its founders (Etienne Léro, Guy Tirolien, Léon G. Damas, Aimé Césaire) integrated in their views several aims of that doctrine to which they were, at the time, adherents. (14) Lastly, due to the pervasive influence of Senghor, the writings of Leo Frobenius, Father Tempels, l'Abbé Kagame and others who articulated the lost empires and the mythological realm of Africa, Négritude locates its spiritual roots in the ancestral continent. (15)

As to the first strain, Fanon and Sartre have simply stated the situation that we find from one end of the Black American novel to the other: the Black man in the company of the White man is first and foremost seen and defined as Black and he is thus shackled with the pejorative connotations, the irrational fears, blackness conjures in Western culture. (16) The individual Negro, whether his name is Rena Warwick, Bob Hayes, Bigger Thomas or Lutie Johnson, may deny or object to the typecasting, engage in searing pathos or suicidal revolt — but there is no way to escape from being made into an object. Succumbing to despair, unable to bear the weight of this condition, some resort to suicide (the Clotels), others to surrealist absurdism (Ellison's protagonist). But if the Black man is to continue living, existing amidst an alienated environment, conscious that existence precedes essence, he recognizes, as a first step, how he is seen by the "other", which is the primary merit of Ellison's protagonist: "And yet I am what they think I am." (p.329) This intellectual stance — a cleansing of the mind and heart through awareness — is the individual's, not the group's. Blackness must not be seen as something to be escaped from or to deny. If only because of its high visibility, it cannot be hidden; therefore it must be affirmed in the face of negation. (17)

If that is all there is to Négritude, one can understand how it has been referred to, in some circles, as a reverse form of racism. (18) Further, what is one to do with this "awareness"? Contemplate it in sterile narcissistic fashion? Négritude would then merely be the carbon copy of a European intellectual movement, quite worthy of being rejected by writers steeped in a reality different from that conditioned by twenty centuries of Western civilization.

At this stage the second strain comes in. Négritude maintains a connection between the individual and the group; not unlike Sartre's and Camus' appeals to "engagement" and "solidarité", but in a more immediate visceral fashion. Because the individual Negro's victimization is so due to his identification with a despised group (one is tempted here to paraphrase Sartre's line, "C'est l'anti-sémite qui fait le juif": it is the racist who creates the Negro), he cannot but equate his individual condition with the group's. (19) And this results in the need for action as group consciousness takes over where individual contemplation leaves off. Revolt accompanies therefore existential recognition in the works of Césaire, Fanon, Damas, and Roumain. In the area of the Black novel we can see how individual alienation, when identified with the collective state of economic deprivation, culminates in violence of the most brutal sort. As Wright says, Bigger can be multiplied, so that his revolt becomes the potential one of twelve million Biggers (the Black population of the U.S. in 1940, p.84). Furthermore, the sentiment of revolt contained in Négritude was meant to be extended beyond the printed page. When Césaire warned that his "grand cri nègre [ébranlera] les assises du monde" he meant to forecast the end of colonialism in the West Indies and in Africa. (20) Fanon heeded the cry and went to Algeria. It echoed in the precipitous dismemberment of the French colonial empire in the early sixties. Similarly, Bigger's or Ras the Exhorter's cry had its echo in the wave of riots that shook many American summers in the sixties; and the Black Panthers' most articulate spokesman, Eldridge Cleaver, has expressed his deeply-felt admiration for both Richard Wright and Aimé Césaire. (21)

But revolt is double-edged. At times, it foreshadows a positive liberation for the individual and the group. One thinks here of Senghor who became the first president of his country, Sénégal. When successful only in literary metaphors it makes for expatriate writers turning hopelessly bitter (Wright) and embattled politicians turning for solace to writing historical dramas and hermetic poetry (Césaire). (22) History is a cruel judge when we consider Wright's misreading of the future on two significant occasions (his trip to Ghana on the eve of independence, and the first conference of Negro writers and artists), and Césaire's cry, which echoed in Africa, and, to some degree, in America, but not in his own island, to this day a French "overseas department".

Moreover, in the past forty years, since Négritude's self-conscious emergence, there has been a surfeit of revolt and violence manifested in wars: Spanish, Second World, Korean, Algerian, Middle East, Biafran, and Vietnamese, not counting East European uprisings, ethnic skirmishes, sundry assassinations, and the list goes on. In so far as Black Americans are concerned, revolt is a thing of the past. Now that there is a foot firmly past the door of the society of affluence (as a result, to a great extent, of revolt) there has occurred a change of tactics. In the light of the enormous progress achieved since Wright's revolt, the felt presence of the Black American in most spheres of the overall American society, the cultural celebration of an African heritage, a fundamental truth emerges. The synthetical third stage Sartre envisioned in Négritude's dialectical movement, that of Négritude's disappearance in a society devoid of racial consciousness, is proven to be wrong on several scores (Sartre says, "... dans une société sans races ... la Négritude est pour se détruire, elle est passage et non aboutissement, moyen et non fin dernière"). (23)

We have to go now into the background of the concept of "integration" in order to demonstrate that, fifty years after its inspiration in the Negro Renaissance, Négritude is being articulated anew in America. Integration, the scheme of bringing the Negro into the mainstream of American society as a way of alleviating and correcting the socio-economic injustices that have their roots in the institution of slavery, is a notion that can be traced all the way back to the Abolitionist movement, then through Lincoln's Emancipation Act, the period of Reconstruction, Franklin D. Roosevelt's New Deal and the WPA projects, Truman's order desegregating the armed forces, the Supreme Court 1954 decision on school desegregation, and the Civil Rights movement, up to the present day. But where does the matter of culture come into the socio-economic scheme? What of Black culture (that is an outlook, an historical experience of self, a particular lifestyle) in the great American mainstream? Are the writings of Hughes, Toomers, Cullens, Wrights merely works of 'protest', reducible to the mere sociological fact of indicating the Negro's distemper in the face of deprivation? Unbelievably (somewhat understandably) no one, at the time, seems to have given much thought to such questions, since no one questioned the concept of integration (except the White supremacists, of course, but for quite a different purpose). What with all the socio-economic denials segregation implied, integration became a catch-all and be-all for people who were proving thus the rightness of Aristotle's phrase that one cannot think or contemplate abstract values on an empty stomach. Only Baldwin seems to have glimpsed the cultural issue when he wondered how there could be integration with a burning house, in *The Fire Next Time*. (24) But he did not follow through, as he chose rather to predict more fire and brimstone on a guilt-ridden America.

However, had anyone taken the time to peruse a book such as Glazer and Moynihan's *Beyond the Melting Pot* (or observed the time-honoured New York reality reflected in the book), the fact of an America not really divided on racially-simplistic terms (Black and White) but along *ethnic* lines would have stood out. (25) Given this fact, the following question should have been asked: does integration culturally mean assimilation into the lifestyle of the Italo-, Polish-, Chinese-, Jewish-, Wasp-, or the Spanish American? One had to wait until 1967 for an in-depth discussion of this matter by a Black intellectual. Thirteen years after the Supreme Court's

156

decision, Harold Cruse's *The Crisis of the Negro Intellectual* presented a reasoned argumentation, based on solid historical and sociological foundations, that exploded the shibboleths of shallow integration and witless nationalism cultivated by the Negro intellectual whose crisis lay precisely in his failure to articulate the specificities of Black American culture, given the notion of ethnicity in America. (26) A year later, Stokely Carmichael and Charles Hamilton conveyed, in *Black Power,* that in political terms cultural autonomy is nothing less than the "bloc" concept essential to American politics: "Traditionally, each new ethnic group in this society has found the route to social and political viability through the organization of its own institutions with which to represent its needs within the larger society." (27) Discovering that they did not really wish to be carbon copies of Italian-, Jewish-, Polish-, WASP-Americans, and since they had to be hyphenated Americans, as the others, the Blacks grew in the awareness that they had to relate to their ancestral land, Africa:

> More and more black Americans are developing this feeling. They are becoming aware that they have a history which predates their forced introduction to this country. ...It is absolutely essential that black people know this history, that they know their roots, that they develop an awareness of their cultural heritage. (28)

So they chose to be "Afro-Americans." And this is where myth enters, as we come to the third strain in our analysis.

The works of C.G. Jung and his disciples point to the concept of the "collective unconscious", whereby the individual psyche is seen as an historically-molded product of group experience. The result is the "unconscious memory" that primordially conditions the make-up of the individual, or the group, in his, or its, day-to-day behavioural pattern and outlook. (29) Northrop Frye, the influential Canadian critic, in his *Anatomy of Criticism* and other works, has applied Jung's and Freud's insights to the lore derived from the Judeo-Christian origins of Western culture. The Bible thus stands as the source of recurring myths, symbols and archetypes in the Western imagination. (30) T.S. Eliot, one of the dominant influences in twentieth century literature and criticism, has, in his *Notes Towards the Definition of Culture*, analyzed the composition of the term and framed it into the concept of "organicism." By which Eliot means that culture cannot be discussed in isolation, whether in speaking of an individual, a class, or a political group; nor can it be separated from spiritual beliefs. Culture, to Eliot, is a whole that embraces the past and the present history of a society; it is the product of interaction between the varied classes, institutions, regions and groups in that society. Because of the availability of the past, through learning, institutions, kinship and set of

157

beliefs, knowledge of tradition, in which culture is grounded, enables the individual to grasp the ordering, if not the meaning, of existence. Without the consciousness of tradition, culture is a vain word. (31)

In all three writers we find the common view that the writer, or the individual, who wants to orient himself, to possess an outlook about self and others, who cares to have something significant to say to other humans, must apprise himself of what he and his kins have been through the ages. Ordinary behaviour can be explained by reaching for the core of the "tribe's" experience. Culture defined thus, as the depository of collective experience, can be ignored only at the expense of a people's humanity. No people, nation, or society can hope to survive without such an awareness.

Significantly, a similar view of culture secures the positive side of Négritude. Says Senghor: "c'est l'ensemble des valeurs culturelles du monde noir." (32) One must distinguish between these cultural values. African traditional culture, which is what Senghor has in mind, in its reliance on the presence of ancestors, the intense feeling of kinship maintained by a "life force" that pervades the telluric realm and shapes the communal structure of society (legitimizing the hierarchy of priests, elders, heads of tribe and family), is irretrievably lost to the Blacks who were brought to the Americas. (33) (Even in modern Africa it is put to a hard test.) Some of the "exiled" Blacks' cultural values may ultimately reach back to Africa (as the findings of Herskovits in the South of the U.S. point out, and as can be seen in the folk religions of the West Indies and Brazil, in Voodoo, Macumba, Obeah). (34) But, Négritude, being principally a philosophy born of exile, primarily articulates cultural values organically tied to that state. They derive from the consciously remembered past of uprootment, the Middle Passage, the experience of slavery. Denying that the "pulsations de l'humanité s'arrêtent aux portes de la nègrerie," (35) Négritude argues that these cultural values are further present in the various modes of adaptation in an alien environment through the course of the centuries, whether in folklore or in history. Such a perspective sustains Césaire's celebration of Haïti, the first autonomous nation carved out by the exiled African: "Haïti où la négritude se mit debout pour la première fois et dit qu'elle croyait à son humanité..." (36) And he claims the legendary Haitian hero, Toussaint Louverture, as his own:

> Ce qui est à moi
> c'est un homme seul emprisonné de
> blanc
> c'est un homme seul qui défie les cris
> blancs de la mort blanche
> (*Toussaint Toussaint*
> *Louverture*) (37)

And there lies also, in the exiled Black's transcendence over his state, Senghor's praise of the Negro Renaissance:

> Que veulent les chefs de la nouvelle école? Une "Renaissance nègre," *Negro Renaissance*. Il ne s'agit plus d'infériorité non plus que de supériorité ni d'antagonisme, mais de différence profonde. La personnalité nègre s'est affirmée dans le passé; l'expérience de l'esclavage n'a fait que l'enrichir en profondeur. Il s'agit, dans le présent, d'exprimer cette personnalité en beauté; de définir un des aspects les plus humains de la condition humaine. (38)

Clearly, beyond its initial stance of revolt, Négritude is an affirmation. Through hardship grows the consciousness of the deeper layers of the human condition. Pain and suffering, when endured and overcome, cannot be merely a negative source of bitterness, revolt or protest but a positive powerful metaphor for all humanity. (39) This is what Ellison has in mind when he has his protagonist conclude: "Who knows but that, on the lower frequencies, I speak for you." (p.503) Further, this belief explains his impatience with Irving Howe's reduction of the Black experience (in the novels of Wright, Baldwin and Ellison) to the negation of protest:

> Evidently Howe feels that unrelieved suffering is the only "real" Negro experience, and that the true Negro writer must be ferocious.
> But there is also an American Negro tradition which teaches one to deflect racial provocation and to master and contain pain. It is a tradition which abhors as obscene any trading on one's own anguish for gain or sympathy; which springs not from a desire to deny the harshness of existence but from a will to deal with it as men at their best have always done. It takes fortitude to be a man and no less to be an artist. (40)

Howe's misreading can be excused, however, when one considers that no less than Jean-Paul Sartre, much to the dismay of Fanon, while praising Négritude was, in fact, burying it as the negative middle term in Hegelian dialectics, a "racisme anti-raciste." (41) Is the presentation of pain experienced by a Black man racism on the Black man's part, because he explores the pain? Sartre ignores the question. But, as if to prevent such distortions, Césaire had warned: "ne faites point de moi cet homme de haine pour/qui je n'ai que haine." (42) And Fanon had concluded:

> Moi, l'homme de couleur, je ne veux qu'une chose:
> Que jamais l'instrument ne domine l'homme. Que cesse à jamais l'asservissement de l'homme par l'homme. C'est-à-dire de

moi par un autre. Qu'il me soit permis de découvrir et de vouloir
l'homme, où qu'il se trouve.
Le nègre n'est pas. Pas plus que le Blanc.
Tous deux ont à s'écarter des voix inhumaines que furent
celles de leurs ancêtres respectifs afin que naisse une authentique
communication. (43)

All of which brings us again to the contemporary Black American's
search for his cultural roots, his attempts at re-appropriating his heritage.
This search is a resumption of a philosophy that came to be when it asked
itself questions similar to those which arose after the euphoria of integration
in the U.S. In affirming his heritage, his cultural identity, as a condition to
successful integration, the Black American proves the erroneousness of
Sartre's view of Négritude's disappearance (in the third synthetical stage of
its dialectical movement) in a "société sans races." Likewise, the belief that
Négritude ended with the decolonization process in Africa, in the early
sixties, is proven to be wrong. (44) We are witnessing a re-assertion of the
fact that Négritude was never Africa's philosophy or that of indigenous
Africans. Because it represents culture, that which "makes life worth living",
in the words of T.S. Eliot, (45) the renewed claims of Négritude should
flourish in the U.S. There is at present an increasing consciousness of the
pluralistic composition of the society, due to the forceful affirmation of
cultural diversity rooted in ethnicity.

The present stage of the Black American experience, then, is that of the
Shakespearean Caliban looking into himself, striving for a central core of
experience antedating Prospero's grip on his psyche. At this stage, the Black
writer is primarily unconcerned with psychological trials, social and
religious revolt. He cannot care less to be called a "foul-mouthed, base
slave" if he is secure about his identity. And he is, to the extent of reaching
now for depths in his being, his past, bringing forth a re-channelling of
creative energies; this turning inward is not static but full of vitality. It gives
meaning, articulation, to a positive set of references that stands in contrast
to the erstwhile psychological malaise, the sentiment of nihilistic revolt, and
vague spiritual yearning. The "core of experience" contains all this. And
here Sartre's image of the committed Black writer as an Orpheus who
descends into himself to repossess and bring to the surface of existence the
core of his culture, the Eurydice of his négritude, is once more applicable.
(46)

Richard Wright's *The Outsider* (1953) is the story of Cross Damon, a
drop-out from college, who, as the novel begins, works as a night clerk in a
Chicago post office. He is introduced as a misfit, a malcontent, who resorts
to drinking and fornicating to dull the sense of dread and despair that grips
him and turns him into a walking picture of meaninglessness. Damon is
married, but separated from his wife and four children. He seduces a

sixteen-year old girl who becomes his mistress. But Damon still wallows in despair. Psychological malaise takes a quite concrete form when he learns of his mistress' pregnancy and of her intentions to force him to marry her by denouncing him for statutory rape. Damon's job is in jeopardy since the girl's threats force him to borrow on his pension fund for an abortion. On his way to see her with the money, Damon is involved in a subway accident where he is mistakenly taken to be one of the fatal victims. Seizing the occasion to escape from his identity and his web of problems, he decides to leave for New York, but not before killing a fellow-worker whom he fortuitously meets. In New York, Damon takes a number of new names and joins the Communist party. The remainder of the book tells of the Stalinist methods of the New York cell, Damon's inability to escape his sense of futility, his revolt against the Party and his killing of two of its officials, as well as the landlord of an apartment building. The book closes with Damon's murder by avenging Party henchmen, just as he is about to be arrested following the discovery of his true identity.

The novel, it would not be unfair to say, is a collage of Existentialist and Marxist viewpoints experienced by a character who seems to be a latter-day intellectualized Bigger Thomas. And this makes for a strange book, the pale remake of a classic. Reflecting Wright's undiluted experiences with the Communist party in the forties, particularly the Stalinist methods and crass opportunism that drove away many members and sympathizers, as well as his adoption of a self-conscious existentialist ethic (an undeniable reflection on the Sartre-Simone de Beauvoir circle which lionized him early in his Parisian exile), this book may be helpful as autobiographical material. (47)

Damon is not a character but a mouthpiece for Wright's ideas. The party members, Damon's wife and mistress, the West Indian waiter who dabbles also as a Party organizer, notwithstanding Ely Houston, the hunchback District Attorney of New York, are obvious puppets lacking in credibility. With the exception of the Negro ghetto of Chicago, a replica, to a certain degree, of the one in which Bigger lived, setting is nonexistent. Organically, the book is divided into two parts, the Chicago and the New York scenes, which correspond to the two ideological poles of Existentialism and Marxism that are in fact the dramatic centres of the novel. This does not make for unity of design, or structural cohesion.

But, if only on the level of intention, there is an argument at work, giving some sense to the novel. And it is Wright's view of the Negro as archetype for man's universal condition. The "outsider", Damon, much like Camus' Meursault, represents absurd man. It is Wright's contention that the experience of the Negro, or that of any oppressed minority group, may be seen as symbolic of man's universal despair. This belief is explicitly stated early in the novel, as a character says:

For four hundred years these white folks done made everybody on earth feel like they ain't human, like they're outsiders. They done kicked 'em around and called 'em names [and there ensues a catalogue of racial epithets used in regard to Blacks, Chinese, Japanese, Mexicans, Jews and Hindus.] (p.27)

Later on, talking with Houston, the D.A., Damon, who is deserting two women and five children after committing murder, a menial clerk whose major activities have been up to now drinking and fornicating, is made to muse thus about man's fate:

Aren't all cultures and civilizations just screens which men have used to divide themselves, to put between that part of themselves which they are afraid of and that part of themselves which they want to try to preserve? Aren't all of man's efforts at order an attempt to still man's fear of himself? (p.137)

There is a "déjà vu" feeling upon reading such a statement, compounded by hollowness. These pitfalls recur when similar words are used by Ely Houston, a hunchback who might have been credible in his understanding of man's wanton cruelty. But this is a New York District Attorney speaking?

Negroes, as they enter our culture, are going to inherit the problems we [Whites] have, but with a difference. They are outsiders and they are going to *know* that they have these problems. They are going to be self-conscious; they are going to be gifted with a double vision, for, being Negroes, they are going to be both *inside* and *outside* of our culture at the same time .. Negroes will develop unique and specially defined psychological types. (p.129)

Such statements, if lacking artistic credence, at least reveal Wright's vision of a post-revolt attitude on the part of the American Negro. However, in addition to the lavish description of four violent murders, this vision is undermined by its being framed by unassimilated European Existentialism. Wright did not live to integrate his correct insight of the Negro's 'double vision' into a philosophy indigenous to his heritage. His failure here must no doubt be correlated with his inability to transcend (even and *foremost* in his Parisian exile) the early traumas of his Mississippi upbringing and the later one of his adulthood in Chicago and New York. One has to conclude that their legacy of bitterness so impressed his outlook as to render him unable to relate to a deeper cultural experience, however exposed he was, albeit late in life, to the exponents of Négritude and African rebirth with whom he fraternized in Paris in the fifties.

William Demby's *The Catacombs* (1965) is another product of

162

European exile and illustrates its vagaries on a writer's outlook. If Demby's first novel, *Beetlecreek* (1950) could be labelled an "existentialist" novel (but a redeeming one), his second defies all categories, unless we are ready to call it a pre-Truman Capote "non-novel novel". At the outset we are told that this is a novel centred on two characters: Demby, the novelist, a twenty-year resident of Rome, who is going to write a novel (the one we have in our hands) about Doris, a Black dancer who has a feature role in a film being shot in Italy (*Cleopatra*, starring Elizabeth Taylor and Richard Burton, no less!). The use of this non-imaginative fact introduces the second aspect of the intended novel: an investigation of the time element rendered in the very structure of the book.

The synchronic time factor is the period 1962-1964. In addition to the filming, the author makes abundant use of newspaper headlines and stories, refers to the media (he and his wife work in television and the film industry, and so do their friends), better to convey the turmoils of the actual world during that period. The agony of the Algerian war, Marilyn Monroe's suicide, the 1963 March on Washington, Kennedy's assasination, not to mention the Cuban missile crisis, are all there. Through all this the author hopes to represent the timelessness of art, contrasted with the timeliness of these events; thus producing a sober reflection on the cyclical pattern of human history. And here one supposes is the significance of the storyline. Doris is presented in an imagery of vitality, sensuality, so that she becomes symbolic of fertility in a world devoid, because of its violent temper, of these qualities:

> Doris bursts into the room like an explosion of sunflowers. As always, her astonishing nightclub-dancing vitality intimidates me ... in her stormy freshminted presence, my soul shrivels ...
> Doris laughs and the dust particles giving aural substance to the sun's rays churn and mill about like a storm of migrating birds ... crosses her long, forest-tapered legs. (pp.11-12)

She becomes the mistress of an Italian Count, to whom she is introduced by Demby. The Count is, apparently, a typical member of the decadent Roman aristocratic class Fellini portrayed on the screen in *La Dolce Vita*. He is a blasé, world-weary character, separated from his wife who is barren; and he panders his title to an American firm in return for a Public Relations post. The Count becomes alive, however, and regains a measure of vitality in his dalliance with the Negro girl. Eventually he impregnates her, and their affair ends upon his imminent departure for an overseas assignment with his wife with whom he is reconciled.

Demby's intent is this: Doris stands for renascent Africa, or the ancient Arabic civilizations (the significance of the frequent substitution of Moor

163

for Negro by the "mistaken" Italians), and the Count stands for Roman Western civilization in the process of dying. We are told that the Count's father was an Africanist whose tireless field work, away from Europe, eventually brought about his wife's death. The Count, moreover, has a sister, a missionary in Africa. Both the sister and the father are said to have wrestled (the sister still is) with the deep significance of Africa which to them represents an "idea", a "dream", that, if penetrated, would allow for a momentous insight on life. Whereas the father never managed to conceptualize his insights in a learned study, and the sister almost succumbs, in Kurtzian fashion, to the "dream" surrounding her (she is saved when she discovers its humanistic import), the Count, succeeds in grasping, through Doris, the synthesis of the "dream" and the reality: hence the symbolism of his fathering a child, for he has reached the source of life in Doris' fertility. As his wife, who has been talking with the Count about the meaning of Africa, says, recognizing the symbolism (allegorically tainted) of her husband's achievement: "Last night I dreamed of a name for your child... She shall be a girl... Her name shall be Annunziata." (p.154)

In the larger framework of the book, the meeting of Africa and Europe represents the ironies of time. In a Viconian manner, Demby alludes to the cyclical movement of history through his two characters: the fall of the Roman "dream" of civilization is paralleled by the rise of the "dream" of Africa. Insofar as the Count gets a new lease on life from his relationship with Doris, Demby indicates where an aged Europe might replenish its sources: in the African "dream" world of myths, rituals and symbols.

However, formally, there are drawbacks: Demby fails to keep a constant focus and interest on what should have been the centre of his novel, the relationship between the Count and Doris. Not satisfied to let the frequent intrusion of the actual world of contemporary strife speak for itself, Demby's *persona* takes over as a looming and bothersome shadow over the proceedings. It is no small wonder, indeed, that with all the newspaper clippings and the amount of platitudinous details, Demby did not succeed in defeating his novel's very purpose. A book meant to investigate the time dimension in human history and life (as Proust and Eliot showed), the interweaving of cultures through the media and spiritual needs (as Dos Passos showed in *Manhattan Transfer*) need not turn into an overblown collage or yield to an exercise in narcissism.

Possibly, this book demonstrates in the last analysis that Demby's twenty-year exile was turning sour, not unlike Wright's own exile. (Significantly, at the end of the book, we are told of his impending return to the U.S.) At any rate, *The Catacombs* is a symbolic novel. The American Negro dancer portrays an almost convincing Eurydice (the book's final scene is the Count's descent into the "catacombs" with Doris whom he loses there). But the Roman catacombs cannot really be the appropriate metaphor for hell.

LeRoi Jones                                    (Wide World)

America is, apparently, for the Black American; America is the hell LeRoi Jones wishes to explore in his short poetical novel, *The System of Dante's Hell* (1966). The book opens with the paradoxical statement, "But dante's hell is heaven." (p.9) This arouses the startled reader's attention. As he remembers the chart of the nine circles, appropriately divided according to the degree of guilt (incontinence, violence, fraudulence, treachery, *et al.*) and goes on with his reading, the reader realizes that the Dantesque reference is only meant as irony, for there are no Beatrice and Virgil here, and the public framework of Dante's high medievalism has been thoroughly subverted to an intensely private existential one. The paradoxical statement becomes meaningful when Jones tells us in concluding: "I am and was and will be a social animal. Hell is definable only in those terms ... Hell in the head. The torture of being the unseen object, and, the constantly observed subject ... Hell is actual, and people with hell in their heads." (pp.153-154)

Hell, then, is used in a Sartrian context. This brings us back to the beginning statement again. How can even a Sartrian hell be heaven? Here we get into the second strain that structures the spiritual journey: the recreation, through memory, of the primal molds of the artistic sensibility. Jones is double throughout: Sartrian or Beckettian in a sterile present, or in the past seen through immediate consciousness; Joycean in his representation of sensibility through the sounds, smells and moods of birth and growth in the Black ghetto of Newark.

Because Jones is foremost a poet, a dealer in half-tones rather than bright light, in moods rather than confrontations, in feelings rather than vociferations, in the deeper recesses of the imagination and the senses rather than the surface immediacy of socio-political realities, the ghetto life he recreates is certainly not Bigger's, or the "invisible man's". Determined to reach for the "smithy of his soul", for the recreated "conscience of his race", (48) Jones can proclaim in the closing lines of his journey what he ambiguously announced as "heaven": "Once as a child, I would weep for compassion and understanding. And Hell was the inferno of my frustration. But the world is clearer to me now, and many of its features, more easily definable." (p.154)

But let us start at the beginning. There is no storyline to speak of, nor are there characters. Taking no doubt his artistic inspiration from the author of *Portrait of the Artist as a Young Man*, Jones presents his youth and adolescence in the ghetto of Newark, the friends he had, the early sexual promiscuities, the meaning of the streets and the "blocs" of the city, his departure from a sensitive rapport with the world upon entering college, his infatuation with and eventual rejection of the Black middle class. Finally, the concluding section relates his enrollment into the Air Force and his visit, on a furlough, to the bordello district of Shreveport, Louisiana. Rock bottom is reached in this nadir sphere of experience, and death, in the figures of Black hoodlums, greets the Narrator on his way out of the inferno. The last chapter is a commentary that throws light on the previous proceedings.

Let us review the two poles: hell as a metaphor for the Negro's condition, and hell as the heaven the artistic sensibility fashions at the outcome of the Orphic quest. The first aspect represents the historical, psychological and social malaise that has been the lot of the Negro. This shared experience is the type of hell of which Jones is conscious when he speaks from a present standpoint, albeit as a modern intellectual. Thus his language and imagery of despair and dissatisfaction are those of Beckett, Sartre and Eliot: "The weight of myself... No air gets in... Nothing to interest me but myself... Nothing remains with me... except myself to each, as to himself... The prodigal lives in darkness... I am, as you are caught. Here, is where we die." (p.11, p.13, p.15, p.24, p.31, p.35) Indeed one hears Beckett's Malone when we are told: "Flesh to flesh, the cold halls echo death. And it will not come." (p.54) But Beckett is cast aside when the personal pronoun is used in direct interrogation: "Who created me to this pain?" (p.112) The forcefulness of the question leads to the integration of intellectual and visceral pain: Jones' pain as the Negro's. This is the hell that, Orpheus-like, the Black writer descends to apprise himself of: "Natives down the street. All dead. All walking slowly towards their lives. ... That they suffered and cdn't know it. Knew that somehow, forever. Each dead nigger stinking his same suffering thru us. Each work of blues some dead face melting. Some life drained off in silence" (p.11, p.125) — all the way to the last circle in the inferno. And this is the significance of the bordello scene:

> The place was filled with shades. Ghosts. And the huge ugly hands of actual spooks. Standing around the bar, spilling wine on greasy shirts. Yelling at a fat yellow spliv who talked about all their mothers pulling out their drinks. Laughing with wet cigarettes and the paper stuck to fat lips... A smell of despair and drunkenness... Their frightening lives. (p.128)

These "frightening lives" should not frighten away the poet. Since they define him, he must see himself through them. But how? How to present creatively this consciousness? Certainly not through vain-glorious forms of protest. Jones, conscious of his négritude, does not shy from availing himself of experiences that, to some degree, parallel his: Yeats' and Joyce's. Stephen Dedalus meets with Orpheus in Jones' recreation of his past, in an art form which becomes both form and content of a sensibility. Jones accomplishes two tasks: first, a personal statement on the nature of art; second, a collective one in showing through "frightening lives" the Dedalian conscience of his race.

Because "I am left only with my small words... against the day" (p.45), words are used and transformed for the picture of a sensitive state. The Newark ghetto, like Dedalus' Dublin, is felt, not described:

The breakup of my sensibility... The walks there and back to
where I was. Night queens in winter dusk. Drowning city of
silence. Ishmael back, up through the thin winter smells. Conked
hair, tweed coat, slightly bent at the coffee corner. Drugstore,
hands turning the knob for constant variation. Music. (p.9, p.11)

The epiphanies, to be sure, are in line with the character of ghetto life: the
comradeship of street gangs; the suggestive power of street names (Belmont
Ave., Raymond Blvd.) and city sections (North ward, South ward); the gang
fights; the sexual promiscuity that breeds fifteen-year old unwed mothers.
Language distillates these harsh realities, as in the following description of a
fight between rival gangs at a party:

He came back with six guys and a meat cleaver. Rushed down
the wooden stairs and made the whole place no man's land. Dukes
took off the tams and tried to shove back in the darkness. Ladies
pushed back on the walls. Orioles still grinding for the snow.
"Where's that muthafucka." Lovely Dante at night under his
flame taking heaven. A place, a system, where all is dealt with... as
is proper. "I'm gonna kill that muthafucka." Waved the cleaver
and I crept backwards while his mob shuffled faces. "I'm gonna
kill *some*body." Still I had my coat and edged away from the
center (as I always came on. There. In your ditch, bleeding with
you. Christians.) (p.99)

Undoubtedly, there is a deliberate contrast between the harsh scatology of
murderous violence and the narrator's deflating detached comments
("Lovely Dante..."); an ironic view of the proceedings ("A place, a
system...") that blurs the realism as it transmutes the tension of the moment
into a sensitive experience. So that instead of an impression of crude
violence we are left rather with a filtered one, a "privileged moment" in the
lifestyle of the ghetto.

A number of other scenes, sordid in possible implications (one thinks
of a prostitute thrown out of a moving car) are equally defused through the
prism of Jones' language. If hell can be so envisaged, as a molding centre of
reference reaching deep into one's sensibility, it is in truth "heaven". Jones
convincingly concludes his book with the summation of a barren
consciousness redeemed through the workings of art. For the poet has
reinvented his sensibility:

Hell is actual, and people with hell in their heads. But the pas-
toral moments in a man's life will also mean a great deal as far as
his emotional references. One thinks of home, or the other
"homes" we have had. And we remember w/love those things

bathed in soft black light. The struggles away or toward this peace is Hell's function. (p.154)

A similar recognition is central to the last novel of this analysis: Paule Marshall's *The Chosen Place, the Timeless People* (1968). Set in the Caribbean, it opens with the arrival on Bourne Island of an American Jewish anthropologist, Saul, his WASP wife, Harriet, and his assistant, Allen. They are to work on a Foundation (the Centre for Applied Social Research) development project designed to lift the island from economic morass. They are received by Merle, a very Black woman, who owns the guest-house where they are to stay. Soon enough they are introduced to the traditional Caribbean lifestyle of mass poverty lorded over by an educated Black élite and a land-owning mulatto bourgeoisie more attuned to the taste of luxury acquired through their British orientation than to the local realities. The hot-house culture centred on parties given by the élite and the colony of foreigners is described. Other hackneyed island pursuits are witnessed, and, in the end, the promise of success for the economic project remains only a promise. Saul's plans are thwarted by his wife who engineers his recall. But the island was fated to remain what it always was, timeless to itself and to the outside world.

So far there seems to be nothing particular to that novel that a Graham Greene or Alec Waugh had not dealt with before. But there is a design at work beneath the clichés. In a big book that could have been cut by half, Mrs. Marshall is after a central "core of experience" against which all her main characters are tested and which the "timelessness" of the island and its people symbolizes. The myth at work is that of Cuffee Ned, a legendary Black slave who led a successful insurrection against the colonial masters. For three years the people lived free until Cuffee Ned's capture and beheading. Cuffee Ned was an "Obeah man" who relied on the African gods of his ancestry for guidance: "(for Cuffee had been that also, both seer and shaman to the people, the intermediary between them and the ancient gods" p.284).

Significantly, when we first meet Merle, she has just suffered a severe mental breakdown brought about by her dismissal, by the local school board, for having lectured on the legend of Cuffee Ned: "'... She was telling the children about Cuffee Ned and things that happened on the island in olden times. ... . Well, they fired her in no time flat. ...But the thing had her so upset her head went clean out again.'" (pp.32-33) But it is in the climactic third part of the novel the myth appears wedded to the design. During the marathon two-day celebrations of Carnival, all the main characters' lives come to a decisive test as a result of which their fate is sealed. The chief feature in the public rituals is the recreation of Cuffee Ned's odyssey, as rival bands of marchers incarnate the historical antagonists in a highly-charged atmosphere that stills time and place in mass catharsis and in a moment of truth for each of the principals.

Harriet has volunteered to march in one of the pageants. She gets caught up among the Cuffee Ned Marchers and is seized with terror amid the surrounding blackness. She hysterically contemplates being thrown off the docks towards which the rambunctious crowd is driven. She recovers, as the apprehended threat never materializes, for it is Marshall's intent to indicate that the terror that seized Harriet is her unsettling experience of being suddenly confronted with repressed truths in her past. Harriet is from a "main line" Philadelphia family whose founder, three generations removed, was active in the slave trade. With the money derived from such exploitation the Foundation is financing her husband's project. An historical movement of retribution is at work; of course not really in favour of the slaves' descendents, but against those of the slave masters. It is the consciousness of this, it seems, that eventually drives Harriet to her death.

In the evening of that same day, when Harriet had a glimpse of her demons, Saul and Merle are releasing theirs. Saul tells of his experience of alienation as a Jew which lies behind his professional wanderings aimed at bringing help to underprivileged peoples. He tells of the toll taken by fate: his first wife's death, eight months pregnant, in the wilderness of Honduras. His marriage to Harriet, it is implied, is a tentative attempt at dulling his experience of malaise. That it is a failure is shown in what he recognizes in Merle. For Merle has experienced also the descent into hell. And she proceeds to unveil the harsh truths underlying her façade of brash loquaciousness: her sojourn as a student in England; the sexual promiscuities that led her to lesbianism; her marriage to an African destroyed by her London benefactress when the latter revealed her past to her husband; her return to Bourne island to soothe her wounds, reopened by her dismissal. As a result, Merle is subject to fits of depression from which she escapes in posturing ("...I've had to pay with my sanity for the right to speak my mind so you know I must talk" p.11 — as she says early in the book). But now, ironically, she has found her Orpheus, in Cuffee Ned's night, in the person of the Jew. From such a recognition, as Saul later would have his wife understand, the two start a liaison.

Following the carnival, Saul regularly visits Merle, a fact which soon becomes public knowledge for the "timeless people" who welcome in Saul one of their own. Harriet grows increasingly impatient with island life, and the most innocuous details (such as children refusing her gestures of generosity) add to the unsettling experience among the marchers. The product of a family, a culture, rooted in taking from others, Harriet is unable to give of herself to people. This inability grows into a psychological state of dissatisfaction that leads her back to her archetypal roots of destruction, which ultimately explains her suicide. It is interesting to note how the symbol of blackness signals the wish for destruction. As Harriet confronts her husband with his unfaithfulness, she does not attack him so much

170

on the level of marital values as for his having embraced the "terror" of blackness: "I think... of your touching someone like that and I can't understand it" (p.430). Blackness, whether it has to do with the colour of someone's skin or not, as long as it stems from the Manichean Puritan mold (fundamental to Harriet's outlook, in her "main line" lineage), has to be stamped out, destroyed. This Saul, as a Jew, understands. This consciousness, originating in centuries of persecution by the likes of Harriet, is soon buttressed when Harriet, pulling on her family's strings, successfully engineers Saul's recall from the project. At that point Saul articulates the savage truth from which Harriet never recovers: " '*What is it with you and your kind, anyway?*... If you can't have things your way, if you can't run the show, there's to be no show, is that it? ... You'd prefer to see everything including yourselves, come down in ruins rather than 'take down', rather than not have everything your way, is that it?' " (p.454)

Ironically, Harriet *is* the evil she sees in others. She is thus identified by Merle as Harriet offers her money to get her away from the island. This in an earth-shaking outburst, as Merle assigns to Harriet the recurrent pattern of evil she is familiar with since her British sojourn, and calls to witness the environment (the "chosen place") that welcomed her back from Hades:

> '...England now,' she was shouting, her voice at a scathing pitch. 'Did you hear her? Does she have any idea of the hell I saw in England? Why, that's the last place in this world I want to see again. Canada. Africa. My passage paid to the ends of the earth. Get thee gone, Satan, and here's enough money to stay gone. Oh, God, this woman must be trying to set out my head again coming over here this afternoon talking about money.
>
> 'Money! always money! But that's the way they are, you know,' she cried, informing the sea, the long wearily sloping veranda, the house with its ancient ghosts, of the fact. 'They feel they can buy the world and its wife with a few raw-mouth dollars. But lemme tell you something m'lady'— her face, streaked white from the tears brought on by her laugh, dropped close; it was only a dark featureless blur in Harriet's remote gaze — 'I can't be bought. Or bribed. ...' (p.441)

Because Bourne Island is the center of self where truth lies, it is an appropriate metaphor for hell and Merle serves well as Marshall's Eurydice. That Marshall's "chosen place" is the humanism of Négritude is proven in the recognition that binds Saul and Merle. She seems to say that in reaching deep into oneself one attains the plateau of universality, if only because of the communality of suffering. Some individuals, some cultures, can but derive a positive meaning from an Orphic quest; others, the self-righteous, as Conrad points out in *Heart of Darkness*, expose themselves to self-destruction. "This place", in fact, is the truth of self whose danger is sensed by Harriet, but whose inescapability destroys her: "...'I mean this place. It's this place, can't you see that, where nothing you do seems to matter. It's this place!,' She spoke wildly, irrationally, her eyes dark gray, suggesting that the mind behind them had gone dark also.'*This place*'"(p.429). Kurtz calls it "the horror..." (49)

By contrast, Merle has been strengthened by the quest, and the book closes with her departure to rejoin her husband and daughter in Africa. Her route is thus charted:

> And she was not taking the usual route to Africa, first flying north to London via New York and then down. Instead, she was going south to Trinidad, then on to Recife in Brazil, and from Recife, that city where the great arm of the hemisphere reaches out toward the massive shoulder of Africa as though yearning to be joined to it as it had surely been in the beginning, she would fly across to Dakar and, from there, begin the long cross-continent journey to Kampala. (p.471)

A fine parting ironic shot, up-ending the historic Golden Triangle of the Atlantic slave trade that lies at the root of both Négritude and the Black American experience.

1  Jean-Paul Sartre, *No Exit*, p.47.
2  Jean-Paul Sartre, *Existentialism and Humanism*, p.26.
3  *Ibid.*, p.156.
4  Albert Camus, *Le Mythe de Sisyphe*, p.15.
5  *Ibid.*, p.90
6  See Daniel Aaron, *Writers on the Left*, pp.335-345; for a fuller account, see Wilson Record, *The Negro and the Communist Party*.
7  See Konrad Lorenz, *On Aggression*, pp.iv-xix.
8  Chester Himes, *If He Hollers Let Him Go*, p.205.
9  Max Dorsinville, "Levels of Ambiguity in the African Novel", *Canadian Journal of African Studies*, pp.213-225.
10  Janheinz Jahn, *Neo-African Literature*, p.22.
11  See René Dépestre, "Les Métamorphoses de la Négritude en Amérique", *Présence Africaine*, pp.19-33.
12  For a full account of the movement, see Lilyan Kesteloot, *Les Ecrivains Noirs de Langue Française*, pp.25-201.
13  I am referring, of course, to his preface, "L'Orphée Noir", to Senghor's *Anthologie de la Nouvelle Poésie Nègre et Malgache de Langue Française*.
14  See Kesteloot, pp.53-62.
15  For the influence of Frobenius' *Histoire de la Civilisation*

*Africaine*, see Kesteloot, pp.101-103: for the influence of Father Tempels' concept of "force vitale" in Bantu philosophy, see Senghor's "L'Esthétique Négro-Africaine" in *Négritude et Humanisme*, pp.203-205.

16 Fanon refers thus to the West Indian's first experience of racial consciousness in Europe: "Et puis il nous fut donné d'affronter le regard blanc. Une lourdeur inaccoutumée nous oppressa... Dans le monde blanc, l'homme de couleur rencontre des difficultés dans l'élaboration de son schéma corporel." *Peau Noire, Masques Blancs*, p.109. Sartre adds: "Et puisqu'on l'opprime dans sa race et à cause d'elle, c'est d'abord de sa race qu'il lui faut prendre conscience." "L'Orphée Noir", *Ibid.*, pp.xiii-xiv.

17 "Ainsi est-il acculé à l'authenticité: insulté, asservi, il se redresse, il ramasse le mot de "nègre" qu'on lui a jeté comme une pierre, il se revendique comme noir, en face du blanc, dans la fierté." Sartre, p.xiv; see also Frantz Fanon, *Les Damnés de la Terre*, p.159. "Le concept de négritude par exemple était l'antithèse affective sinon logique de cette insulte que l'homme blanc faisait à l'humanité."

18 Sartre, *Ibid.*

19 Jean-Paul Sartre, *Réflexions sur la Question Juive*, p.84.

20 Aimé Césaire, *Les Armes Miraculeuses*, p.156.

21 See his "Notes on a Native Son" in *Soul on Ice*, pp.96-107.

22 For an account of Wright's sour later years in Paris, see Chester Himes' reminiscences in "My man Himes: An Interview with Chester Himes", *Amistad*, pp.85-91.

23 Sartre, "L'Orphée Noir", p.xii.

24 James Baldwin, *The Fire Next Time*, pp.127-130.

25 Nathan Glazer and Daniel P. Moynihan, *Beyond the Melting Pot*, p.v.

26 Harold Cruse, *The Crisis of the Negro Intellectual*. Cruse, however, fails also to articulate a positive definition, being more concerned with establishing the shortcomings of the Negro intelligentsia. Cruse was an early exponent of Négritude as a cultural set of reference for the American Negro; see "Rebellion ou Révolution", *Présence Africaine*, pp.42-61: see also, "An Afro-American's Cultural Views", *Présence Africaine*, 31-43.

27 Stokely Carmichael and Charles V. Hamilton, *Black Power*, p.44.

28 *Ibid.*, p.38.

29 See Carl G. Jung's "On the Relation of Analytical Psychology to Poetic Art" in *Modern Continental Literary Criticism*, pp.284-288.

30 Northrop Frye, *Anatomy of Criticism*, p.353.

31 T.S. Eliot, *Notes Towards the Definition of Culture*. See also, for its application to the work of art and the artist, "Tradition and the

173

Individual Talent", *Selected Essays*, pp.3-11.

32  Léopold Sédar Senghor, *Négritude et Humanisme*, p.9.
33  See C.L.R. James, "The Atlantic Slave Trade and Slavery", *Amistad*, pp.120-164.
34  See Erika Bourguignon, "Afro-American Religions: Traditions and Transformations", *Black Americans*, pp.207-219.
35  Aimé Césaire, *Cahier d'un Retour au Pays Natal, pp.61-62.*
36  *Ibid.*, p.44.
37  *Ibid.*, p.45-46.
38  Senghor, *Négritude et Humanisme*, pp.107-108.
39  Césaire, *Ibid.*, pp.39-40.
40  Ralph Ellison, *Shadow and Act*, p.119.
41  Sartre, "L'Orphée Noir", p.xiv. For an examination of Sartre's view in the context of Hegelian "negativity" which explains the antithetic middle term in its positive sense but does *not* take away the negative moral leftover in Sartre's use of the term "racisme", see W.A. Jeanpierre, "Sartre's Theory of 'Antiracist Racism' in his Study of Négritude", *Black and White in American Culture*, pp.451-454.
42  Césaire, p.75.
43  Fanon, *Peau Noire, Masques Blancs*, p.207.
44  See for example the introduction to *Modern Poetry in Africa*, pp.25-26.
45  Eliot, *Notes*, p.26. As a result of the first Congress of Negro Writers and Artists, in 1956, at the Sorbonne, a branch of the Society of African Culture headed by Alioune Diop, the publisher of *Présence Africaine*, was created, the American Society of African Culture, to extend into the U.S. the spirit of Black solidarity. The spirit of Négritude, as a self-conscious movement and philosophy, in the U.S., concretely took form in 1959, in the first (American) Negro Writers Conference convened by AMSAC. See the papers that were delivered in *The American Negro Writer and His Roots*, particularly Samuel Allen's "Négritude and its Relevance to the American Negro Writer", pp.8-20. In 1965, a second Negro Writers Conference was held, during which young writers such as LeRoi Jones, Paule Marshall, John O. Killens, took control of the proceedings. See Cruse's account in *The Crisis of the Negro Intellectual*, pp.498-519. I think the significance of the creation of AMSAC and the two conferences is of doubtless importance for the factual connection between the formal Paris origins of Négritude and its equally formal introduction in America, and also for what was being foreshadowed in the involvement of Jones and Marshall — of which more later.
46  Sartre, "L'Orphée Noir", p.xvii.

47  Compare with Wright's account of his experience in the Communist party, "I Tried to be a Communist", *Atlantic Monthly*, pp.48-56; 61-70.

48  James Joyce, *Portrait of the Artist as a Young Man*, p.253.

49  Joseph Conrad, *Heart of Darkness and the Secret Sharer*, p.147.

# QUEBEC SELF

# ARTICULATION

That the poet, or the writer, is, in Wordsworth's words, "a man speaking to men" (1) proves to be a fact throughout the history of French-Canadian literature. From the poet Octave Crémazie, in the 1860's, to Paul Chamberland, in the 1960's, we have, in the creative imagination in Quebec, a mirror reflective of a people's anguish, a pervasive sense of exile consequent to a fateful historic clash between England and France. Since this literature is, according to Robidoux and Renaud, "née de l'histoire et par l'histoire," (2) it follows that up to recent times it has functioned as an arena for actual and pressing problems or issues to be discussed.

Thus we find its beginnings marked by the controversy sparked by the 1839 Durham Report: F.X. Garneau writes a history of the French-Canadian people to prove that they have one, while the *Mouvement Littéraire de Québec* self-consciously calls for the creation of an indigenous literature to disprove Durham's second assertion. (3) When the clergy assigned a redemptive role to French Canada, whereby the French Canadians were to live on the land rather than in the cities, strive for survival by having large families, and sublimate all secular concerns in faith; when, indeed, the famous "revenge of the cradles" became the rallying cry of a nation, literature complied with the inspiring figures of Maria Chapdelaine, Menaud, the archetypes of the land, the family and the faith. Similarly, when in the 1880's Curé Labelle led a crusade for the opening of new territories in Québec's hinterland, this "back to the soil" reassertion, although a painful failure from the start, nonetheless came to occupy an important place in a number of agrarian novels and pamphlets, namely Antoine Gérin-Lajoie's *Jean Rivard* cycle, Arthur Buies' notebooks, C.H. Grignon's *Un Homme et son Péché*, Ringuet's *Trente Arpents* and other works. A structural analysis of literature and society in Quebec would point

177

out that, while the preoccupations of *L'Ecole Littéraire de Montréal*, or *La Relève*, had little correspondence with popular tastes, they nonetheless conveyed the temper of a deracinated bourgeoisie. Lastly, when from the forties to the sixties, a strong gust of revolt blows over both literature and society, it is not surprising to observe a striking correlation between the concerns found in Lemelin's and Roy's novels and the conscription crisis of the last World War; nor one between such novels as *Le Cassé, Prochain Episode*, or books of poetry like *Terre Québec, Pays Sans Parole*, (4) and the rise of F.L.Q. violence. Perhaps the *Parti Pris, Liberté*, and Hexagone groups were the first to identify Quebec's dilemma in the context of colonial acculturation and to call for, as a consequence, the same visceral, cathartic revolt occurring in societies more frankly victims of imperialism and colonialism. But, in spite of their assertions, they were not the first to open their eyes to *le pays* and to assume it in their writings. If anything, literary history in Quebec has always functioned as handmaiden to social history. Jean-Charles Falardeau, the Laval University sociologist, writes:

> La littérature a été avant tout un instrument de combat social ou politique, un refuge, une soupape de sûreté. Rendre compte de la littérature canadienne-française c'est, dans une large mesure, récapituler l'aventure de la collectivité humaine pour qui elle a été un cri ou une évasion. (5)

As a consequence, the level of literature from the beginnings to the contemporary period demonstrates an art that is more *mimetic* ("represents appearance rather than truth, and nourishes ... feelings rather than ... reason") and *pragmatic* ("the work of art [is looked at] chiefly as a means to an end, an instrument for getting something done, and [the pragmatic theory] tends to judge its value according to its success in achieving that aim"); rather than *expressive* ("the artist himself becomes the major element generating both the artistic product and the criteria by which it is to be judged") and *objective* ("the work of art [is regarded] in isolation from all ... external points of reference, [is analyzed] as a self-sufficient entity constituted by its parts in their internal relations"), to use M.H. Abrams' well-known categories. (6) But the poet, in Shelley's words, is "a nightingale, who sits in darkness and sings to cheer its own solitude with sweet sounds; ...." (7) If the writer is "the unacknowledged legislator of the world," (8) his lot is nevertheless a solitary one. Because he is a "prophet" and a "seer", in Shelley's terms, he cannot expect his contemporaries to recognize his truths. Though his truths may leave "men entranced by the melody of an unseen musician," (9) his audience sits in ignorance of their meaning, and the power of poetry remains unrecognized. There lies the dilemma: art is, of course, social by nature since it is addressed to man; but its medium (craft, technique) is not. The message is supposedly social, but

178

the medium is private. How to reconcile this fundamental ambiguity? The history of literature illustrates the pendulum swing of writers who confronted it: the populism of a Wordsworth *v.* the elitism of an Eliot; the assertiveness of a Byron *v.* the sense of privacy of a Keats; Chaucer's worldliness *v.* Sidney's courtliness. More often than not, though, great poetry has always found its subject in the tension, the striving-for-balance, exerted by these would-be opposite poles. One thinks of Shelley's "To a Skylark", Yeats' "Among Schoolchildren", Tennyson's "Lady of Shalott" whose allusive common resolution in the face of warring claims is echoed in Arnold's turning to his muse, his only security in a world "where ignorant armies clash by night", on the one hand, and beguiled by sea-like deceptive appearances, on the other hand:

> Ah, love, let us be true
> To one another! for the world, which seems
> To lie before us like a land of dreams,
> So various, so beautiful, so new,
> Hath really neither joy, nor love, nor light
> Nor certitude, nor peace, nor help for pain; (10)

It is too soon to affirm that the post-revolt French-Canadian writers have realized the truth and implications of T.S. Eliot's dictum, that art is a parting away from emotions rather than a dwelling in them. (11) But there are certain signs, not the least of which being recent events in Quebec's political life, which point to a maturing process. If the events of October 1970 seem to have served somewhat a purpose, it would appear to be the culmination in literature of that self-questioning which at first took the form of *le pays* celebration. This culmination could be thus formulated: where does literary exaltation end and social irresponsibility begin? Where does violence celebrated in literature end and violence in the streets begin? Where is the dividing line in assigning responsibility or non-responsibility? The Montreal police, perhaps the world's most scholarly force (!) spoke to this dilemma in its own fashion when it echoed Plato's beliefs that a well-ordered society could do without artists by jailing Gaston Miron, Gérald Godin, Pierre Vallières, Pauline Julien and other artistic types during the October Crisis.

The powers-that-be thought that, thus, mindless echoing of revolutionary cries could be subdued. That the Draconian invocation of the War Measures Act succeeded in suppressing the rhetoric of dissent, let alone its social basis is, of course, debatable. But the irony is that, since 1967, during a time when Quebec separatism received its most respectable support in a sonorous note of impoliteness from De Gaulle, the literary temper was undergoing a decisive process of change. Paul Chamberland, one of the founders of *Parti Pris* and the foremost young poet of the post-

Duplessis era, published, in 1967, his last book of poetry, *L'Inavouable*. A long, narrative and symbolistic poem told by a narrator named Désiré, the "unnamable" refers to the agonies of failure and disillusionment experienced by Désiré who once saw himself committed to the liberation (at least through *la parole*) of his land. And it concludes on two levels: one, that it is not through language a land is to be liberated but through action ("je sais qu'aujourd'hui ce n'est point la parole qui confère le sens mais l'acte") (12); second, and more important, Désiré indicates that his quest henceforth will be inward, in the soul ("cette voix sourde qui parle en moi, je l'entends"). (13) Like countless other poets before him, and under all climes, Chamberland had come to a crossroads where he had to choose between politics and art. And he chose neither one. Chamberland has foresaken *engagé* poetry in favour of an obscure, precious and mystical type of writing influenced by the so-called counter-culture and Eastern philosophies, becoming thereby Quebec's own Allen Ginsberg. (14)

A few days before the events of October 1970, another young poet, of the generation after Chamberland's, had this to say about the commitment to *le pays* he was heir to: "Finie la vieille thématique. Ecrire quelque chose sur le pays, ça ne donne plus rien....Le pays, je m'en chrisse [fiche]." (15) More recently, in March 1971, the literary critic of Quebec's biggest daily, *La Presse*, an institution which is to Quebec what *The New York Times* is to the U.S., had to admit that:

> Le temps des écoles littéraires qui réunissaient des auteurs autour d'une préoccupation esthétique, morale ou sociale particulière, est à peu près disparu....Des livres paraissent qu'il est difficile de situer; peut-être doit-on y voir un signe de diversité, qui serait à son tour un signe de richesse. La littérature québécoise, en somme, s'est démocratisée; ouverte à tous, elle reflète tout. (16)

Assuming that Martel is correct, what does this new 'openness' in the literature, and particularly the novel, imply in the context of our analysis? It would seem that a mode of classification becomes imperative so as to escape redundancy and to put in sharper focus the present state of Quebec's literary evolution.

First, there are social novels still, in the tradition of Lemelin and Roy, portraying proletarian French Canadians trying to make ends meet: one thinks of the work of Victor-Lévy Beaulieu and Jean-Jules Richard. Second, gothic novels but with Quebec for setting and the large family and Church tradition as *foci* for horror — the irremediable wallowing in incest, fratricide, dehumanization, wanton violence and cruelty regularly produced by Marie-Claire Blais, whom Edmund Wilson no less somewhat extravagantly praised to the world. (17) Suffice it to name one of her dozen novels, *Une Saison dans la Vie d'Emmanuel* which, in 1965, won the Prix

Médicis in France. Third, baroque novels using verbal invention to mystify the reader, in tales that are: pretexts for the display of arcane erudition (Hubert Aquin's *Trou de Mémoire* [1967], *L'Antiphonaire* [1969]); or designed to translate a never-never land of fancy (Réjean Ducharme whose *l'Avalé des Avalées* was received with claims of genius in Paris, in 1965, but whose successive *l'Océanthume, Le Nez qui Voque, La Fille de Christophe Colomb* [1966-1969]) soon exhausted curiosity; or baroque novels, which present a Lautrémont-like quest for the *fantastique*, without however the Frenchman's ingenuity (Jacques Renaud's *En d'Autres Paysages* [1970]). Fourth, there is Jacques Ferron, a satirist in a class all by himself, who takes his inspiration from the folklore of provincial bourgeoisie. Ferron excels in the short story, the form *par excellence* for his talent, which he un-fortunately over-stretched in a long, pompous and dull novel like *Le Ciel de Québec* (1969).

Of course, these are only the main currents since 1965, and inevitably arbitrary at that. It goes without saying that there is, in addition, the conventional novel with little to recommend itself other than the satis-faction of the would-be author. Is there anything, however, in the four categories mentioned above that pursue or enlighten the themes we have been discussing? It would seem not. Either there is repetition, rehashing of commonplaces with little of the original's brilliance, or there is an outlook that belongs to world literature and as such should be measured against its standards (consequently, Aquin's formal exercises pale next to those of Gide, Joyce or, closer, Robbe-Grillet; Blais' cult of the bizarre was, of course, the province of "the romantic agony" of the late nineteenth century). Yet, there seems to be a fifth current which appears as a logical continuation to the themes analyzed so far: that of what I would call the "novels of am-biguity", reflecting the consciousness of the complexity of life the French Canadian never had access to when either the cult of Messianism or *le pays* meant a belief in simple creeds and answers, a reduction of life to religious or secular dogma.

The concept of ambiguity at work in the novels of that last group can be defined thus: to be aware of living a condition that is not easily identifiable; to reach for answers and to find a multiplicity of questions instead; to be conscious of the heterogeneity of life, of the relevancy of numerous parallels to any one unique experience. The ambiguous hero comes as a cousin of the absurd hero, but with the following differences: the former is, historically, a later development, a product of the post-Second World War dismemberment of the old empires and nation-states; more often than not, he is a product of decolonization, in fact if not in cultural conditioning. This last word brings us to the second difference: the ambiguous hero's emergence parallels the fruition of mass technology, particularly the mass media, in the post-industrial era. Whereas the absurd or existential man could dwell in his inner ruminations or go out into the world to find

181

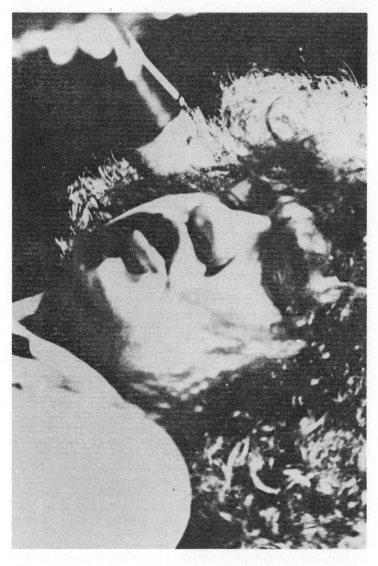

Robert Charlebois                    *(Cinémathèque Québécoise)*

meaning, commitment, in a "just war" (whether the China and Spain of Malraux, Hemingway's Spain, or Mailer's Southeast Asia), in a constant worldly "quest" (the Celinian journey, Graham Greene's blasé man) — even when the end result is a nightmarish witnessing of one's helplessness in the process of self-disintegration culminating in silence, as is the case for Beckett's anti-hero — the ambiguous man is constantly surrounded by, and finds himself a prisoner of, pictures and sounds of a world filled with horror (e.g. Vietnam), where his only function seems to be that of passive spectator of history.

For man, feeding on such images and sounds, there has been an "extension of the senses", as McLuhan says, and it results in his being brought full circle to the primal environmental aural-tactile-visual sense of kinship whereby there practically exists no dichotomy between inner and outer worlds, the individual and the group. (18) But another form of ambiguity arises precisely — and that is one of the drawbacks of McLuhanism — when in *practice* there can be no return to a preternatural Edenic state. McLuhan man is as much a victim of history's burden as Sartrian man. McLuhan's failure to grasp the ramifications of his theories in the perspective of politics and economics, as D.F. Theall indicates in *The Medium is the Rear View Mirror*, points to the necessity of discussing the fact that technology, however sophisticated, is used in a social context to whose values it must be held accountable. (19) The ambiguous man, heir to a humanist tradition that has culminated in a philosophy of despair, a participant in the new world of the media, finds ambiguity resting squarely in his being placed at the crossroads of old and new cultures, forms and outlooks — and yet being unable to choose. A creature of "the global village" of technology, he is not a prey to heroism since he is too well-informed as to the odds of such an attempt. If he is, on the other hand, a possible prey to cynicism, this danger is compensated by the openness of view, the sense of tolerance which the awareness of the complexity of life has forced on him. He is, in the final analysis, the classic man-in-the-middle, one who has left behind a traditional way of life, who would seem to be in the process of building a new set of values, but while doing so he severely questions their effectiveness: perpetual doubt besets that man. He has thrown away the past and consigned the present and the future to an active state of becoming inspired by the technique of the media. It is as if, long confined to a static culture, the would-be new culture refuses any allegiance calling for bases, foundations, and thrives on change, movability, instability, much like the action of the camera which has become the icon of a new age, contemporary culture. (20)

Within a context of change, flux, interpenetration of all national modes of life through the media, we find the ambiguous hero in the post-revolt French-Canadian novel.

Jacques Godbout's *Le Couteau sur la Table* (1965), written by one who is also a film-maker (as is wont to be the case for many modern writers; one thinks of Robbe-Grillet, Mailer, Van Peebles, even Beckett), illustrates, as Luc Granger's *Ouate de Phoque* (1969), written by a former Radio-Canada disk-jockey, our premise of the media's influence on the changing outlook in Quebec. Godbout's book is the most ambiguous of the two. Published at the height of the *pays* craze, and incorporating newspaper items relating the first F.L.Q. cell's activities (and first fatal killing) it was thought to be like *Prochain Episode*, a prophetic book, to be read less for what it said than for what it left unsaid open-endedly. Again, one will not repeat enough the vagaries to which a long tradition of mimetic art and mimetic criticism in Quebec leads. It seems obvious, though, to anyone who carefully reads the book that there is an abrupt change of pace starting with the last chapter (precisely the one referring to the F.L.Q. activities and closing with the narrator's threat, a knife left ready for a ritual of violence).

Built upon the cinema technique of rapid shots, panoramic view, close-ups, use of soundtrack — all of which are incorporated in Robbe-Grillet's concept of the "New Novel" (21) and borrowing the sense of *immediacy* of cinema, Godbout focuses his lenses on a French Canadian who is initially stationed on an Air Force base in the Canadian Prairies and acquires a mistress in the person of a voluptuous and rich blonde named Patricia. If another blonde, Aquin's K, could on the one hand symbolize Quebec, and on the other hand, when associated with H. de Heutz, the Establishment, here there is no uncertainty: Patricia *is* the land of abundance, the blonde radiancy of affluence, the well-fed, well-shed and well-bred product of an Anglo-Saxon culture that knows not the sense of indecision, constant self-doubting and self-questioning beholden by the member of a minority group, such as her lover. Thus the narrator wishes not merely to possess Patricia sexually but to partake psychologically as well of her secure identity:

> (Encore aujourd'hui je n'arrive pas à m'expliquer ce besoin que j'avais d'une femme qui me fût à ce point étrangère. A cette époque d'ailleurs je me plaisais à répéter machinalement en baisant la pointe de son sein: une peau nordique, puis promenant mes lèvres sur son visage: des yeux du nord, des cheveux d'un blond nordique, une langue du nord, comme si pour le prix d'un tel mannequin j'allais pouvoir m'acheter une identité.) (p.36)

He endlessly celebrates his mistress' blondeness and beauty, obviously the better to convey the archetypal attraction she represents (the 'outside' world so feared, yet not so fearful). And she, exasperated by his perpetual doubts and questions, by his constant drawing of parallels about Vietnam, the Civil Rights movement in the U.S. and assorted strifes, tells him to stop feeling sorry for himself and enjoy if not her, at least what he is experiencing through their liaison:

—Ça ne t'emmerde pas chéri de porter comme ça le monde entier sur tes épaules? *I mean come on get that chip off your shoulder!* Je ne suis pas une raciste moi, mais les seuls nègres que j'ai connus étaient porteurs à bord des trains. *I can't get upset like you...* Ça te coupe vraiment l'appétit? (pp.28-29)

Fed up with the service, the narrator bolts camp and a long leisurely train ride follows which leads him from the Prairies to Quebec. In Montreal, he works in a drugstore and Patricia attends McGill University. A fight takes place between the two lovers and they break up for a while. He goes out with a French-Canadian girl, Madeleine, and meets with old friends whose conversations about *le pays* bore him to death. When Madeleine dies in a motorcycle accident, the narrator is shaken out of his complacency long enough to start a new romance, though a brief one, with Madeleine's sister. But, following an impulse conditioned by his long-standing admiration for Jack Kerouac, the narrator leaves Quebec and sets out on an American tour. We are told little of his experiences in the U.S., except that he identified with Jews, Negroes, Poles, Puerto Ricans and assorted other ethnic groups, depending on the company of the moment. But all to no avail: America fails him, and Kerouac's sense of "beat" no longer stands for "beatitude" but, literally, the same metaphysical fatigue with which the narrator returns to Quebec. His return coincides with the explosion of the first F.L.Q. bombs in Montreal (in 1963). And the novel ends with his quoting of related news items and the threat of possibly murdering Patricia with the knife left on the table.

This is the bare plot. But enough has been said to show how Godbout has touched on a variety of themes: the desire to flee Quebec; the association between land and woman; the nagging psychological malaise; and the last resort to revolt and violence. All these attitudes are held together by the quest for identity which leads the narrator from Patricia's, or Anglo-Saxon America's arms to *le pays*. Ideologically, the implied embrace of F.L.Q. terrorism can be explained with regard to the date of publication of the novel. But, aesthetically, from the Jamesian point of view, the implications are quite different.

The narrator's 'voice' until the last chapter (three pages) is decidedly that of the ambiguous man. A man who early in his liaison with Patricia, in the Prairies, tells us:

(Il n'y a pas si longtemps ces évènements [civil rights demonstrations in the States] nous eussent parus impossibles ou au bout du monde, ou encore nous n'en aurions rien su; aujourd'hui si l'on passe à la baignoire les membres du parti socialiste de l'Union nationale des forces populaires, à Agadir, c'est comme si cela se pratiquait à deux rues d'ici. [L'homme universel est né et

185

nous ne nous en sommes pas aperçus.]) (p.26)

The affirmation is clearly of a universal conscience created by the impact of the media; a conscience shaped as world identity while at the same time it dulls the urge for involvement in any particular cause or issue. This last sense is conveyed in the worldly-wise, or world-weary, tone maintained by the narrator. For instance, impatient with his friends' endless boring political discussions, he reflects:

> Mais la grande, l'épuisante peine que nous prenions à tout vouloir nommer! défaites et pays! accrochait une lueur identique aux jours qui passaient. Du matin au soir nous cherchions avec entêtement les signes de l'asservissement, l'indice récent de l'abrutissement général, jusque dans les statistiques, les almanachs, les horoscopes. (p.110)

Or he sardonically tells of his American peregrinations, in the pursuit of Jack Kerouac's mystique: "je voulais me faire accepter à tout prix des déshérités..., devenir nègre avec les nègres, Juif parmi les marchands de fourrure, Italien, Irlandais, m'annihiler encore; c'était à rire; travail inutile où l'orgueil se déguisait en humilité contrite" (p.151).

If the narrative voice is important, so is the climate of indecision, ambiguity throughout his relationship with Patricia-*cum*-America. Neither this nor his involvement with America-*cum*-Kerouac justifies or motivates the following concluding paragraphs in the wake of referring to F.L.Q. violence:

> Pour détruire la volière, choisir.
> *Inimi/ni maï, ni mo, catch a nigger by the toe, if he hollers let him go, Inimi/ni mai, ni mo.* Choisir à poings fermées.
> (La haine est venue, comme une saison. Le printemps est venu, comme une gifle; personne ne peut lutter contre le vent, les saisons, la lumière blanche, la neige ébouriffée des rafales.)
> (Je ne te ferai aucun mal, si tu ne dis mot, Patricia. D'ailleurs il ne te servirait à rien de te débattre ou de crier, ou même de parler de nos amours anciennes. Le couteau restera sur la table de la cuisine. Aucune trace de sang sur le tapis.
> A peine ton corps vibrant et doux qui s'agitera, à peine ton souffle qui) (pp.157-158)

Yet this last resort to violence may be explained by the media's impact. Early in the novel, the narrator reads a newspaper report on a civil rights demonstration in the U.S. referring to the violence of Southern policemen using electric cattle prods to break up a band of Negro marchers: "Des

pour écouter la radio! Alors pourquoi ce ton d'ORACLE chez la plupart des speakers. Et cette fausse diction. Cette "voix" dé-naturée inhumaine "bidon". Cette "incapacité-à-communiquer" autrement que par "le commercial" perpétuel, la prédication-du-sourire-de-service? Y a donc personne pour s'en rendre vraiment compte? (il est vrai que... le "niveau de scolarité" étant assez peu élevé dans ce pays-qui-eût-pu-être-nôtre (3 accents circonflexes... ça fait joli au-dessus des caractères. 'vez pas), les antennes n'ont guère eu la possibilité de s'allonger... Mais, c'est pas not' radio qui pourra améliorer les choses. Et quant à la télé ben là, vraiment, vraiment... vraiment pas la peine de s'y attarder. D'abord ça coûte tellement cher, même en "sépia" — UNE EMISSION SEPIA DE RADIO-CANADA! — que la commandite est inévitable. Tandis qu'avec la radio, une certaine démocratie est encore plausible, sinon possible. Ça reste du domaine du "pensable"...) Donc, W.B.A.I., New York, chapeau!

C'est comme pour les revues aux E.-U. Les périodiques financés de la même façon. Par les seuls lecteurs. Où l'on n'accepte de réclame sous aucune forme et où l'on donne, par contre, la liste des noms des "donateurs", pour la plupart professeurs dans diverses universités. En parcourant l'une de ces listes j'ai remarqué, entre autres noms, celui de Linus Pauling... "THE MINORITY OF ONE" (subtil, ce nom...), "independant monthly for an american alternative. Dedicated to the eradication of all restrictions on thought"... avec en épigraphe au dessus du "générique", cette citation de George Orwell, vétéran (mort de tuberculose il y a quelques années) de la Guerre d'Espagne: "There was truth and there was untruth, and if you clung to the truth, even against the whole world, you were not mad".

—Pourquoi faire un tel plat de c'qui s'passe "à l'étranger" (I hear you whisper)... Ben, mondieu c'est simple! En manchette, dans la Presse du vendredi 3 mai '68 on pou-

229

policiers à cheval font grimacer de douleur un noir en lui touchant le dos avec des bâtons à aiguillon électrique, lesquels servent normalement à aiguillonner le bétail." (p.25) He reads about other demonstrations and quotes Martin Luther King on the subject of the Birmingham Church bombing of 1963 which took the lives of four little Black girls. Interestingly, immediately following this, we have the narrator's previously quoted statement on the media's creation of universal man. But let us turn to the concluding note on violence. The narrator says, before quoting two newspaper reports (one in English, one in French) on the accidental killing of a nightwatchman by an F.L.Q. bomb: "J'ai tout expliqué à Patricia; elle n'a pas compris; mais au fond *cela n'a aucune importance*. Nous sommes des millions à comprendre, enfin à peu près." (p.155) To understand what? Not that "la haine est venue" and that violence is a purifying ritual that all true revolutionaries must be willing to undertake (as the young middle-class members of the first F.L.Q. cell thought Fanon was saying), but, rather, since our narrator is *not* the revolutionary type (unless one is ready to equate Hamlet with Malraux' Chen), the power of images now crisscrosses the T.V. tube in the living room and the reality in the streets. So that it is perhaps technological man's fate not to be yet able to separate what numerous summer riots and racial confrontations in the States have shown: the correlation between images of violence on the screen, dreams of violence, and the urge to do violence in the streets. (22) Contrary to the process carried on by the novelists and poets of revolt in Quebec, and in line with the narrator's ironic assessment of his search for identity in the States, there is no *actual* comparison between the violence meted out to the Blacks and that which Quebec radicals feel entitled to use; nor is there any common ground between a Martin Luther King and the obscure terrorists of the F.L.Q. Such *facts* seem to matter little, though. Or so it seems in a world culturally conditioned to respond to images and sounds of international media, rather than the traditional shibboleths of tribe, clan and nation. And since violence seems to rule our lives more than ever in history — or one is more *aware* of it than ever — the most remote village in Quebec is no longer immune from exposure, nay participation, as shall be seen later in Roch Carrier's novel.

It is a matter that one had better leave for meditation or conclude with a question: when is one form of resistance justifiable, because of its organic roots (the Civil Rights movement in the U.S.), and when is another, to a significant extent, the effect of exposure to the media? It is a query which Godbout, an urbane and sophisticated artist, certainly meant to dramatize, without purporting to provide any simple answer.

That the media's impact need not solely result in the pursuit of violence is demonstrated in a confessional type of fiction that heavily borrows from the technique of elliptical, oracular prose common to radio. A "novel", in the formal sense of the word, Luc Granger's *Ouate de Phoque* (1969) is not. One looks in vain for a well-structured plot, the existence of characters, or

188

some well-defined dramatic conflict, in this book which narrates a young disk-jockey's experience while working in a small Chicoutimi radio station — the reading that he does in his spare time and the trouble that he gets into with the administrators for lack of punctuality and his fondness for playing American and avant-garde French recordings; the very same troubles that beset him when he makes it to "the top", working for Radio-Canada, the state-owned radio and television network. When the narrator is dismissed from this latter position (as he was in Chicoutimi), he, like Godbout's narrator, leaves for the U.S. in search for identity if not for immediate contact with that environment he is in tune with through the media. He returns to Quebec, gets his Radio-Canada job back, loses it again, and the book ends with the narrator's profession of disbelief in the fashionable values of *le pays*, the French-English confrontation, and Radio-Canada's purist notions about the question of culture. By implication, and by direct references, there is the affirmation that here is an anarchistic, liberated and uncommitted soul who does not know where he stands about anything; for there, it seems, lies humaneness in the post-industrial world.

If all this seems confusing, it is; moreover, when the narration is sandwiched between extended notes, comments taken from tapes of the narrator's programmes and when we are told of the conception of some of the book's chapters ("J'ai improvisé ça devant mon magnétophone, après quoi je l'ai tapé. Toute une d'jobbe [un job], believe you me. De toute manière il m'eût été fastidieux de 'composer' ça" p.254). Nonetheless, what is important, as in Godbout's book, is the narrative voice, the sensibility expressed throughout, shaped by the medium of radio and the culture of the technological age. The narrator acts more as a reflector than as an interpreter of the new culture; he is both detached and involved. The interpenetration of polarities makes for irony, ambivalence and always ambiguity. This is evident when the narrator is faced with the *pays* celebration. How can he be concerned with a spatially-oriented involvement when his very medium denies the barriers of space and the frontiers of religion, race and language?

> OPTION-QUEBEC? Well...maybe. Je ne demanderais pas mieux, mais...I have the keen and somewhat obsessive feeling that EV'RYTHING is going on NOW and FOR THE WHOLE WESTERN WORLD, "south of the border." Je n'arrive pas à croire que "le" québec (qui n'est,pour l'instant, qu'une abstraction) puisse échapper au "dread" qui pèse sur l'Amerique et sur l'occident-en-général. Bien sûr que non je n'ai "rien d'autre à proposer", ce qui en dégoûtera plus d'un... Je ne me reconnais pas de nationalité, au sens "nation-état" du terme; ni canédiune ni kébékoâ. (pp.251-252)

It is not the situations in which the narrator is placed that define his sensibility, since he is pretty much confined to his studio booth. The quality of language used, the inflections, intonations, the modulations given to a phrase, a thought, the choice of words is what matters. What happens is a marked contrast in the constant alternation of French and English, the impossibility for the narrator to commit himself to any one particular language. Reflecting the bilinguism and biculturalism of his province, Quebec's ambiguous position as a pocket of French culture amid an English-speaking continent, he is hybrid in speech as well as in thought, and he assumes this duality:

> Et quant à cette question de l'anglaise-et-du français-back-and-forth, ben ciboire, tant que j'aurai la "citoyenneté" (passeport, droits de l'homme and so on) canadienne, c'est mon droit le plus strict de m'adresser à mes com-patriotes dans l'une ET l'autre des deux langues ci-devant officielles, et personne ne peut m'INTERDIRE de parler l'anglais non plus que de parler le français. Et personne ne peut me CONTRAINDRE à parler l'anglais non plus qu'à parler le français. (p.254)

To be sure, from the evidence of some passages of strict description, we know that the narrator is capable of writing in an honoured French tradition. But, precisely, the different level used to express his consciousness is symptomatic of the ambiguity of the land and, more important, the matter of culture in the post-industrial age. The linear form of French represents the old humanist tradition that has culminated in the Sartrian, Beckettian, philosophy of despair:

> Un vent qui apporte des quatre coins de son ciel noir tous les germes de la désespérance universelle, un vent qui vient écornifler les fenêtres aveugles des édifices-à-bureaux, pour débouler ensuite dans la rue, en piqué, à l'endroit exact où vous offrez votre pauvre nuque de 'civil' anonyme et sans défense. (p 171)

Whereas the non-linear, broken, syncopated form where English is mixed with French, slang with "Joual," stands for the nascent, post-humanist culture "full of sound and fury" that may yet signify something:

> Je devais bientôt "avoir des ennuis" avec ces messieurs de la salle des nouvelles (salle des dépêches, si vous "aimez" mieux...) et là encore, avec un "chef de service." The man in charge. (In charge, TO A CERTAIN EXTENT...) That cat did not "appreciate" my tone of voice when I would read the newscast. On me reprochait entre choses mon ironie, mon "manque d'intérêt!?! ÇA là,

VRAIMENT là, FRANCHEMENT LA...ben X% Z(!) ? % % XC
!!! Ah j'te dis, j'les trouve PARFAS. "Manque d'intérêt"... Non
mais, alors quoâ les gârs, vous m'charriez ou quoi? ... Yeah, I'm
hip. (pp.212-213)

The narrator would rather relate to a consciousness that ignores historical
conditionings and nationalistic obsessions. Modern Pop music, the rhythm
and pace of contemporary big-city life reflected in the personality of the
arbiter of present culture (the disk-jockey, or T.V. "personality"), among
others, are the sources of his sensibility. Admittedly, it dwells in a certain
facile tenderness, a pedestrian poetry of simple emotions and not-deepened-
enough experiences. But there need not be an apology, since this sensibility
is deliberately geared toward its own values and beliefs. For a French
Canadian who is only too conscious of the strictures of his society, both past
and present, the shock of recognition found in Bob Dylan's and Léo Ferré's
rejection of old forms and affirmation of a new humanism based on simple
sentiments and feelings, can be quite a powerful one.

One can very well fault Granger for negating the very form he uses to
communicate. Granted the concerns he wishes to convey are valid, it could
be asked, need they be presented in a mode so lacking in structure, design
and even coherence? The same argument has been levelled at McLuhan, of
course, and the reply is that the book form can be remolded to convey an
aesthetic experience that is primarily tactile, visual or/and audile. A long
tradition in Western culture, further, bears this out; whether one has in
mind the world of medieval *amanuenses*, Counter-Reformation poets the
likes of Crashaw, Gongora and Marino, notwithstanding the emblematic
tradition at work in Herbert's poetry, or Mallarmé's concept of *Le Livre*,
Apollinaire's and the Surrealists' inventiveness in 'sensorizing', so to speak,
the written word. This is not to say that Granger's attempt is comparable
either in subject matter or in achievement to these precedents; but an aesthetic objection based on his rejection of the book convention would be a
tenuous one. Altogether, juxtaposed to the works analyzed so far, Granger's
is an unassuming, refreshing and truly liberated work, were it only for its
humour. If laughter is, as it is said, the politeness of despair, then Granger's
book seems to suggest that it is a politeness that should be acquired and
cultivated.

Laughter, whether as a politeness or, perhaps, as the one statement of
reconciliation in an ambiguous world is likewise central to the last novel of
our analysis, Roch Carrier's *La Guerre, yes Sir!* (1968). In contrast to a
number of novels that ended with a note of departure from the land of exile
*(Le Cassé, Bonheur d'Occasion, Trente Arpents* and others), Carrier's
novel, like *Prochain Episode, Ouate de Phoque, Le Couteau sur la Table,*
operates rather in a return to Quebec whereby the protagonist is to assume
the land in all its ambiguity. His novel is particularly close to Godbout's in

191

that both utilize the motif of a sexual relationship between a French and an English Canadian. (Groulx, of course, had used a similar motif, but for quite different purposes.) More than any other writer before him, however, Carrier works with the marriage motif between English and French Canadians better to render through a succession of ironies, contrasts and paradoxes a situation which is the leaven of human experience. *Ouate de Phoque* used the irony of mixed media for the baring of one's sensibility. In *La Guerre* the reservoir of folk humour and the vernacular serves as liberating mode from existential confinements and interrogations which are quite acute, though belied by the book's surface comedy.

The novel opens with the first level in the overall marriage motif: Amélie's marriage to Henri in a small village lost in the winter hinterland of Quebec during the last World War. The War forces a triangle onto this marriage in the person of Arthur who, hiding from military duty, finds refuge not only in Amélie's and Henri's house, but in Amélie's arms as well. Soon enough, Arthur has supplanted the legitimate husband's role, and this fact, replete with comic effect, is important to bear in mind since this marriage *à trois* introduces the two other levels in the marriage motif in an accretion of ambiguity. We are next presented with the marriage that gives its title to the book, and which is the source of dramatic conflict. Six English-Canadian soldiers, none of them conversant in French, are escorting home to his final rest a dead French-Canadian comrade, Corriveau, a native of the village. Third, on that same train, a newly married couple is also returning home to the village: Bérubé, a French-Canadian enlisted man, with his bride, Molly, a blonde (yet another one!) English-Canadian prostitute whom he married since, faithful to the tenets of his religion, had he had sexual intercourse without the bonds of marriage, it would have been a most serious sin of the flesh....

These three levels are joined in the climactic moment of the book: the wake held for the dead soldier. The sexual energy and robustness indicated in Amélie and Molly (females with overdeveloped mammary glands; an endowment frequently referred to that reveals an almost authorial fixation); the sexual inhibitions contained in Henri, Bérubé and other villagers; the characters' submission to their Church-assigned role; the latent hostility between French and English Canadians fed by the war issue and by traditional fears and ignorance (the villagers do not speak a word of English; the English-Canadian soldiers not one of French) — everything finds release in that long night which turns out to be an extended pagan ritual, a ceremony where most elemental energies burst out; and comedy lapses into ugliness. Gathered in the Corriveau home, the 'mourners' feast their palates on meat pie and apple cider; and as the night progresses ribald jokes and curses are exchanged, appetites are wetted and an orgiastic revelling is in progress fanned by the men's contemplation of Molly's cuvaceous forms. But by the time Molly appears in a skimpy négligée, a vicious fight is taking place between her husband and Arsène who, drunk as a lord, celebrates the courage and bravery of military life. For this, Bérubé mercilessly beats him to a pulp, ostensibly to impress his anti-war feelings upon him. For good measure, he tells Molly to climb Arsène's shoulders who is made into a mock infantryman on parade:

> —Gauche... Gauche... Droite! Danse, puante vermine. Danse!
> Vivent la guerre et ses soldats! Danse. Gauche droite! Voici un obus!
> Bérubé le frappa au derrière.
> —Voici une grenade.
> Bérubé le gifla.
> —Voici une bombe.
> Bérubé lui soufflait de la salive à la figure. (p.86)

The significance of the image of Molly astride Arsène maintains the balance between sex and violence, the poles between which the novel oscillates; the two being primitive urges long repressed by the Church. At this stage, the English-Canadian soldiers who have been keeping an uneasy watch over the coffin are shocked and outraged by the French Canadians' peculiar 'customs' in honouring their dead. The following description pictures quite well the contrast which in effect might summarize that between two cultures and civilizations, the Dionysian Gallic "joie de vivre" and the Apollonian Anglo-Saxon insistence on decorum and propriety:

> Les Anglais longs et maigres examinaient le double menton des French-Canadians, leur ventre gonflé, les seins des femmes gros et flasques, ils scrutaient les yeux des French Canadians flottant inertes dans la graisse blanche de leur visage, ils étaient de vrais porcs, ces French Canadians dont la civilisation consistait à boire, manger, péter, roter. (pp.90-91)

The soldiers thereupon chase everybody out into the cold. This action precipitates the ironic eruption of war in the village. The villagers, after the first moment of surprise, cease their internecine banters and quarrels to focus on the significance of their having been routed by English soldiers (observe the ironic catalogue of their assessment, which is Carrier's way of subtly alluding to the Messianic tradition): "qui n'étaient ni du village, ni du comté, ni de la province, ni même du pays, des Anglais qui n'étaient même pas des Canadiens mais seulement des maudits Anglais...." (p.100) They then finally muster the sense of community and aim at seeking revenge in a fists-and-feet attack. The "war" would have remained a mock epical one, typifying a trivial motive — like the war between the Sylphs and assorted spirits in Pope's *Rape of the Lock* — were it not for the note of pathos

193

introduced by Henri's action. Henri, the deserter who came home to find he has to share his conjugal bed with a draft dodger, crazed by his wife's indifference and his hatred for war which he can no longer contain when he sees the arrival of Corriveau's coffin, grabs a rifle, joins the rabble and fires the one shot of the "war", killing an English-Canadian soldier. Just as it began, the "war" abruptly ends.

The sobered French Canadians go on to bury their dead Corriveau, chastened by the Curate's eulogy, a man whose tongue "ressemblait, lorsqu'il ouvrait la bouche, à un crapaud qui n'osait sauter". (p.115) Bérubé, who during the battle has responded to his training and fought the villagers most fiercely ("Il devait frapper plus fort que les gens du village et plus fort que les Anglais s'il voulait que quelqu'un le respectât" p.108), is ordered by the Sergeant to carry the dead English soldier with the remaining soldiers. And as they leave the village, Molly follows, ironically, still in her white wedding dress.

Who has won the war? seems to be the question left at the end of the book. And the implication is, how can a war be won or lost when you still have to live a marriage situation? Whether it is Henri, who sought salvation by killing out of frustration; Bérubé, who beats senselessly a compatriot to prove his peace sentiments, who hates war, but is forced, the moment he hears the Sergeant's order, to turn against his compatriots and set out to prove his superior brand of bellicosity; or the village itself, which harbors Henri, the deserter, Arthur, the draft dodger, and presumably stands in its remoteness as an oasis amidst the folly of mankind — they all prove, in the end, that they are not immune from life's profound ambiguity. The war between English and French, where foes and friends seem to be so clearly identified, is mock epical and absurd at that. More profoundly, in a book which at times is indecisive in its choice of focus, Carrier demonstrates, in the final analysis, that war as symbolic of enmity is but the complement of the amity contained in the marriage motif.

The book opens with the three-fold proposition of amity (the three levels of marriage earlier discussed), goes through events which threaten to destroy, or seem to have destroyed it (e.g. Corriveau); and culminates, finally, in the war episode which symbolically seems to imply total destruction. Ironically, though, this enmity (Molly v. Bérubé; Bérubé v. the villagers; Henri v. the soldiers; the French v. the English) is but the transposition, on a lesser scale, of that which everyone is concerned to dissent from: the war. And because in its microcosm the spirit of enmity is the transitory reverse of amity (maintained throughout by Molly's and Amélie's generous forms if not embraces), Carrier seems to be showing in the novel's final image ( Molly following her husband, and Bérubé the English soldiers — two *exempla* of French-English marriage), the inescapable solidarity of mankind, the ties that bind all actions so long as they are human. If such is the specificity of the human order, that amity and enmity
194

are correlated, then such an outlook based on the same awareness of life's pluralism, as seen in Godbout and Granger, makes for the ambiguity of the contemporary French-Canadian novel. Which is not a mean feat in the long process of maturity.

1 William Wordsworth, "Preface to 'Lyrical Ballads' ", in *Romanticism*, p.77.
2 Réjean Robidoux and André Renaud, *Le Roman Canadien Français du Vingtième Siècle*, p.10.
3 See *Lord Durham's Report*, p.150.
4 *Terre Québec* is Paul Chamberland's well-known second volume of poetry; *Pays Sans Parole* is one of Yves Préfontaine's books of poetry.
5 Jean-Charles Falardeau, *Notre Société et son Roman*, p.48.
6 M.H. Abrams, *The Mirror and the Lamp*, pp.9-26.
7 Percy Bysshe Shelley, "A Defence of Poetry", in *Romanticism*, p.87.
8 *Ibid.*, p.97.
9 *Ibid.*, p.87.
10 Matthew Arnold, "Dover Beach", in *Romantic and Victorian Poetry*, p.350.
11 "Poetry is not a turning loose of emotion, but an escape from emotion; ... ." See T.S. Eliot, "Tradition and the Individual Talent", *Selected Essays*, p.10.
12 Paul Chamberland, *L'Inavouable*, p.64.
13 *Ibid.*, p.118.
14 See Paul Chamberland, "Manifeste des Enfants Libres du Kébek", *Ellipse*, No. 8-9 (1971).
15 Roger DesRoches, *La Presse*, p.C2.
16 Réginald Martel, *La Presse*, p.D3.
17 In terms such as, "...; she may possibly be a genius". See Edmund Wilson, *O Canada, An American's Notes on Canadian Culture*, p.148.
18 Marshall McLuhan, *Understanding Media: The Extensions of Man*, p.20.
19 D.F. Theall, *The Medium is the Rear View Mirror*, pp.43-49.
20 McLuhan, *Understanding Media*, pp.248-259.
21 Alain Robbe-Grillet, *For a New Novel*.
22 See the "Kerner Report", an investigation of the root-causes behind the urban riots of the summer of 1967 more formally titled, *Report of the National Advisory Commission on Civil Disorders*, pp.362-366, pp.377-378; see also, Otto N. Larsen, ed., *Violence and the Media*, especially Fredric Wertham's comments.

# CONCLUSION

After examining the dominant themes and attitudes in the literatures of Quebec and Black America, particularly as they appear in the most 'open' form possible, that of the novel, one may resume — and conclude if possible — the central concern introduced at the outset of this essay. Black American and French-Canadian literatures, like African, West Indian, South American — and even American — literatures, emerge as late developments in the context of Western culture. They suggest, consequently, a problem for literary criticism and literary history. To my knowledge, although these literatures are increasingly being read and taught, especially for the past quarter of a century, there has been no critical and theoritical attempt at defining the relationship of these literatures in an overall context. I posited, in the introduction, two key symbols as foundations for this context; those of Caliban and Prospero. The tentatîve definition suggested for these literatures was that of "Caliban Without Prospero". The time has come for a detailed discussion of this definition which now can be substantiated by the novels analyzed.

To say 'Caliban Without Prospero' implies, of course, the converse, 'Caliban With Prospero'. Let us start with the last proposition. Prospero, in Shakespeare's play, is our symbol for the cosmopolitan Renaissance man of culture. He is the man secure with the knowledge he is issued from the womb or the cradle of Western civilization. Whether he is a Frenchman or an Englishman, a Spaniard or an Italian, he can point to achievements in thought, language and literature begotten in his national culture as well as inherited from a common store or reservoir which is Roman and Greek. Thus bred, nurtured and polished by a T.S. Eliot-like sense of "tradition" and "culture", he looks askance at that which stands outside his background and labels it "uncivilized". Such a fate befalls Caliban, whose speech decidedly sounds foreign to Prospero's ears, whose geographical emplacement is non-European, and whose habits stand out in jarring contrast to Prospero's. Immediately a certain relationship is envisaged and the terms dictated by Prospero: Caliban, a "thing of darkness", must be enlightened and brought 'up', if possible, to Prospero's level. We have at the outset a situation of imbalance: one is up and the other is down; one is civilized and the other is not; one is the arbiter and articulator of "culture" and the other is beholden to the arbiter; one is light and the other is dark; one is metropolitan, the other is provincial; one is cosmopolitan , the other is colonial. Always, suffice it to say, from the perspective of Prospero. But to what extent is Prospero entitled to such claims? What is Caliban implying, in the play, when he alludes to Prospero's misrepresentation of truth?

In terms of Hellenistic and Roman syncretism, from which evolved a repertoire of myths, beliefs, sagas and archetypes from which all of early Europe could partake, there undoubtedly existed a unity of European culture. Considering the unitary function of the Church of Rome in the Middle Ages whether, strictly speaking, in the influence of rituals, eschatology, cosmology and heraldry, or, via secular ramifications, in the Crusades, the spirit of romance and chivalry — again the parallelisms between, say, the *Romance of the Rose, Troilus and Criseyde,* and *Niebelungen,* point to a common European culture. Even developments that straddle the late Middle Ages and the early Renaissance, such as *The Faerie Queene, Orlando Furioso, Gerusalemme Liberata,* buttress this fact. One could go on to show how an examination of Shakespearean, Jonsonian, Miltonic sources reveal 'borrowings' from a common reservoir. From then on, using such terms as "influences", "receptions", and "relations" it appears to be a never ending task for the comparatist to study the ties between Richardson and Diderot, Voltaire and Newton, Coleridge and Schiller, Carlyle and Nietzsche, Romanticism, the Baroque and Symbolism as trans-national occurrences. But, by the time we have substituted 'borrowings', 'influences', 'relations' for 'unitary', a definite change seems to have taken place. For with the late Renaissance rise of secular philosophy, the Baconian call for the "advancement of learning" and its echo in Cartesian systematic doubting, on to the Newtonian breakthrough in the field of physics and mathematics and the extreme Materialists of the Enlightenment, there definitely is a scission within the great European design; one that Paul Hazard finds culminating in the eighteenth century as *La Crise de la Conscience Européenne.* (1) Further, a "dissociation" of sensibility that Eliot sees starting with Milton in England, in the seventeenth century, (2) logically gives way in the late eighteenth century and for most of the nineteenth, to interest in folklore, local colour, myths, beliefs, habits peculiar to a people. From centring on a people's particularities to those of the individual's sentiments and feelings, there is but a step, which Romanticism gingerly takes. So that by the time we

200

witness the sorrows of young Werther, the anguish of Chateaubriand's René, Wordsworth's kinship with Nature, and the Byronic cult of the self, we can scarcely speak of European culture in the same terms as in the Middle Ages or as in the Greco-Roman period. Indeed the 'cult of the self' which symbolizes more than anything else the significance of Romanticism in standing in absolute contrast to the 'public cult' of earlier periods in European culture and literature, might well serve as the end point for validity in Prospero's claims (a validity that first came under questioning during the Renaissance, as earlier seen). With the Symbolists, the 'cult of self' becomes even more rarefied in mythology and language that are essentially private. From the self, interest shifts to the intricacies of verbal signs. And these two characteristics, the Self and the Word-as-Sign, seem to be the modern preoccupations of European literature, whatever the labels: Dadaism, Surrealism, Chosisme. Indeed, a very continuous line seems to run from the Romantic wallowing in the self, albeit in the irrational, to the Existentialist feeling of imprisonment with the self, albeit rational; or, yet, the Symbolist preoccupation with the portents of language as sign-words and the modern Structuralist attempt at detecting the imports of a civilization in its sign-symbols.

The historical movement in European culture appears, consequently, as one going from the general to the particular, from the public to the private, from the organic to the specific. It is no coincidence that it is precisely at the moment when the unitary basis of European literature has definitely disintegrated, in the nineteenth century, that there arise the literatures that interest us: 'post-European' ones, by which I mean literatures that come to be outside of Europe, and although the products of descendants of Europeans (partly or wholly), nonetheless are expressive of emergent nationalities, or group consciousness: America, Haiti, Quebec, South America. Rooted in countries colonized by Europeans, literature first emerges as colonial artifact: voyagers' reports, diaries, missionaries' narratives, tales to titillate the metropolises. More important, though, even when written by the newly born nationals, the nascent literature is crippled.

In all these countries, whether we are speaking of America, French or English Canada, Haiti or Argentine and Brazil, there is the primary situation of cultural dependence. One could substitute the term 'relation' or 'influence' for dependence; but, because of the terms upon which such a relationship is structured, this dependence is vitiated and warped from the start. For, we have a literature mimicking another, indigenous writers hypnotized by the cult of metropolitan 'models'. No matter how original James Fenimore Cooper's and Washington Irving's imagery of the North American wilderness and their insights as to its auguries (and the same can be said about the cult of native lore in the literatures of South America, English and French Canada, Haiti), a primary feature nonetheless stands out, a recurrent pattern appears. All these writers may be using setting, characters, stories, congruent with their non-European habitat, but they are still integrating these materials in an outlook which in Europe is already passé: Romanticism. (3) When the 'Parnasse' is discovered in Quebec, Haiti and South America, when Symbolism reaches American shores, these movements already have been replaced for decades by Surrealism and Dadaism. To continue, when Naturalism comes to dominate American letters in the twenties and thirties, after an early ushering in the late nineteenth century (Twain for example), it is a belated occurrence; Emile Zola has been dead for some time, in France, by the time Dreiser publishes *An American Tragedy*. One could go on: Existentialism reaches Quebec in the mid-fifties when it raged in France a decade earlier; Surrealism reaches it in the late forties when its apogee had been attained twenty years earlier; Robbe-Grillet's 'chosisme' is 'in' in America in the early sixties, at the very moment when it was dying in France.

What I am getting at is obvious: the 'Caliban With Prospero' relationship is a warped one because the post-European writer, so long as he tries to function ever so self-consciously in the 'mainstream' of Prospero's culture, is bound to fail, or to experience the type of frustration that long made the consciousness of the French Canadian, the American (Black and White), the West Indian or the South American writer one of *exile*. Thus we can see the striking parallels of Henry James', Ezra Pound's, T.S. Eliot's infatuation with a European notion of "civilization", the lost Generation's attempt at losing itself in Paris of the twenties, the earlier mentioned Quebec writers who emigrated to France, the phenomenon of a Julio Cortazar, Miguel Asturias, Alejo Carpentier, Richard Wright, Aimé Césaire, Chester Himes, Léon Damas *et al.* all of them long-time residents of France. It is an attempt at 'securizing' oneself, which is understandable considering the fact that these writers knew the feeling of exile in their native lands, one stemming from the dilemma of having to follow in European footsteps; but one that contains its weight of sadness, to be sure, if we listen to cries such as the Haitian poet's Léon Laleau, which no doubt echo in Prufrock's "what shall I do":

> Ce coeur obsédant qui ne correspond
> Pas avec mon langage et mes costumes
> Et sur lequel mordent, comme un crampon,
> Des sentiments d'emprunt et des coutumes
> D'Europe, sentez-vous cette souffrance
> Et ce désespoir à nul autre égal
> D'apprivoiser avec des mots de France
> Ce coeur qui m'est venu du Sénégal? (4)

Or it is a sadness that takes its toll in the number of suicides and psychological aberrations in the history of French-Canadian literature, (5) underscoring the fact that post-European literature was coming to be in the nineteenth century, saddled with a European weight of 'tradition' and 'model' from which Europe itself at the time was moving away. A study of literary history suggests that the very evolution of European literature logically justifies the existence of a post-European literature not blithely mimicking but pursuing the process of miniaturization of literature as expression of a people in what it holds to be its authenticity and specificities. A number of causes may explain why this did not take place from inception, including the arrogance of metropolitan critics, the meekness and lack of audacity of post-European writers, and the peculiar trials inherent to the birth and early growth of national literatures and national consciousness.

If the first stage in all these literatures is one of imitation, the attempt at identifying and articulating particular lores and historical experiences nonetheless is germane to the foundation of indigenous expression. The American experience, blessed with the fortune of politics and economics, and a unique formation as a mass society, soon materialized in investigations of native themes such as the Frontier values, the agrarian myth, the pursuit of happiness, and the Protestant ethic, which are all woven in the grand tapestry of the American Dream. In this century, in the works of Fitzgerald, O'Neill, Lewis, Dos Passos and Miller, these came to dominate and define American literature. Added to other specificities such as regionalism, the question of ethnicity, these concerns contribute to make American literature, the first, albeit unconsciously, Calibanic or post-European expression to escape the Prospero syndrome. In the short span of less than a century, 'mainstream' American literature functions now in a Prospero relationship vis-à-vis the literature of some of its major ethnic groups, such as the Blacks, now the new Calibans in the process of asserting themselves. It is a peculiar irony of history that, whereas it took Europe a number of centuries to move from a unitary outlook to a fragmented one, America has come to a similar stage in so brief a period.

Haitian literature comes to this second stage when American intervention in Haiti brings about a militant affirmation of national consciousness. (6) In literature this is translated by stressing the distinctiveness of Haitians more indebted to their African descent than to French colonization whose legacy had been, up to the twenties, celebrated in attempts at reproducing colonial Hugos, Lamartines and Chateaubriands. When students from Martinique, Guadeloupe, French Guyana, and French-speaking Africa come to an understanding in Paris that what they have in common is not just that they all spoke French and were indebted to French largesses, but, the process of acculturation they had all gone through to reach a stage of alienation, their disenchantment and anger produced the recognition of their négritude. From that stage, in the early thirties, a literature of the French islands and French-colonized Africa was born.

203

The most troubled ethnic group in the U.S. was vainly trying to gain society's acceptance through the elitist tenets of the "Talented Tenth", the cultivation of the Southern agrarian myth and concept of gentility (the 'tragic mulatto' syndrome is a result); while appealing to Christian ethics, the morality of their "masters" (the Slave narratives, the Abolitionist movement), and remaining the butt of dehumanizing stereotypes and the object of buffoonery which even some Black writers revelled in (the Minstrel tradition). At long last, the juxtaposition of a nascent cultural interest in Africa (the writings of Frobenius, the discovery of African art in the West), and the influence of city-life, gave birth to the Negro Renaissance which, though mostly a hedonistic craze, planted the seeds for the literary self-assertion we find starting with Wright, and the cultural pride which inspired the Négritude writers in Paris.

Similarly in French Canada, self-assertion comes late, after decades of trying to 'integrate' into an overall mainstream with little success. When socio-economic conditions force a transplant from the rural to the urban setting, the signs of revolt appear, conveyed in the consciousness of having been delusioned for too long; the sons revolt against their fathers. Further, revolt culminates in a cultural movement celebrating the land.

Belatedly, to be sure, these post-European literatures, most often when placed in a particular socio-historical context, of which they become the reflection, reveal the consciousness of their specificity, and their reluctance to continue imitating. A study of their literary history often is one of their political history, at that period. Is it possible to formulate, with the evidence gathered through examination of two of these post-European literatures, a theoretical base for Calibanic literature? Since, presumably, Prospero's aesthetics does not apply for Caliban's peculiar brand of experience, can we find *descriptive* features in the literatures of French Canada and Black America that would seem to point to a theory, perhaps an aesthetics, for these new literatures?

One is immediately struck by three characteristics which seem to ordain the cultural expression in Quebec and Black America: an initial stage of *sadness*, corresponding to an agricultural economy; a second of *anger*, paralleled by the rise of industrialization; a third of *reflection*, occurring in the post-industrial, technological age. It is a movement from passion to intellection, from sentiments to rationality, visceralness to cerebralness. Let us examine each:

*Sadness* is the mood characterizing the inability to live with the consciousness of division within the self, inasmuch as the characters in the early novels, in both literatures, are incapable of *choosing*, of willing themselves out of hybridity. Tragedy is the form such inability takes. In the novels of Brown, Chesnutt and Johnson this matter of choice is made particularly poignant since the blight of slavery, or racism, is such that there is really little room for personal election on the part of the Black pitted against the odds of his colour. That is to say, the choice is indeed limited when the caste and class system dictates one's precise location in the hierarchy of the genteel South. But it is specifically upon that thin line of a particular skin shade, shape of nose and lips, texture of hair, that the Renas and the Clotels stake their lives. They think they are choosing to be "White" and not "Black", but the lesson in all these novels is that the misfortune of being born Black and a slave is light compared to the tragedy of being born half-White and half-Black, thus straddling slavery and freedom, racism and tolerance. Fate is always responsible, in the end, for here are these mixed-blood, who quite humanly in the face of adversity try to survive and protect themselves by attempting to "pass" (although racism is an insurmountable barrier) but, yet, are constantly denied ultimate satisfaction since a "chance meeting" (*The House Behind the Cedars*), a "mistake" (*Clotel*), or "remorse" (*Autobiography of an Ex-Coloured Man*), all willed by Fate, can destroy them.

Tragedy likewise takes its toll in Maria Chapdelaine's inability to choose the urban life over the rural, Lorenzo Surprenant over Eutrope Gagnon, personal happiness over her mother's footsteps; she also is ruled over by an implacable Fate that dictates that "nothing must change" if the French Canadian is to survive on the American continent. But it is an implied tragedy, it shies from showing its extent; which is not the case in *Menaud*, where "staticism", the consciousness of rigid tradition, now takes its toll in the complete divorce existing between a man's ideals and the realities he refuses to acknowledge. Here also the dominant temper is Menaud's refusal to *choose* the present over the past, the fact of industrialization against the anachronism of *le pays en haut*, and, more important, to accept the implied consequences of such a choice: that the ideal world of *Maria Chapdelaine* he is obsessed with, the motto "nothing must change", may have contained in its very resiliency the making of its own destruction. Menaud, of course, never gets around to reflecting, let alone willing; thus we see the destruction of his ideal world paralleled by his son's death, his attempt at destroying his daughter, Maria, and lastly, his own destruction through insanity. That tragedy, in all these novels, Black American and French-Canadian, is rooted in the characters' dependence on sentiments, idealization and mythicizing — while, by contrast, the 'world' against which they are pitted is harsh, concrete and evident — is buttressed in Ringuet's novel, *Trente Arpents*. Euchariste Moisan does everything to perfection according to the Messianic myth: his land is fertile and plentiful; his brood abundant; he is a dutiful Catholic who has given two of his twelve children to the Church, and who even accepted with equanimity his wife's death in labour. But everything 'caves in'; ultimately through no fault of his own, but because Fate, is would seem, has willed the end of a lifestyle that is to disappear with the advent of industrialization. His family is destroyed, his land parcelled and he himself ends up in exile in the U.S.

205

The first stage, then, of post-European literature is one of intense 'inadequacy' between the individual and the 'world' (by which I mean Nature as well as human society), of non-relationship between the inner and the outer self, of conflict. Always this conflict rests in a sentimental vision of self and the world, which jars with the unsentimental realities the characters are brought to confront. It is reflective, one supposes, of a period in the life of a collectivity at its birth; the trials and traumas of the infantile stage. It indicates the gestation of group consciousness left to its own articulation. *Sadness* is the feeling generated by this early and unprepared confrontation with the 'world'. The character of defeat is so strong at that stage that one wonders whether Caliban can really function without Prospero (translated in literary critical terms: is such 'young' literature of any value?). Lastly, this is the period where the temptation to return to metropolitan models is strongest. This lacking in assurance is fueled by the presence of native critics whose standards are "universal" (meaning European) and who deem as unworthy of their attention anything "local". (One thinks of Braithwaite and Brawley in the U.S.; Marcel Dugas, Jean Ethier-Blais in his early period, and even Jean LeMoyne in Quebec; Dantès Bellegarde in Haiti.) (7)

*Anger* erupts as the active mode opposite to the passive one of *Sadness*. It is the stage of assertion arising from the realization that a nadir state has been reached. The Calibanic man, caught in the "soft" side of his passions, adopts a "hard" stance directed at the Other he feels is responsible for his vital incapacity (racism in the U.S.; the consequences of Conquest for Quebec), or at the "feminine" part of himself he now loathes (the revolt against religion in both literatures; self-hatred in the U.S.; the legacy of the fathers in the urban environment in Quebec). In aesthetics, it is the realization of acculturation, the growing consciousness that art, before achieving the universal, is always rooted in the particular; the recognition that the expression of an indigenous culture is thwarted when it has to resort to imported models and depend on metropolitan approval for success or failure. It is at this stage, indeed, that the Calibanic writer grasps consciously or unconsciously his situation in the evolution of Western aesthetics: that to engage oneself in the articulation of native expression is the logical extension of the nineteenth-century European recognition of cultural pluralism rooted in diversity of self-expression. The Black writer discovers his négritude (the Negro Renaissance); he invents a set of images, he applies to literature a rhythmic pattern attuned to his lifestyle and rejoices in the pleasure of authenticity. The French-Canadian writer commits himself to the investigation and celebration of his native land, affirms his Americanness of spirit and de-emphasizes his French origins. More than anything else, he discovers a novel sense of identity: no longer a French Canadian (a composite, hybrid term), he now is a "Québécois". In both cultures a central preoccupation with authenticity emerges, symbolized in the "invisible man's" confronting the significance of Rinehart, in Ellison's

206

novel, for example; or Aquin's equally nameless hero's confrontation with the shadows of his dispossessed self.

But, this is still the stage of passion, not intellection. The all-destroying anger of a Caliban, who has discovered the extent of the delusion under which he has been kept, typifies it. Bigger Thomas stands out. His uncompromising pride in his actions is set against Dalton, the 'friend of the Negro', who yet is a slumlord, owner of the abject lodgings in which Bigger lives — is introduced as symbolic of the type of double-faced oppression under which Bigger has to live. Apparently a free man, Bigger is in fact still in bondage, with the exception that the "massa" is now more subtle in his lordship. Bigger's killing of Dalton's blonde daughter allegedly serves as retribution for all the tragedies suffered in the South. Similarly, Norton, in Ellison's novel, represents the same type of oppressor as Dalton: the slave master hidden behind the veneer of philanthropy. When polar opposites such as his accidental exposure to incest on a tour with the protagonist, and, in the structure of the novel, the formidable figure of Ras the Exhorter, are pitted against him, it is clear Ellison means to convey that violence begets violence. A host of other minor figures representative of the "massa" archetype are present in the novels of Attaway, Himes, Petry, Gardner, Smith and others, and next to them stand out in contrast the defiant figures of revolt of Big Mat, Bob Jones and Lutie Johnson, who refuse either to 'keep to their place' or to wallow in self-conscious helplessness in the face of adversity. Since the figure of the Preacher is a reminder of defeatism and resignation, he is, in *Native Son, Cane, Blood on the Forge,* and other novels, the object of scorn and violent rejection by the self-assertive protagonist. So that, although there is an undeniable positive side to the movement of revolt — one thinks of the roots of Négritude in the Negro Renaissance; the imagery of *Cane* and *Home to Harlem* — which of necessity had to follow in the light of tragedy, it nonetheless becomes so vehement as to threaten to engulf Caliban in a self-destructive course.

A similar awareness grows out of the release through anger found by the sons revolting against the world of the fathers in the French-Canadian novel. Though positively-rooted in such novels as *Au Pied de la Pente Douce* and *Bonheur d'Occasion*, this anger takes a quasi-nihilistic tone, if not a Romantic lyricism all of its own, in the novels of the sixties influenced by Frantz Fanon's theories of violence. To be sure, it is quite clear that the conditions materially experienced by Ti-Jean, in *Le Cassé*, and psychologically, by the protagonist in *Prochain Épisode* indicate that local conditions in Quebec were fertile enough for such a cult. The danger which appears, though (and which occurs similarly in the Black novel), is the tendency to subscribe wholeheartedly to feelings of oppression for which an Other is blamed but which, all too often, are at least partially self-inflicted. But, in the end, as in the Black novel, because of the aesthetic implications contained in such visceral revolt — from whence a creative explosion occurs

207

in celebrating the land in luxurious and deeply-felt imagery, in positing the roots for renewal with the self in mature form and more importantly, in the self-confidence and assurance whereby a distinctive and unapologetic new literature is produced, some of the aberrations of revolt in Quebec society are put into context.

*Anger* being a transitory stage — although an essential one for the individual in his claims to existence, and for the formation of a new aesthetics — it must lead to a more reflective and sober stage if it is not to sour and disintegrate in self-destruction. We reach then the state of *reflection* in post-European literature, the most problematic of the three since it is indicative of a maturing process, a statement that the young literature has progressed enough so that it is able to reflect upon itself and assume and assess its deficiencies and merits without the need ·for braggadocio and shallow repetition. This stage is a tentative one (because not enough evidence is yet available, and because of the all too facile tendency to fall back on the tried-and-true formula of revolt). But it can be defined, nevertheless, aesthetically, as the stage when Black literature, for instance, in America seems to grow conscious that if it is to have lasting value it must relate to the common experience of Négritude; and when Quebec literature recognizes the inescapable ambiguity of its Gallic heritage wedded to an American outlook. No easy solution is available, for such a condition is tied to a reflective, and not emotional or spiritual, view of self. It is predicated upon the ultimate recognition that if one's particular situation is investigated deeply enough — the Orphic quest in Black literature; the unrestrained consciousness of the 'world' in Quebec — then the very articulation of one's specificity mutates into the universality of the human experience. Richard Wright certainly portrays this mutation when *Native Son* and *The Outsider* are juxtaposed. From Bigger's unyielding revolt we come to Cross Damon's consciousness of the metaphor of the Negro's condition. William Demby and LeRoi Jones likewise utilize the descent into the self, whether in the metaphor of *The Catacombs* or that of the Black ghetto of Newark, to gain awareness of self whereby, in Jones' words, hell is discovered to be indeed heaven. Not surprisingly, both Jones and Wright share an existentialist outlook to temper and order their quest. Paule Marshall utilizes the metaphor of the island to conclude with the necessity of the universal contained in the particular: how Merle, a victim of racism, shares a common human experience with Saul, also a victim of racism, although White.

In Quebec, the consciousness of a world outlook conditioned by the impact of the media which, then, renders inadequate any limited preoccupation with geographical borders and, by implication, with any hot-house lifestyle, makes for a mature sense in the novels of Jacques Godbout and Luc Granger. Here, instead of a descent into the self (no doubt because of the different historical experience), we have an opening towards other selves. Instead of introspection, we have extroversion; but the result is the

208

same: the embracing of the human experience. The narrator of Godbout's novel is McLuhan's audile-tactile man who hears and sees the echoing or the reverberation of world manifestations, thus finds himself unable to pick up the knife of violence which the spirit of revolt wants him to. Witnessing his separatist friends' endless celebration of *le pays* and the glories of independence, he hears echoes of the Black movement in the States. In the end, when a nightwatchman has been killed by an F.L.Q. bomb there occurs a structural relationship in the novel which is a most powerful comment: the Montreal bombing echoes the Birmingham bombing referred to earlier which killed four little Black girls. Well aware of the deep malaise which leads to such acts in Quebec, the narrator would rather try to understand the phenomenon of Jack Kerouac's attempt at turning his French-Canadian heritage of "beat-ness" into the beatitude of self-discovery. This, for the narrator, is a never-ending task that takes him from the loving arms of an English-Canadian heiress to a retracing of Kerouac's journey in the U.S., but in vain. Escape into America being not the answer, the narrator assumes life's ambiguity, returning to Quebec, convinced that it is by being a witness made wise by the consciousness of polarities, ironies and the elusiveness of events that meaning — if it is ever to be attained — must be sought. If Granger's novel accomplishes an itinerary similar to Godbout's, Roch Carrier's is set in the earlier period of rural entrenchment and "state of siege" mentality, particularly as it came to a head in the conscription crisis during the last World War. But he too conveys a post-revolt state of mind where life's ambiguity is dramatized. War is rejected by the villagers, yet a state of disorder is created in their midst. Suspicious of English-speaking Canadians, they are shown to be really uneasy with themselves in the climactic wake scene where obsession with sex, religion, violence, ethnic pride, death, sense of the family are all released in a feast which is the Dionysian urge that a culture has long been kept from celebrating. Thus, the obstacles to the French Canadian's cultivation of the vital in life, the energetic and the pleasurable, were always within and not without. It is the ambiguity of a culture (germane to the ambiguity of the ancient Dionysian myth) that it had to be shown this while paying homage to the dead, shown that the powers of life could be affirmed in the presence of death.

If one word may serve to summarize this third stage, it would have to be: complexity. The awareness of the complexity of life, of its heterogeneity, and the Calibanic artist's ability to render it honestly and soberly is different from the pathos of the beginnings and the recourse to revolt in the median stage. It is all the more remarkable since it occurs as a logical progression in post-European literature, i.e. something organically tied to a particular experience which called for self-expression and articulation.

After describing the three stages of post-European literature from the evidence gathered, a final question has to be considered: can there be articulated a *normative* set of values for post-European literature? In sum, can it be argued that there is a particular imagery, a recurrent symbolism, a mythical lore and a rhythmic use of language, and speech specific to post-European literature?

First, one distinction should be made which can be reduced to the conventional notion of form and content. By which I mean that the content of a particular image or symbol, the meaning of a myth in post-European literature, can hardly escape partaking of the universal human experience of love, death, birth, loneliness, pain. Because the content is always concerned with passions, appetites, senses and moods, one cannot imagine such fundamental human experiences to 'contentually' change whether in European or post-European, Asian or Indian literature. If meaning, therefore, is always universal, a post-European aesthetic can only be justified on the level of form. And there the function of language emerges as supreme.

The call for use of the extreme vernacular in Quebec (*joual*), Black American (ghetto English), Haitian (Creole) and African (Swahili, Wolof, among a few hundred) literatures may sometime in the future lead to the foundation of a new aesthetic where myth, symbol and image may have a quite novel structure because they are rooted in the rhythm of each particular vernacular. (8)

One only wonders, though, if such attempts can be more successful than the late nineteenth-century call for the creation of an Irish Gaelic national literature? And how different, and aesthetically warrantable, when it is considered that in Black American literature, for instance (and Haitian too, for that matter), the use of dialect is an old and controversial issue indeed? (9) One only has to think of the disrepute into which Paul Laurence Dunbar's work has fallen to be aware of the pitfalls of such an enterprise. (10) How different, in fact, such a would-be "new" literature from the Romantic interest in folklore, native myths and beliefs which led to the creation of national literatures and a return of interest in the Middle Ages? Admittedly, one could surmise that there is, as a matter of fact, a definite precedent therein; that, even at the cost of parcelling cultures and literatures to Babelian limits, the theorists of vernacular literatures are pursuing the revolution in aesthetics led by the Romantics. However, since achievements in Creole, *Joual* and ghetto English are still minimal and do not constitute a substantial body of literature, the whole matter, however theoretically possible, individually electrifying, is in too formative a stage for critical evaluation. There is the possibility of self-defeat in the post-European artist's, or critic's, refusal to recognize the formidable achievements and viability in using and in investing with his own store of feelings and concepts a 'standard' language which he 'educated' to his own sense of reality and experience. The current success and promising future of post-European literature are there to be seen in the curricula of universities and high schools as well as in publishers' figures.

A stage of reflection where the universal is reached through descent into the self, or through overture towards other selves, corresponds, in the last analysis, to that of present European literature, where concern with the individual was arrived at after initial unravellings of public values and common revolt. A descriptive theory of post-European literature, as I have aimed at articulating in this essay, can lead to a possible synthetical stage of reconciliation between Caliban and a a re-educated Prospero.

1 Paul Hazard, *La Crise de la Conscience Européenne 1680-1715.*

2 "In the seventeenth century a dissociation of sensibility set in, from which we have never recovered; ... ." T.S. Eliot, "The Metaphysical Poets", *Selected Essays*, p.247.

3 See Alberto Zum Felde, *La Narrativa en Hispanoamerica*, pp.37-72; Leslie A. Fiedler, *Love and Death in the American Novel*, pp.168-205; Gérard Tougas, *Histoire de la Littérature Canadienne-Française*, pp.10-11; Lilyan Kesteloot, *Les Ecrivains Noirs de Langue Française*, pp.31-32; Naomi Garrett, *The Renaissance of Haitian Poetry*, pp.18-52.

4 Léon Laleau, "Trahison", *Anthologie de la Nouvelle Poésie Nègre et Malgache de Langue Française*, p.108.

5 One thinks of Emile Nelligan, Saint-Denys Garneau, Sylvain Garneau and their tragic fate; more important is the consciousness of alienation, "le sens de l'exil", that imposes such levy, see Jean Ethier - Blais, "Exils", *Littérature Canadienne-Française*, Conférences J.A. de Sève 1-10, pp.115-140.

6 Jean Price-Mars, *Ainsi Parla l'Oncle*, pp.187-194, p.235; "L'Etat Social et la Production Littéraire en Haïti", *Conjonction*, pp.51-52.

7 See Darwin T. Turner, "Afro-American Literary Critics: an Introduction", *The Black Aesthetic*, pp.64-65, p.71; Jean Ethier-Blais, "Exils", pp.122-126; Dantès Bellegarde, *Haïti et son Peuple*, p.62; Jean LeMoyne, *Convergences*, pp.101-108.

8 Gérald Godin, "Le Joual et Nous", *Parti Pris*, pp.18-19; I am thinking of the echo of Godin's credo in the present proletarian plays of highly-regarded young playwrights such as Michel Tremblay and Jean Barbeau. See also, in the case of ghetto English, LeRoi Jones, "The Black Aesthetic", *Negro Digest*, pp.5-6; also in the same issue of *Negro Digest*, for an evaluation of the Jones-influenced Black poetry of the sixties, written by Don L. Lee, Sonia Sanchez, Nikki Giovanni *et al.*, see Carolyn M. Rodgers' "Black Poetry — Where it's at", pp.7-16; in the case of creole, see Félix Morisseau-Leroy, "La Littérature Haïtienne d'Expression Créole, son Devenir", *Présence Africaine*, pp.46-55; Jacques Zéphyr, "Les Problèmes de Contact Entre le Français et le Créole en Haiti", *Bulletin Annuel*, French viii, Modern Language Association,

pp.21-32; lastly, see Senghor's reply to the call which goes unabated, mainly from the younger European-educated African élite, for an actual "africanization" of literature rather than rely on what, practically-speaking, is rather vague in present-day Africa (the reference is, of course, to Négritude), "Le Français Langue de Culture", *Négritude et Humanisme*, pp.358-363.

9  See Robert A. Bone, *The Negro Novel in America*, pp.38-43, p.66.
10  See Addison Gayle Jr., "Cultural Strangulation: Black Literature and the White Aesthetic", *The Black Aesthetic*, pp.45-46.

LIST OF

# WORKS CITED

*A. PRIMARY SOURCES*

1. The Black American Novel

Attaway, William. *Blood on the Forge.* New York: Doubleday, Doran and Co., 1941.

Baldwin, James. *Go Tell it on the Mountain.* 1953; rpt. New York: Signet, 1963.

Brown, Cecil. *The Life and Loves of Mr. Jiveass Nigger.* New York : Farrar, Straus and Giroux, 1969.

Brown, William Wells. *Clotel, or the President's Daughter.* 1853; rpt. New York: Collier, 1970.

Chesnutt, Charles Waddell. *The House Behind the Cedars.* 1900; rpt. New York: Collier, 1969.

Demby, William. *Beetlecreek.* 1950; rpt. New York: Avon, 1967.

Demby, William. *The Catacombs.* New York: Pantheon, 1965.

DuBois, W.E.B. *Dark Princess.* New York: Harcourt, Brace and Co., 1928.

Ellison, Ralph. *Invisible Man.* 1952; rpt. New York: Signet, 1964.

Fauset, Jessie R. *Plum Bun.* New York: Frederick A. Stokes, 1928.

Himes, Chester. *If he Hollers Let him Go.* New York: Doubleday, Doran and Co., 1945.

Himes, Chester. *Pinktoes.* 1962; rpt. London: Arthur Barker Ltd., 1965.

Johnson, James Weldon. *The Autobiography of an Ex-Coloured Man.* 1912; rpt. New York: Hill and Wang, 1969.

Jones, LeRoi. *The System of Dante's Hell*. 1963; rpt. New York, 1966.

Kelley, William Melvin. *Dem*. New York: Collier, 1967.

Larsen, Nella. *Quicksand*. New York: Knopf, 1928.

Larsen, Nella. *Passing*. New York: Knopf, 1929.

Marshall, Paule. *The Chosen Place, the Timeless People*. New York: Harcourt, Brace and World, 1969.

McKay, Claude. *Home to Harlem*. 1928; rpt. New York: Avon, 1951.

Petry, Ann. *The Street*. 1946; rpt. New York: Pyramid, 1966.

Smith, William Gardner. *The Last of the Conquerors*. New York: Farrar, Straus and Co., 1948.

Thurman, Wallace. *The Blacker the Berry*. New York: Macaulay, 1929.

Toomer, Jean. *Cane*. New York: Boni and Liveright, 1923.

White, Walter. *Flight*. New York: Grosset and Dunlap, 1926.

Wright, Richard. *Native Son*. 1940; rpt. New York: Signet, 1964.

Wright, Richard. *The Outsider*. New York: Harper, 1953.

2. The French-Canadian Novel

Aquin, Hubert. *Prochain Episode*. Montréal: Cercle du Livre de France, 1965.

Aquin, Hubert. *Trou de Mémoire*. Montréal: Cercle du Livre de France, 1967.

Aquin, Hubert. *L'Antiphonaire*. Montréal: Cercle du Livre de France, 1969.

Aubert de Gaspé, Philippe. *Les Anciens Canadiens*. 1864; rpt. Montréal: Fides, 1963.

Beaulieu, Victor-Lévy. *Jos Connaissant*. Montréal: Editions du Jour, 1970.

Bessette, Gérard. *Le Libraire*. 1960; rpt. Montréal: Cercle du Livre de France, 1966.

Blais, Marie-Claire. *Une Saison dans la Vie d'Emmanuel*. Montréal: Editions du Jour, 1965.

Carrier, Roch. *La Guerre, Yes Sir!* Montréal: Editions du Jour, 1968.

Desmarchais, Rex. *La Chesnaie*. Montréal: Editions de l'Arbre, 1942.

Ducharme, Réjean. *L'Avalée des Avalés*. Paris: Gallimard, 1966.

Ducharme, Réjean. *Le Nez qui Voque*. Paris: Gallimard, 1967.

Ducharme, Réjean. *L'Océanthume*. Paris: Gallimard, 1968.

Ducharme, Réjean. *La Fille de Christophe Colomb*. Paris:

Gallimard, 1969.

Ferron, Jacques. *Le Ciel de Québec.* Montréal: Editions du Jour, 1969.

Godbout, Jacques. *Le Couteau sur la Table.* Montréal: Editions du Seuil, 1965.

Granger, Luc. *Ouate de Phoque.* Montréal: Parti Pris, 1969.

Groulx, Lionel. [Alonié de Lestres.] *L'Appel de la Race.* 1922; rpt. Montréal: Granger, 1943.

Harvey, Jean-Charles. *Les Demi-Civilisés.* 1933; rpt. Montréal: Editions de l'Homme, 1962.

Hémon, Louis. *Maria Chapdelaine.* 1915; rpt. Montréal: Fides, 1964.

Lemelin, Roger. *Au Pied de la Pente Douce.* 1944; rpt. Québec: Institut Littéraire du Québec, 1953.

Renaud, Jacques. *Le Cassé.* Montréal: Parti Pris, 1964.

Renaud, Jacques. *En d'Autres Paysages.* Montréal: Parti Pris, 1970.

Ringuet. *Trente Arpents.* Paris: Flammarion, 1938.

Roy, Gabrielle. *Bonheur d'Occasion.* Montréal: Société des Editions Pascal, 1945.

Savard, Félix-Antoine. *Menaud Maître-Draveur.* Québec: Librairie Garneau, 1937.

## B. SECONDARY SOURCES

Aaron, Daniel. *Writers on the Left.* New York: Avon, 1965.

Abrams, M.H. *The Mirror and the Lamp: Romantic Theory and the Critical Tradition.* 1953; rpt. New York: Norton, 1958.

*American Assembly.* *The United States and Canada.* Ed. John Sloan Dickey. Englewood Cliffs,N.J.: Prentice Hall, 1964.

AMSAC. *The American Negro Writer and his Roots.* New York AMSAC, 1960.

Aquin, Hubert. *Point de Fuite.* Montréal: Cercle du Livre de France, 1971.

*Archives des Lettres Canadiennes.* Edité par Centre de Recherches de Littérature Canadienne-Française de l'Université d'Ottawa. Tome III. Montréal: Fides, 1964.

Arnold, Matthew. "Dover Beach". *Romantic and Victorian Poetry.* Ed. William Frost. Englewood Cliffs, N.J.: Prentice-Hall, 1965.

Auerbach, Erich. *Mimesis, The Representation of Reality in Western Literature.* New York: Anchor, 1957.

Bacon, Francis. *The Advancement of Learning.* Ed. W.A. Wright.

Oxford: Clarendon Press, 1963.

Baillargeon, Samuel. *Littérature Canadienne-Française*. 3rd ed. rev.; Montréal: Fides, 1957.

Baldwin, James. *Nobody Knows My Name*. New York: Dell, 1963.

Baldwin, James. *The Fire Next Time*. New York: Dell, 1964.

Baldwin, James. *Notes of a Native Son*. New York: Bantam, 1964.

Bellegarde, Dantès. *Haïti et son Peuple*. Paris: Nouvelles Editions Latines, 1953.

Blais, Jean-Ethier. "Exils". *Littérature Canadienne-Française*. Conférences J.A. deSève. Montréal: Presses de l'Univ. de Montréal, 1969.

Bone, Robert A. *The Negro Novel in America*. 2nd. ed., 1965; rpt. New Haven, Conn.: Yale Univ. Press, 1969.

Booth, Wayne C. *The Rhetoric of Fiction*. Chicago: Univ. of Chicago Press, 1967.

Borduas, Paul-Emile. *Refus Global*. Saint-Hilaire, Qué.: Mithra-Mythe, 1948.

Bourguignon, Erika. "Afro-American Religions: Traditions and Transformations." *Black Americans*. Ed. John F. Szwed. Washington: U.S.I.S., 1970.

Browning, Robert. "Caliban Upon Setebos." *Selected Poetry*. Introd. Horace Gregory. New York: Holt, Rinehart and Winston, 1956.

Brunet, Michel. *La Présence Anglaise et les Canadiens*. Montréal: Beauchemin, 1958.

Butcher, Margaret Just. *The Negro in American Culture*. 1956; rpt. New York: Mentor, 1971.

Camus, Albert. *Le Mythe de Sisyphe*. Paris: Gallimard, 1964.

Carmichael, Stokely and Charles V. Hamilton. *Black Power: The Politics of Liberation in America*. New York: Viking, 1967.

Casgrain, H.D. *Oeuvres Complètes*. Montréal: Beauchemin, 1896.

Césaire, Aimé. *Les Armes Miraculeuses*. Paris: Gallimard, 1946.

Césaire, Aimé. "Culture et Colonisation". Présence Africaine. Nlle Série, Nos. 8-10 (1956); rpt. in *Liberté*, 5, No. 1 (1963), 15-35.

Césaire, Aimé. *Cahier d'un Retour au Pays Natal*. 2nd ed., 1956; rpt. Paris: Présence Africaine, 1960.

Césaire, Aimé. *Ferrements*. Paris: Editons du Seuil, 1960.

Césaire, Aimé. *Cadastre*. Paris: Editions du Seuil, 1961.

Césaire, Aimé. *La Tragédie du Roi Christophe*. Paris: Présence Africaine, 1963.

Césaire, Aimé. *Une Saison au Congo*. Paris: Editions du Seuil,

1967.

Césaire, Aimé. *Une Tempête*. Paris: Editions du Seuil, 1969.

Chamberland, Paul. "De la Damnation à la Liberté". *Parti Pris, 1,* Nos. 9-10-11 (1964), 53-89.

Chamberland, Paul. *Terre Québec.* Montréal: Déom, 1964.

Chamberland, Paul. *L'Afficheur Hurle.* Montréal: Parti Pris, 1965.

Chamberland, Paul. "Dire ce que je Suis". *Parti Pris, 2, No. 5 (1965), 33-42.*

Chamberland, Paul. *L'Inavouable.* Montréal: Parti Pris, 1967.

Chamberland, Paul. "Manifeste des Enfants Libres du Kébec". *Ellipse.* No. 6 (1971), 48-52.

Chamberland, Paul. and Allen Ginsberg. *Ellipse.* No. 8-9, (1971).

Chaput, Marcel. *Pourquoi je suis Séparatiste.* Montréal: Editions du Jour, 1961.

Cleaver, Eldridge. *Soul on Ice.* New York: Dell, 1970.

Conrad, Joseph. *Heart of Darkness and the Secret Sharer.* New York: Signet, 1962.

Costisella, Joseph. *L'Esprit Révolutionnaire dans la Littérature Canadienne-Française de 1837 à la fin du XIX Siècle.* Montréal: Beauchemin, 1968.

*Crémazie.* Ed. Michel Dassonville. Montréal: Fides, 1956.

Cruse, Harold. "An Afro-American's Cultural Views". *Présence Africaine,* No. 51, (1964), 31-43.

Cruse, Harold. "Rebellion ou Révolution". *Présence Africaine,* No. 51, (1964), 42-61.

Cruse, Harold. *The Crisis of the Negro Intellectual.* New York: William Morrow Co., 1967.

Davidson, Basil. *The African Genius.* New York: Atlantic-Little, Brown, 1970.

Dépestre, René. "Les Métamorphoses de la Négritude en Amérique". *Présence Africaine,* No. 75 (1970), 19-33.

Desbiens, Jean-Paul. *Les Insolences du Frère Untel.* Montréal: Editions de l'Homme, 1960.

Descartes, René. *Discours de la Méthode.* 1637; rpt. Paris: Librairie Larousse, 1934.

DesRoches, Roger. *La Presse,* 3 Oct. 1970, p.C2.

Dorsinville, Max. "La Négritude et la Littérature Québecoise". *Canadian Literature,* No. 42 (Autumn 1969), 26-36.

Dorsinville, Max. "Levels of Ambiguity in the African Novel". *Canadian Journal of African Studies,* 5, No. 2 (1971), 213-225.

Dorsinville, Max. "Pays, Parole et Négritude". *Canadian Literature,* No. 51 (Winter 1972), 55-64.

Durham, Lord. *Lord Durham's Report.* Ed. G.M. Craig. Toronto: McClelland and Stewart, 1963.

Eliot, T.S. *Notes Towards the Definition of Culture*. New York: Harcourt, Brace and World, 1949.

Eliot, T.S. *Selected Essays*. New York: Harcourt, Brace and World, 1960.

Ellison, Ralph. *Shadow and Act*. New York: Signet, 1964.

Ellison, Ralph and James Alan McPherson. "Indivisible Man". *The Atlantic,* 236, No. 6 (1970), 45-60.

Falardeau, Jean-Charles. *Notre Société et son Roman*. Montréal: HMH, 1967.

Fanon, Frantz. *Peau Noire, Masques Blancs*. Paris: Editions du Seuil, 1952.

Fanon, Frantz. *Les Damnés de la Terre*. Paris: François Maspéro, 1961.

Felde, Alberto Zum. *La Narrativa en Hispanoamerica*. Madrid: Aguilar, 1964.

Fiedler, Leslie. *Love and Death in the American Novel*. 2nd ed.; New York: Dell, 1966.

Frazier, E. Franklin. *The Negro Church in America*. Liverpool: Liverpool Univ. Press, 1964.

Frobénius, Léo. *Histoire de la Civilisation Africaine*. 3rd ed.; Paris: Gallimard, 1936.

Frye, Northrop. *Anatomy of Criticism: Four Essays*. Princeton, N.J. Princeton Univ. Press, 1957.

Garrett, Naomi. *The Renaissance of Haitian Poetry*. Paris: Présence Africaine, 1963.

Gayle, Addison Jr. "Cultural Hegemony: The Southern Writer and American Letters". *Amistad*, No. 1 (1970), 1-24.

Gayle, Addison Jr. "Cultural Strangulation: Black Literature and the White Aesthetic". *The Black Aesthetic*. Ed. Addison Gayle Jr. New York: Doubleday, 1971.

Glazer, Nathan and Daniel P. Moynihan. *Beyond the Melting Pot: the Negroes, Puerto Ricans, Jews, Italians, and Irish in New York City*. Cambridge, Mass.: M.I.T. Press, 1963.

Glicksberg, Charles I. "The Alienation of Negro Literature", *Phylon*, No. 1 (1950), 49-58.

Godin, Gérald. "Le Joual et Nous". *Parti Pris,* 2, No. 5 (1965), 18-19.

Goldmann, Lucien. *Pour une Sociologie du Roman*. Paris: Gallimard, 1964.

Greene, Graham. *The Power and the Glory*. London: Penguin, 1964.

Gross, Seymour L. "Stereotype to Archetype". *Images of the Negro in American Literature*. Ed. Seymour L. Gross and J.E.

Hardy. Chicago: Univ. of Chicago Press, 1966.

Hazard, Paul. *La Crise de la Conscience Européenne 1680-1715.* Paris: Hatier, 1934.

Hébert, Anne. *Le Tombeau des Rois.* Québec: L'Institut Littéraire du Québec, 1953.

Herskovits, Melville. *The Myth of the Negro Past.* Boston: Beacon, 1956.

Hill, Herbert, ed. *Anger and Beyond.* New York: Harper and Row, 1966.

Himes, Chester. "My Man Himes: An Interview with Chester Himes". *Amistad,* No. 1 (1970), 85-91.

Howe, Irving. *A World More Attractive.* New York: Horizon, 1963.

Jahn, Janheinz. *Muntu: An Outline of the New African Culture.* 1958; rpt. New York: Grove, 1965.

Jahn, Janheinz. *Neo-African Literature: A History of Black Writing.* 1966; rpt. New York: Grove, 1969.

James, C.L.R. "The Atlantic Slave Trade and Slavery". *Amistad,* No. 1 (1970), 120-164.

James, Henry. *The Future of the Novel.* New York: Vintage, 1956.

Jeanpierre, W.A. "Sartre's Theory of 'Antiracist Racism' in his Study of Négritude". *Black and White in American Culture.* Ed. Jules Chametzky and Sidney Kaplan. Amherst, Mass.: The Univ. of Massachusetts Press, 1969.

Jones, D.G. "La Vraie Révolution est celle de l'Imagination". *Ellipse,* No. 6 (1971), 91-97.

Jones, LeRoi. "The Black Aesthetic". *Negro Digest,* XVIII, No. 11 (1969), 5-6.

Joyce, James. *Portrait of the Artist as a Young Man.* 1916; rpt. London: Penguin, 1965.

Jung, Carl G. "On the Relation of Analytical Psychology to Poetic Art". *Modern Continental Literary Criticism.* Ed. O.B. Hardison. New York: Appleton, 1962.

Kane, Sheikh Hamidou. *L'Aventure Ambiguë.* Paris: Julliard, 1961.

Kesteloot, Lilyan. *Les Ecrivains Noirs de Langue Française: Naissance d'une Littérature.* Bruxelles: Univ. Libre de Bruxelles, 1965.

Laleau, Léon. "Trahison". *Anthologie de la Nouvelle Poésie Nègre et Malgache de Langue Française.* Ed. Léopold S. Senghor. Paris: P.U.F., 1948.

Lamming, George. *The Pleasures of Exile.* London: Joseph, 1960.

Lapointe, Renaude. *L'Histoire Bouleversante de Mgr Charbonneau.* Montréal: Editions du Jour, 1962.

Laporte, Pierre. *Le Vrai Visage de Duplessis.* Montréal: Editions de l'Homme, 1962.

Laroche, Maximilien. *Le Miracle et la Métamorphose: Essai sur les Littératures de Québec et d'Haïti.* Montréal: Editions du Jour, 1970.

Larsen, Otto, ed. *Violence and the Media.* New York: Harper and Row, 1968.

Larson, Charles R. "African-Afro American Literary Relations: Basic Parallels". *Negro Digest*, XVIII, No. 2 (1969), 35-42.

Laurence, Margaret. *Long Drums and Cannons.* 1968; rpt. New York: Praeger, 1969.

Laurendeau, André. *La Crise de la Conscription 1942.* Montréal: Editions du Jour, 1962.

LeMoyne, Jean. *Convergences.* Montréal:HMH, 1961.

Littlejohn, David. *Black on White: A Critical Survey of Writing by American Negroes.* New York: Grossman, 1966.

Lorenz, Konrad. *On Aggression.* New York: Bantam, 1967.

Lubbock, Percy. *The Craft of Fiction.* London: Jonathan Cape, 1921.

Lukacs, Georg. *La Théorie du Roman.* Paris: Editions Gonthier, 1963.

Marcotte, Gilles. "Une Poésie d'Exil". *Canadian Literature*, No. 2 (Spring 1959), 32-36.

Marcotte, Gilles. *Une Littérature qui se Fait.* Montréal: HMH, 1962.

Mannoni, D.O. *Psychologie de la Colonisation.* Paris: Editions du Seuil, 1950.

Margolies, Edward. *Native Sons: A Critical Study of Twentieth Century Negro American Authors.* New York: Lippincott, 1969.

Martel, Réginald. *La Presse,* 6 Mar. 1971, p.D3.

Mbiti, John. *African Religions and Philosophy.* London: Heinemann, 1969.

McLuhan, Marshall. *Understanding Media: The Extensions of Man.* New York: Signet, 1964.

Memmi, Albert. *Portrait du Colonisé.* Paris: Corrêa, 1957.

Moore, Gerald. "The Politics of Negritude". *Protest and Conflict in African Literature.* Ed. Cosmo Pieterse and Donald Munroe. London: Heineman, 1969.

Moore, Gerald and Ulli Beier, ed. *Modern Poetry in Africa.* London: Penguin, 1966.

Morisseau-Leroy, Félix. "La Littérature Haïtienne d'Expression Créole, son Devenir". *Présence Africaine*, No. 17 (1958), 46-55.

Mphahlele, Ezekiel. *The African Image.* London: Faber and Faber, 1962.

Myrdal, Gunnar. *An American Dilemma: The Negro Problem*

*and Modern Democracy.* 1964; rpt. New York: Harper and Row, 1952.

Préfontaine, Yves. *Pays Sans Parole.* Montréal: Hexagone, 1960.

Préfontaine, Yves. *Quatre Figures Martiniquaises.* Diss. Univ. de Montréal, 1966.

Price-Mars, Jean. *Ainsi Parla l'Oncle.* Port-au-Prince: Compiègne, 1928.

Price-Mars, Jean. "L'Etat Social et la Production Littéraire en Haiti". *Conjonction,* No. 34 (1951), 51-52.

Record, Wilson. *The Negro and the Communist Party.* Chapel Hill: Univ. of North Carolina Press, 1951.

*Report of the National Advisory Commission on Civil Disorders.* New York: Bantam, 1968.

Rioux, Marcel: "Aliénation Culturelle et Roman Canadien". *Recherches Sociographiques.* Québec: Université Laval, 1964.

Robbe-Grillet, Alain. *For a New Novel.* New York: Grove, 1965.

Robidoux, Réjean and André Renaud. *Le Roman Canadien Français du Vingtième Siècle.* Ottawa: Univ. d'Ottawa, 1966.

Rodgers, Carolyn. "Black Poetry - Where it's at". *Negro Digest,* XVIII, No. 11 (1969), 7-16.

Rousseau, Guildo. *Jean-Charles Harvey et son Oeuvre Romanesque.* Sherbrooke: Cosmos, 1969.

Sartre, Jean-Paul. *Existentialism and Humanism.* London: Methuen, 1948.

Sartre, Jean-Paul. "Orphée Noir". *Anthologie de la Nouvelle Poésie Nègre et Malgache de Langue Française.* Ed. Léopold S. Senghor. Paris: PUF, 1948.

Sartre, Jean-Paul. *Réflexions sur la Question Juive.* Paris: Gallimard, 1954.

Sartre, Jean-Paul. *No Exit and Three Other Plays.* New York: Vintage, 1956.

Sartre, Jean-Paul. *Qu'est-ce que la Littérature?* Paris: Gallimard, 1966.

Senghor, Léopold Sédar, ed. *Anthologie de la Nouvelle Poésie Nègre et Malgache de Langue Française.* Paris: PUF, 1948.

Senghor, Léopold Sédar. *Négritude et Humanisme, Liberté I.* Paris : Editions du Seuil, 1964.

Shakespeare, William. *Complete Works.* London: Abbey Library, n.d.

Shelley, Percy Bysshe. "A Defence of Poetry". *Romanticism.* Ed. John B. Halsted. New York: Harper and Row, 1969.

Stowe, Harriet Beecher. *Uncle Tom's Cabin.* 1852; rpt. New York: Washington Square Press, 1962.

Sutherland, Ronald. *Second Image: Comparative Studies in*

*Quebec/Canadian Literature*. Toronto: New Press, 1971.

Tawney, R.H. *Religion and the Rise of Capitalism. A Historical Study*. Gloucester, Mass.: Peter Smith, 1962.

Tempels, R.P. *La Philosophie Bantoue*. Paris: Présence Africaine, 1948.

Theall, D.F. *The Medium is the Rear View Mirror*. Montréal: McGill-Queen's University Press, 1971.

Tougas, Gérard. *Histoire de la Littérature Canadienne-Française*. 2nd ed., Paris: PUF, 1964.

Trudeau, Pierre Elliott, ed. *La Grève de l'Amiante*. Montréal: Editions Cité Libre, 1956.

Trudeau, Pierre Elliott. "La Nouvelle Trahison des Clercs". *Cité Libre*, XIII (avril 1962), rpt. in *Le Fédéralisme et la Société Canadienne-Française*. Montréal: HMH, 1967.

Trudeau, Pierre Elliott. "Les Séparatistes: Des Contre-Révolutionnaires". *Cité Libre*, XV (mai 1964), rpt. in *Le Fédéralisme et la Société Canadienne-Française*. Montréal: HMH, 1967.

Trudel, Marcel. *L'Esclavage au Canada Français*. Québec: Presses Universitaires Laval, 1960.

Turner, Darwin T. "Afro-American Literary Critics: An Introduction". *The Black Aesthetic*. Ed. Addison Gayle Jr. New York: Doubleday, 1971.

Vallières, Pierre. *Nègres Blancs d'Amérique*. Montréal: Parti Pris, 1968; trans. *White Niggers of America*. Toronto: McClelland and Stewart, 1971.

Viatte, Auguste. *Les Sources Occultes du Romantisme*. Paris: Champion, 1928.

Vigneault, Robert. *Livres et Auteurs Québécois 1969*. Ed. Adrien Thério. Montréal: Editions Jumonville, 1969.

Wade, Mason. *The French Canadians 1760-1945*. Toronto: Macmillan, 1956.

Wade, Mason. *The French Canadian Outlook*. Toronto: McClelland and Stewart, 1964.

Watt, Ian. *The Rise of the Novel: Studies in Defoe, Richardson and Fielding*. Berkeley: Univ. of California Press, 1967.

Weber, Max. *The Protestant Ethic and the Spirit of Capitalism*. New York: Scribner's, 1958.

Wellek, René. *Concepts of Criticism*. Ed. Stephen C. Nichols, Jr. New Haven, Conn.: Yale University Press, 1963.

Wellek, René. and Austin Warren. *Theory of Literature*. New York: Harcourt, Brace and Co., 1949.

Wilson, Edmund. *O Canada. An American's Notes on Canadian Culture*. New York: Farrar, Straus and Giroux, 1965.

Winks, Robin W. *The Blacks in Canada, A History*. New Haven, Conn.: Yale University Press, 1971.
Wordsworth, William. "Preface of Lyrical Ballads". *Romanticism*. Ed. John B. Halsted. New York: Harper and Row, 1969.
Wright, Richard. "I Tried to be a Communist". *Atlantic Monthly*, 174 (August 1944), 61-70; (Sept. 1944), 48-56.
Wright, Richard. *Black Power*. New York: Knopf, 1954.
Wright, Richard. *White Man, Listen!* New York: Anchor, 1964.
Zéphyr, Jacques. "Les Problèmes de Contact entre le Français et le Créole en Haïti". *Bulletin Annuel*. French VIII. Modern Language Association, No. 14 (1970), 21-32.

# VITA

Max Dorsinville was born in Port-au-Prince, Haiti, 30 January 1943. He left Haiti in 1954 and pursued studies in Montreal, Sherbrooke and New York leading finally to a doctorate in Comparative Literature from the City University of New York. Max Dorsinville is an Assistant Professor of English and Comparative literature at McGill University. A frequent contributor to *Canadian Literature*, he has had critical articles published in *PMLA, Livres et Auteurs Québécois* and other journals. He is currently at work on a comparative study of the figure of "the Outsider" in Quebec and African novels, 1915-1960.